© 2012 by Andrew Sandoval
Bee Gees: The Day-By-Day Story, 1945–1972
First Edition, Paperback—published 2012
ISBN 978-0-943249-08-7
Printed in the USA
Published by Retrofuture Day-By-Day
www.retrofuture.com

All rights reserved. No part of this book may be reproduced or transmitted in any form or by any means, electronic or mechanical, including photocopying or any information storage and retrieval system, without permission in writing from the publisher.

This book is dedicated to "The Loner."

Bee Gees
The Day-By-Day Story, 1945–1972   By Andrew Sandoval

The author wishes to thank Barry Gibb, Robin Gibb and Vince Melouney for their extensive interviews and wonderful music!

Thanks to all those connected with the Bee Gees in the period when this research began: Jimmy Edwards, Robin Hurley and Dick Ashby.

For extensive editorial, emotional and moral guidance: Mark Easter.

For generosity and advice: Joe Brennan, Brian Kehew, Eric Lefcowitz & Bob Stanley.

Extensive research and extraordinary primary source material: Robert Morton Jack.

Over, above and far beyond the call of editorial assistance: Andy Neill.

Invaluable library research: Simon Smith, Doug Hinman, Bob Mehr, Mike Johnson, Wener Wingen, Greg Shaw, Wendy Horowitz, Gordon Carmadelle and Minako Yoshida.

For loan of archival materials: Saul Davis, Alec Palao, Lyric Seidensticker & Geoffrey Weiss.

1972 photos courtesy of Bobby Furst.

Andy Morten and Jon "Mojo" Mills for their inspiration and serialization in *Shindig!*

Extra special thanks to Ken Sharp and Harold Bronson for use of their respective Maurice Gibb interviews.

Page, Simon & Duke who listened with me.

Personal thanks to Arnold Mann, Mark London, Bill Inglot, Kieron Tyler, Mason Williams, Rob Santos, Bill Levenson, Kenn Norman, Matt Lederman, Jim Laspesa, Joe McMichael, Rachel Lichtman and Colin Petersen.

Design & Layout: Stephanie Thompson
Art Direction: Arnold Mann

INTRODUCTION

"Many years ago, I was a simple man..."

I grew up in a home filled with records: at first my parents and later my own. One album that particularly caught my ear growing up in the 1970's was *Bee Gees' 1st*. Despite this being the era when the Bee Gees reached the pinnacle of popularity with a very different set of hits, I heard much more as a child of this LP and *Best Of Bee Gees* (from 1969) than anything else from their vast oeuvre. In ensuing years my fascination for the group only increased, as did the scope of my appreciation of their robust output.

I have always felt their work was worthy of the serious examination afforded to such artists as the Beatles and Beach Boys. With this book—compiled from six years of intensive research and listening—I hope to afford them the long overdue historical context that those wonderful bands have already received many times over. Having poured through hundreds of hours of session reels, volumes of weekly music publications, as well as personally interviewing Barry, Robin and Vince, what has emerged in this book is a unique snapshot of the Gibbs' creative process amidst the hectic chaos of what Barry would later term "first fame."

It was truly one of the highlights of my long career as music historian to have been involved in restoring and reissuing the Bee Gees' early catalog of music. I compiled deluxe editions of their first four albums for the Rhino label, as well as contributing work to some box sets and compilations. For me personally, the crowning achievement was my over-the-top (even by Stigwood standards) three-disc version of their "masterpeace" *Odessa*. To put this in perspective, I have worked on reissues of the Beach Boys' *Pet Sounds*, the Kinks' *Village Green Preservation Society* and Love's *Forever Changes*, and I consider *Odessa* to be among the finest albums of the 1960's.

I must admit, I made myself particularly unpopular with my workmates by pushing for this release for two years while it sat in industry limbo. I laid my career on the line for this music not because of its commercial potential, but rather due to my total belief in the Bee Gees as important creative artists. To my mind, they are by far the most underrated songwriting team to have emerged in the last hundred years. Their output is without equal in both quality and quantity; their gift for melody, seemingly endless.

Despite my devotion and one-of-a-kind perspective into the Bee Gees' music, this book is unauthorized. To be clear, I have not sought further input from the Gibbs or their families, nor is my book intended as a definitive statement on their careers as artists. Most artists have only one life; the Bee Gees have lived several and this is but one chapter. There are certainly volumes more to be written by and about the brothers Gibb. I hope you enjoy mine.

—Andrew Sandoval

FORWARD
by Bob Stanley

The Bee Gees and The Beach Boys were twinned in my head as a child. Not only did the names sound similar, but my Uncle Bill had made me a C90 with the UK-released *Beach Boys' Greatest Hits* on one side and *Best Of Bee Gees* on the other. This was formative stuff. In the music of mid-seventies Britain, there was precious little to excite me. This music from the past sounded a hell of a lot more mysterious and inspiring.

Although chance had paired the groups for me—even now, my two favorite groups in the whole pop canon—it did feel like they were two sides of a coin. While the Beach Boys seemed spring fresh, all about clear blue skies and optimism, the Bee Gees used minor chords and opulent, often oppressive arrangements. They sounded wood-paneled and baroque; this was indoor music and very little light got in. The sleeves of the two albums matched similarly—the Beach Boys' one was high-contrast black and white, as if the sun was so bright it had bleached out their features, but the Bee Gees cover was mustard brown on the front, while the back cover had a murky shot of them standing, unsmiling, on a boat with cloudy skies looming behind them. Unlike the friendlier Beach Boys, the Bee Gees' titles—such as "Every Christian Lion Hearted Man Will Show You" or "New York Mining Disaster 1941"—and their lyrics ("Millions of eyes can see, yet why am I so blind?") seemed dark and unknowable.

By the early eighties, there was a world of difference in the critical perception of the Beach Boys and Bee Gees. While the former had become mired in tragedy and disaster, their catalogue consequently much discussed and dissected, the Bee Gees had, unexpectedly, become the biggest—and then the most widely ridiculed—group in the world. Disco was their commercial making and their critical undoing (though anyone aware of their pre-disco work could easily detect its soulful melancholy in later compositions like "Reaching Out," "How Deep Is Your Love," "Until" or "Heartbreaker"). There was a fine David Leaf book—*Bee Gees: The Authorised Biography*—in 1979 but beyond that it was almost impossible to find any kind of serious discussion of the Gibbs' music. Eventually, by the mid-nineties, things started changing: their late seventies recordings were treated with due respect, and unlikely cheerleaders such as Oasis championed their sixties work.

Andrew Sandoval should be proud of his role in this critical re-evaluation. The book you're reading is the first in which anyone has delved into Barry, Robin and Maurice's music in such loving detail. Now we know that "Portrait Of Louise" from *2 Years On* was a "tribute to the Searchers"; that the intense "I'm Weeping" was written by Robin while he was, incongruously, holidaying in Madeira; and that, even after the thorough Reprise re-issues, there's still a wealth of unheard, unissued Gibb songs from their years in Britain. The titles are all here.

For years I felt privy to a secret world—my Uncle Bill had given me the key, and others were either too embarrassed or too snobbish to walk through the door, put off by the gloss and the high life of the Bee Gees' disco years. But the Gibbs have had more than their fair share of tragedy and disaster since their commercial high water mark; that we will never hear them perform together again is incredibly sad. What they have left us, though, is a catalog of songs almost unparalleled. Their reputation, justly, continues to grow, and it's something this book can only accelerate.

—Bob Stanley is a member of the group Saint Etienne and writes about music for the *Times Of London* and the *Guardian*.

1945

Newlyweds Hugh and Barbara Gibb (married May 27, 1944) move from Manchester, England to the Isle Of Man with their daughter Lesley (born January 12, 1945).

○ Sunday, August 18, 1945
Vince Melouney is born in Sydney, Australia.

1946

○ Sunday, March 24, 1946
Colin Petersen is born in Queensland, Australia.

○ Sunday, September 1, 1946
Barry Alan Crompton Gibb is born in Douglas on the Isle Of Man.

1949

○ Thursday, December 22, 1949
Twins Robin and Maurice Gibb are born in Douglas on the Isle Of Man.

1954

Colin Petersen, once a tap dancer in local variety shows, has now picked up on the drums and receives local recognition for his chops early on. This year he meets and plays for drumming legend Gene Krupa at Brisbane Airport.

1955

In January, the Gibb family returns to Manchester, England. Also this year, the boys start singing together and Barry will receive his first guitar for his birthday ("It was supposed to be a surprise," he will tell *Jackie* in March 1969, "but Mum let the cat out of the bag and told me beforehand and I had to act like it was a surprise when I got it"). Soon after, Barry begins writing his own songs, his earliest composition being "Turtle Dove."

"Barry didn't start writing songs until he was nine," Maurice tells Ken Sharp in 2000, "he started writing a few little things. Then Robin began to write and then me. I started writing songs when I was about eleven. I started getting involved because some of the chords they didn't know. The first instrument I learned to play was guitar. Then I went to bass. Then keyboards.

1956

Colin Petersen attends an open audition for youths applying to star in an upcoming motion picture. After being passed over at first glance, Colin returns to the auditions later and wins the lead in *Smiley*.

1957

Colin Petersen appears in the film, *Strange Affection* (also known as *The Scamp*).

○ Sunday, September 1, 1957
Barry Gibb is gifted a new guitar for his eleventh birthday.

○ December 1957
The Gibb brothers (calling themselves the Rattlesnakes and featuring Barry, Robin and Maurice, plus two of their chums: Paul Frost and Kenny Horrocks) sing live at a local cinema, the Gaumont in the Manchester suburb of Chorlton-cum-Hardy.

They had initially planned to mime to a record owned by the Gibbs' older sister, Lesley, but when the record breaks, they spontaneously busk through a performance regardless. In a 1968 *Fabulous* article, Barry says he played his new guitar and that his brothers had, "...their toy banjos, and we had a skiffle box-bass and no record to mime to."

"There was a record out at the time called 'Wake Up Little Susie' by the Everly Brothers and we thought we'd mime to that," Robin recalled to the *NME*'s Nick Logan in 1967. "We called ourselves the Rattlesnakes. The Saturday morning came, just before Christmas, and we were going up the stairs of the Gaumont when Barry dropped the record! It smashed. We thought: 'Great Everlys! What are we going to do?' Barry had a guitar, which he had taken along to help miming, and he suggested that we go out and really sing.

"So out we went and sang 'Lollipop' by the Mudlarks, and it went down well. We ended up doing five more, including 'That'll Be The Day,' 'Book Of Love' and 'Oh Boy'—and that was how the Bee Gees begun. Our next date was at the Walley Range Odeon, when Maurice and I added banjos."

In October 1967, Maurice offers an alternate version of the story to David Griffiths of *Record Mirror*: "We were supposed to be miming (that was the popular thing then) to a record of 'Young Love' by Tommy Steele. But the idiot in the projection booth dropped the disc and broke it. So we just went and sang the one song we knew—'Lollipop.'"

1958

The brothers Gibb (under various monikers and still with friends filling in) perform at a handful of venues in Manchester, England. In a 1968 *Fabulous* magazine article, Barry mentions, "...personal appearances at the Palatine Cinema, West Didsbury...we got a shilling each for our trouble—or sometimes sixpence."

"We did the Palentine [sic] Theater as Wee Johnnie Hayes and the Bluecats—Barry was Johnnie Hayes," remembered Robin in a 1967 *NME* interview. "We got 5 pounds a week for our act. This was in 1958 and we went on doing matinee performances for about two years."

Another Gibb brother, Andy, is born in March. In August, the whole brood sets sail aboard a ship called the Fairsea for Australia where father Hugh hopes to find better employment opportunities. "They entertained everybody on the boat going out," Hugh tells *Record Mirror* in 1969. "It was a tremendous success. They were only doing it for fun but everybody loved them." In 1967, Robin mentions to the *NME*'s Nick Logan: "We thought up the name the Bee Gees on the boat and also started writing our own material. We lived in Brisbane, where I went to secondary school, and after about a year started the group again." Meanwhile, Colin Petersen makes his final acting appearance of the decade in the film, *A Cry From The Streets*.

1959

In Australia, the Gibb brothers create an unusual gig for themselves selling sodas at a raceway. To entice thirsty spectators, the Gibbs will sing and draw attention to their wares. "We played the Speedway Circus in Brisbane and met a racing driver, Bill Goode, who introduced us to a DJ friend of his," Robin will tell the *NME*'s Nick Logan in 1967. "We did some tapes for his show. He played them and used to get a tremendous number of orders for them but they weren't released as records."

That DJ is Bill Gates, who tells *The Australian Women's Weekly* in 1967: "They had a unique sound even then. We bought them some new guitars and made some tapes for air play. This got them known initially, and then jobs followed in hotels...until problems with their ages arose. At early recording sessions the big problem was keeping the twins from wrecking the place. We'd spend the whole day just mucking around trying to get them organized. At one time we had three songs ready to tape and wanted another. We asked Barry if he had a song written and he replied: 'No, but I'll write one now.'"

Barry Gibb is perhaps the most gifted songwriter of his age group, composing songs with alacrity unequaled.

1960

Having made a name for themselves—the Bee Gees—on radio, the group make the leap to the small screen. "We got on television in Brisbane in 1960 with our show, *Cottie's Happy Hour*, and we got very big in Brisbane," recalled Robin to the *NME*'s Nick Logan in 1967. "The three of us played Surfers Paradise at the Beachcomber Hotel for six weeks, three shows a night."

- March 1960

In Australia, the Bee Gees (as they are now known) appear on television's *Anything Goes*.

- Wednesday, June 29, 1960

The Australian Women's Weekly features an article on the Bee Gees. "My boys have really got the show business bug," says Barbara Gibb in an interview conducted in the family's Cribb Island home. "I can't remember when the boys haven't been singing. On the boat coming to Australia, they entertained the passengers all the way."

"I like to make up the tunes I sing," says Barry. "I get the words from romance magazines and stories my sixteen-year-old sister, Lesley, reads." The paper notes that the brothers have a "make-believe television studio which they've built in their house." "We have a different script every day," says Maurice, "and we're always changing the floor plan and the sets around."

- Saturday, August 12, 1960

In Australia, the Bee Gees are seen on Australian television's *Strictly For Moderns*. "Barry A." is singled out as their leader, and they perform his original, "Time Is Passing."

- Monday, December 26, 1960

In Australia, the brothers open in a pantomime version of *Jack And The Beanstalk*.

1961

- September 1961

Barry quits school as the Gibb family relocates to Australia's Queensland Gold Coast. The Bee Gees are now gigging regularly and thus provide the family income, with father Hugh acting as manager.

1962

• September 1962
Barry makes contact with Col Joye, the first Australian rock and roll singer to have a #1 single nationwide. Joye's backing band, the Joy Boys, feature his brothers Kevin and Keith. Siblings Col and Kevin (whose real last name is Jacobsen), will create an entertainment empire down under. They take interest particularly in Barry's songwriting, and will soon pave the way for Barry's original compositions to be covered by other artists and eventually for the Bee Gees to become recording artists themselves via Australia's Festival Records. The Bee Gees will sign with Festival early in the New Year. "Kevin Jacobsen," writes Barry Gibb in *Fabulous* during 1968, "...*He* was a real top manager. Knew all the wrinkles and the short-cuts. Like getting us a five-year contract with Festival Records that very same day!"

1963

The Gibbs now reside in Sydney and the Bee Gees record for the Festival label imprint, Leedon. The ever-prolific Barry Gibb will compose songs for numerous other Festival releases and the brothers will often guest on other artists' records, a tradition that will carry on throughout their careers.

Meanwhile, Vince Melouney, who worked for two years as a clerk and studied accountancy, is now dedicated to the guitar. This year he forms an instrumental outfit called the Vibratones. Like the Bee Gees, the Vibratones will issue a single on the Leedon label, "Expressway" c/w "Man Of Mystery."

• Saturday, January 19, 1963
In Australia, the Bee Gees serve as openers for Chubby Checker at Sydney Stadium. Also on the bill are locals Johnny O'Keefe, the Dee Jays, the Joy Boys, Warren Williams, Judy Stone, Digger Revell and the Denvermen.

"Chubby was obviously going to close the show," Barry writes in *Fabulous* during 1968. "Johnny couldn't go on immediately before him, so we were thrown in right in the middle of them...Following Johnny O'Keefe was, in a show-business sense, just like having your throat cut. You had to be good, or you'd die a most horrible death! To us, it seemed like facing a firing-squad, but luckily our mixture of songs and comedy went well. We were new, which helped."

• Wednesday, February 13, 1963
In Australia, the Bee Gees appear on *Brian Henderson's Bandstand* performing "Alexander's Ragtime Band" and "My Old Man's A Dustman." This program is telecast in Australia via TCN channel 9.

• Wednesday, March 13, 1963
The Australian Women's Weekly features an article heralding that the trio's first single—"The Battle Of The Blue And Grey" c/w "The Three Kisses Of Love"—is about to be issued by Leedon. The article says the Joy Boys back them and leader Col Joye is considering recording one of Barry Gibb's songs. At home, the brothers are shutter bugs and have used their movie camera and projector to create a "Goon-styled" version of *The African Queen*. Their next home movie project is a horror film.

"We started making records," Barry wrote in a 1968 issue of Fabulous. "First one was 'The Battle Of The Blue And Grey,' but nobody seemed to care who won the battle, and the only plays we got were of the flip, 'Three Kisses Of Love.'"

• April 1963
Col Joye will issue one of Barry's songs—"(Underneath The) Starlight Of Love"—on the B-side of his latest single: "Put 'Em Down." On April 14th, *The Sydney Morning Herald* notes this is one of several new releases employing Festival's upgraded microphones, tape recorders, limiters and "frequency-benders."

• Wednesday, April 24, 1963
In Australia, the Bee Gees appear on *Brian Henderson's Bandstand* performing both sides of their debut release, "The Battle Of The Blue And Grey" and "Three Kisses Of Love" (plus a brief interview).

• Wednesday, May 15, 1963
The Australian Women's Weekly notes that the since moving from Brisbane to Sydney, the Bee Gees have appeared on such television shows as *Bandstand, Sing Sing Sing* and *Saturday Date*. They plan to visit Adelaide soon for more television and personal appearances.

• Thursday, June 6, 1963
In Australia, the trio tapes an appearance on *Brian Henderson's Bandstand* television program performing the Beatles' "Please Please Me" and "Little Band Of Gold." This program will be telecast on June 8th.

• July 1963
A second Bee Gees single—an upbeat stormer named "Timber!" backed with the country-tinged "Take A Hold Of That Star"—is released. Both songs are Barry Gibb originals. The Gibbs also sing impromptu backing vocals on Judy Stone's new single, "It Takes A Lot (To Make Me Cry)."

• Saturday, July 6, 1963
In Australia, the Bee Gees appear on Johnny O'Keefe's television show, *Sing Sing Sing* (seen on ATN channel 7).

The Bee Gees — ~~Barry~~ Robin, Maurice

BIOGRAPHICAL LIFE LINES OF FESTIVAL ARTISTS

Phone No — 752023.

Please complete the following questions carefully, and keep in mind that the information will be used for publicity and other purposes.

FULL NAME... Barry Gibb
STAGE NAME... Bee Gees
PRESENT ADDRESS... 25 ~~Colter~~ Colin St Lakemba
DATE OF BIRTH... 1st Sept 1945   PLACE OF BIRTH... Isle of Man, ~~Eng~~ U.K.
HEIGHT... 5'11"   WEIGHT... 10½ Stone   STANDARD OF EDUCATION... —
SCHOOL... Scarborough Qld/Eng   MOTHERS NAME... Barbara
FATHERS NAME... Hugh   OCCUPATION... Manager of Bee Gees
BROTHERS NAME... Andrew (youngest) + twins Robin + Maurice
SISTERS NAME... Lesley
HOBBIES... Swimming, Football, Water Skiing, Music
T.V. APPEARANCES... Everyone, School BTQ 7 Qld, Brisbane Tonight BTQ 9, Teen Beat BTQ 9, Des Foster Show TCN 9 Sydney, Bandstand TCN 9.
LIVE SHOWS... Stadium Appearances Wel Wheatley, Chubby Checker, Sydney + Brisbane. See Attached White Sheet
HOW DID YOU FIRST START IN THIS FIELD... 11 years ago in England doing Colored Carnival etc. After coming to Aust have 2 contacts with 4BH's Bill Gates who put them on the Road to Stardom.

DO YOU PLAY A MUSICAL INSTRUMENT... Guitar (Barry)
DO YOU COMPOSE... Yes
FAVOURITE LIKES... Tomato Sauce on all foods but ~~not cake~~, 8MM Cine Tape Movies. He makes them.
YOUR AMBITION... To last the Twice as long as Elvis does, to go to USA.
WHAT DO YOU DO FOR RELAXATION... Have a Swim — song writing

ANY FURTHER COMMENTS... Bar, Maurice + Robin are twins and are 14 yrs of age. Robin is 30 mins older than Maurice G

1963

● August 1963
Lonnie Lee & The Leemen issue Barry's song, "I'd Like To Leave If I May," as the flipside of their Leedon label single, "Acres Of Everything But Love."

● Saturday, August 3, 1963
In Australia, the Bee Gees appear on a "western themed" episode of Johnny O'Keefe's television show, *Sing Sing Sing* (seen on ATN channel 7).

● Wednesday, August 7, 1963
The Australian Women's Weekly features a recent photo of the Bee Gees meeting their idols, the Mills Brothers. The venerable vocal group visited Sydney last month for three weeks and encountered the Gibbs at that time.

● Friday, August 16, 1963
In Australia, the Bee Gees tape an appearance for *Brian Henderson's Bandstand* singing "Take Hold Of That Star" and Bob Dylan's "Blowin' In The Wind" (as well as telling some "wind-up doll" jokes). This episode will be telecast on August 19th.

● September 1963
Barry Gibb copyrights a group of new songs—"Breaking Up A Darn Good Thing"; "Here She Comes"; "True True Love"— of which recordings have yet to surface.

● Monday, September 2, 1963
In Australia, the Bee Gees tape an appearance for *Brian Henderson's Bandstand* singing "I Want You To Want Me" and "Hilly Billy Ding Dong Choo Choo" (as well as telling a further set of "wind-up doll" jokes). This program is telecast on September 7th.

● October 1963
A busy month of television and recording dates include the brothers singing backgrounds on Johnny Devlin's single, "Stomp The Tumbarumba" which becomes a local hit. Meanwhile, Tony Brady collaborates with Barry Gibb on his latest single for Australian RCA: "Let's Stomp, Australia Way" c/w "Lucky Me."

● Saturday, October 12, 1963
In the United States, *Billboard* magazine reports that Barry Gibb has signed an exclusive songwriting contract with Belinda Music in Australia.

● Saturday, October 19, 1963
The trio appears on *Brian Henderson's Bandstand* television program performing covers of the Crystals' hit "Da Doo Ron Ron" and the Searchers' smash "Sweets For My Sweet."

● Saturday, October 26, 1963
In Australia, the Bee Gees appear on another episode of Johnny O'Keefe's television show, *Sing Sing Sing* (seen on ATN channel 7).

● November 1963
As the Bee Gees' career as singers and Barry's songwriting catches fire, Noelene Batley records a new Barry Gibb song, "Surfer Boy," which is released as the flipside to her latest single, "Forgive Me," on Festival. In the studio, the trio record backing vocals on four tracks—"Beach Ball"; "You Gotta Have Love"; "You Make Me Happy"; "Hokey Pokey"—eventually issued by Jimmy Hannan in Australia and later in the United States on Atlantic Records (coincidentally a label that will go on to have a strong association with the Bee Gees).

● Saturday, December 21, 1963
In Australia, the Bee Gees appear on the Christmas edition of Johnny O'Keefe's television show, *Sing Sing Sing*.

● Thursday, December 26, 1963
According to *The Australian Women's Weekly*, the Bee Gees open a month long residency at a Sydney nightclub-restaurant today. Their act is said to include comedy numbers and a new arrangement of "Alexander's Ragtime Band."

1964

Vince Melouney's Vibratones have split, paving the way for a new band, the Aztecs. Their first single release—"Smoke Stack" c/w Vince's own "Board Boogie"—is issued by Leedon. By the end of the year, the Aztecs switch from purely instrumentals to having a lead vocalist. They will begin recording and performing with Billy Thorpe (a former child actor born in Manchester, England), and as Billy Thorpe & The Aztecs will become a huge chart success with their second disc together, "Poison Ivy." Vince will adopt a secondary spelling of his surname: Maloney.

- January 1964

In Australia, Barry copyrights two new compositions: "Boy On The Board" and "Run Right Back." Recordings of these tunes have yet to surface, though singer Del Juliana will tape an unissued rendition of "Boy On The Board."

- February 1964

A third single by The Bee Gees—the Mersey-sounding "Peace Of Mind" and the quaint "Don't Say Goodbye"—is issued on Leedon. Also on release this month is "One Road," a single performed by Jimmy Little and penned by Barry. It will become Barry's first Top 10 Australian hit as a songwriter. *The Australian Women's Weekly* (in their February 12th edition) says that Barry composed the song in just two days. Jimmy Little will also cover Barry's "Walkin' Talkin' Teardrop" (issued on his Festival album, *New Songs From Jimmy*).

- March 1964

In Australia, Barry copyrights a new composition, "One Little Blue," though a recording has yet to surface of this song. Also this month, the Bee Gees provide background vocals to a single by Jimmy Hannan: "You Make Me Happy" c/w "Hokey Pokey Stomp."

- Sunday, March 1, 1964

In Australia, the Bee Gees return for another spot on Johnny O'Keefe's television show, *Sing Sing Sing*. Of particular note, another of this episode's guests is Trevor Gordon who, like the Gibbs, is a regular on the music television scene. Trevor is already a family friend, making home movies with the boys (see March 26th & May 27th). Trevor is also a recording artist and will make discs alongside the trio next year and again later in the 1960's.

- Thursday, March 26, 1964

Australian Cashbox writes: "To fill in their leisure hours the Bee Gees have developed a keen interest in amateur movie photography and have purchased all the necessary equipment, brand new, to get the best professional results. They were recently spotted on Bronte Beach complete with two cameras, taking surf shots and beach scenes with Little Pattie and Trevor Gordon as the leading stars." In the same issue, "Peace Of Mind" charts at #52 on the *Cashbox* Big 100 Singles Chart (it was #56 last week) showing that the Bee Gees' latest is getting some play.

- Friday, April 17, 1964

In Australia, Reg Lindsay records Barry's "Scared Of Losing You."

- May 1964

According to a later article in *The Australian Women's Weekly*, the Bee Gees appear this month on QTQ9's television show *Teen Beat* performing "Peace Of Mind."

- Wednesday, May 27, 1964

Jimmy Hannan's "Disc Date" column in *Everybody's* notes: "The Bee Gees are getting very sophisticated about their filmmaking. They have advanced from casual beach shots to a horror film which will be called *The House on the Hill*. Maurice of the Bee Gees is filming it and the cast features the young vocalist Trevor Gordon, John Laws' panel operator at 2GB."

- June 1964

In Australia, the Bee Gees record a set of covers at Festival Studios to be utilized in their now copious television appearances (in this case for Johnny O'Keefe's *Sing Sing Sing*). These include the Dave Clark Five's "Can't You See That She's Mine," the Beatles' "From Me To You," Chad & Jeremy's "Yesterday's Gone," the Hollies' hit of "Just One Look," and George Hamilton IV's final US pop chart hit, "Abilene." The recordings are later found on acetate discs at a garage sale and salvaged for the 1998 release, *Brilliant From Birth* (except "Abilene" which survives, but remains unissued).

Also this month, Johnny Devlin, one of the support acts on the current Beatles tour of Australia, issues a single of covers—

"Blue Suede Shoes" c/w "Whole Lotta Shakin' Going On"—with the Bee Gees singing backgrounds on both sides. Devlin also works with singer Del Juliana on her renditions of Barry's "surfie" sounding "Never Like This" and "Boy On The Board."

• Sunday, June 21, 1964
In Australia, the Bee Gees appear on another episode of Johnny O'Keefe's television show, *Sing Sing Sing* (seen on ATN channel 7) no doubt utilizing some of their recently recorded cover songs.

• August 1964
A fourth Bee Gees single—the Joe Meek-tinged "Claustrophobia" backed with a fine beat number, "Could It Be"—is released to little response. In the August 26th edition of *The Australian Women's Weekly*, the magazine notes that backing on this disc is provided by the Delawares (who hail from Wollongong, N.S.W. but are now in Sydney "attempting to hit the big time").

• Sunday, August 9, 1964
The *Sydney Morning Herald* interviews Vince Maloney (nee Melouney) on the overwhelming success of his group, Billy Thorpe and the Aztecs. "Sometimes it is frightening," says Vince. "There'd be only four bouncers controlling a crowd of 2,000—we knew if they mobbed us we wouldn't have a chance. And the equipment is so expensive we're always worried it will get damaged." Over the past six months, the group has reached the height of Australian success. They've recently toured the country with Screaming Lord Sutch and hope to join him on a jaunt through the United States.

• Friday, August 14, 1964
In Australia, the Bee Gees appear on another episode of Johnny O'Keefe's television show, *Sing Sing Sing* alongside Bryan Davies and Noeleen Batley (both of whom will record Gibb numbers).

• September 1964
Music Maker profiles the trio. "At their present home in Lakemba, a suburb of Sydney, they have a studio under the house, and it is there that they practice and compose songs. For hobbies the boys go swimming, play football, collect records and perhaps, the most unusual of all, is their special pastime of making 8mm 'Goon type' movies—of which the three take part in acting." The magazine further notes the "Bee Gee's [sic] main ambition is to last in popularity as long as the Mills Brothers, and to tour the United States."

Also this month, Barry copyrights a group of new compositions: "I'll Be There"; "My Girl"; "Now Comes The Pain"; "When A Girl Cries." Recordings of these songs have yet to surface.

• Sunday, September 6, 1964
The Bee Gees appear on an Australian version of the British television program, *Thank Your Lucky Stars* performing "Claustrophobia." This episode telecast on ATN channel 7 and hosted by John Bailey will also include the Hollies, the Dave Clark Five, Peter's Faces and Helen Shapiro.

• Friday, September 25, 1964
In Australia, the Bee Gees appear on another episode of Johnny O'Keefe's television show, *Sing Sing Sing* alongside their friends Bryan Davies and Little Pattie. Davies forthcoming single is penned by Barry (see October 1964).

• October 1964
Since their original single releases have failed to make any major chart impact, the trio issues a coupling of cover songs as their next Leedon 45 under the moniker, Barry Gibb And The Bee Gees. "Turn Around, Look At Me" was previously a minor hit for Glen Campbell and "Theme From The Travels Of Jamie McPheeters" was cut by another family group, The Osmonds, who feature in the titular television show. Like their prior releases, this single will meet with little commercial interest.

Also this month, Bryan Davies issues two unique Barry Gibb originals as a single on HMV—"I Don't Like To Be Alone" c/w "Love And Money"—and the ever prolific Barry copyrights a group of new compositions: "In The Middle Of A Dream"; "Leave The Lovin' To The Boy"; "Since I Lost You"; and "This Is The End." However, recordings of these songs have yet to surface.

• Saturday, October 31, 1964
In Australia, the Bee Gees appear on a television program titled *Surf Sound* alongside Noeleen Batley.

1964 • 1965

• **November 1964**
Barry copyrights a group of new compositions—"Boy With A Broken Heart"; "Hey Jennie"; "I Love"; "Mr. Mod Man"; "My Baby Can"; "The One That I Love"; and "You Were Made For Me"—though recordings of these songs have yet to surface.

• **Sunday, November 8, 1964**
The Bee Gees appear for a second time on the Australian version of *Thank Your Lucky Stars* (broadcast by ATN channel 7) to perform their latest single, "Turn Around, Look At Me." This episode hosted by John Bailey will also include the Rolling Stones, Matt Monro, the Roulettes, the Honeycombs, Dave Nelson and the Mojos.

1965

Despite phenomenal success in Australia, Vince Melouney will leave Billy Thorpe & The Aztecs this year to do his own thing. He will become a session guitarist on disc dates and perform in a succession of groups such as Vince & Tony's Two and Tony Worsley & The Fabulous Blue Jays.

Meanwhile, former child actor Colin Petersen joins the group Steve & The Board. The group will record for the Spin label, and Colin will soon find himself socializing with the Gibbs and eventually drumming on some of their recordings. "We originally met in Sydney," Colin will tell *Record Mirror* in 1969. "...I moved to Melbourne with my group but used to fly to Sydney for sessions with them. That's quite a distance—over 600 miles. I used to be out-of-pocket, but I did it out of friendship."

• **January 1965**
Leedon issues a single by Trevor Gordon And The Bee Gees: "House Without Windows" c/w "And I'll Be Happy." Both sides are composed by Barry, while the Bee Gees as a group back Trevor both vocally and instrumentally. Trevor will later form Marbles with Graham Bonnet, and receive further backing from the Bee Gees in the UK during 1968 and 1969.

• **Wednesday, January 27, 1965**
The Australian Women's Weekly publishes an article on Noeleen Batley noting that she will release a new single soon written for her by Barry Gibb.

• **February 1965**
Australian HMV issues another single by Bryan Davies featuring the Barry Gibb composition "Watch What You Say."

• **Friday, February 5, 1965**
In Australia, the Bee Gees are back on Johnny O'Keefe's television show, *Sing Sing Sing*.

• **Monday, February 8, 1965**
The Sydney Morning Herald reports that Vince's current group, Billy Thorpe and the Aztecs, have cut their long hair. Their most recent disc, "Over The Rainbow," hit the top of the charts and sold twenty-thousand copies in the first two weeks of release. Vince will soon depart this unit to form a duo with fellow former-Aztec, Tony Barber.

• **March 1965**
Barry Gibb And The Bee Gees' latest single is a cover of Arthur Alexander's "Every Day I Have To Cry" (which was also a minor hit for Steve Alaimo in January 1963 and more recently covered on an EP in 1964 by Dusty Springfield). The flipside is Barry's "You Wouldn't Know," which features some inspired chord changes and a sound moving ever closer to Beatlesque. The record is a miss, but stylistically the group is now on the right track.

• **Sunday, March 7, 1965**
The Sydney Morning Herald reports that one side of Noeleen Batley's next single—"Baby, I'm Losing You"—is penned by Barry.

• **April 1965**
A second single cut with Trevor Gordon (this time billed solo)— "Little Miss Rhythm And Blues" c/w "Here I Am"—shows that Barry has found his songwriting mojo. Further proof comes from the Stateside release of Barry's first international cover, "They'll Never Know," cut by Wayne Newton for a Capitol label album (*Red Roses For A Blue Lady*). Also this month, Bryan Davies issues a fourth Barry Gibb-penned single, "I Should Have Stayed In Bed."

Barry: "We felt we were getting better and better at what we were doing. But you know, when you haven't made it, you just think, 'Well, maybe they'll like this one or maybe they'll like this one.' So, you're always up against that establishment whether or not you're going to make it, or not. So there was that youthful inexperience: 'Well let's try another song, let's do this one, let's try that one.' I think we were just learning how to make records. It was a little more than just writing and recording. It was, 'How do we make these things really come to life?' We were fired up by the Beatles if not ourselves."

• **Friday, April 9, 1965**
In Australia, the Bee Gees appear on another episode of Johnny O'Keefe's television show, *Sing Sing Sing* alongside their friends Del Juliana, Bryan Davies and Trevor Gordon.

• **May 1965**
Jimmy Boyd issues a cover of Barry's "That's What I'll Give To You" in the United States on the Vee Jay label. The song was discovered by producer Terry Melcher during a recent trip to Australia. Terry is one-half of the surf duo Bruce & Terry, and soon to be better known as producer of the Byrds and Paul Revere & The Raiders.

• June 1965
Tony Brady issues the Barry Gibb song "I Will Love You" as an A-side on Australian Parlophone, while Michelle Rae issues a double-sided Barry-penned country single—"I Wanna Tell The World" c/w "Everybody's Talkin'"—for Leedon. The Bee Gees make a vocal appearance on the B-side, "Everybody's Talkin'."

• Monday, June 14, 1965
In Sydney, the Bee Gees perform in a country and western themed concert at Smoky Dawson's ranch at Terrey Hills. This afternoon charity event, in aid of the Children's Medical Research Foundation, is to include an appearance from James Drury, star of television's The Virginian, as well as the Gibbs' chum, Trevor Gordon.

• July 1965
Another child star of the Australian television scene, ten-year-old Sydney schoolgirl Jenny Bradley, issues a novelty single penned by Barry—"Who's Been Writing On The Wall Again" c/w "Chubby"—on the Leedon label. Unfortunately for Jenny, who had a hit last year with "Everything's Coming Up Roses," this disc is a miss and her television work will ebb. "Who's Been Writing On The Wall" will, however, be revived in late 1966 by Lori (see January 11, 1967).

• August 1965
Meeting the producer (and later arranger) who will change their sound forever, Bill Shepherd, the boys find new ways of working in the studio. In September, they will make a bigger dent in the Australian charts with their single "Wine And Women" c/w "Follow The Wind." Bill Shepherd is a regular on Australian radio during 1965 with his Bill Shepherd Singers ensemble.

Robin: "Bill Shepherd was a producer that came from England in '64 and produced a lot of big hits in Australia for other artists on Festival Records. We met Bill through this because he ended producing some songs for us. What we didn't realize at the time, was that he was a great musical arranger, a musician in his own right. I still think he is one of the best musical arrangers that ever lived."

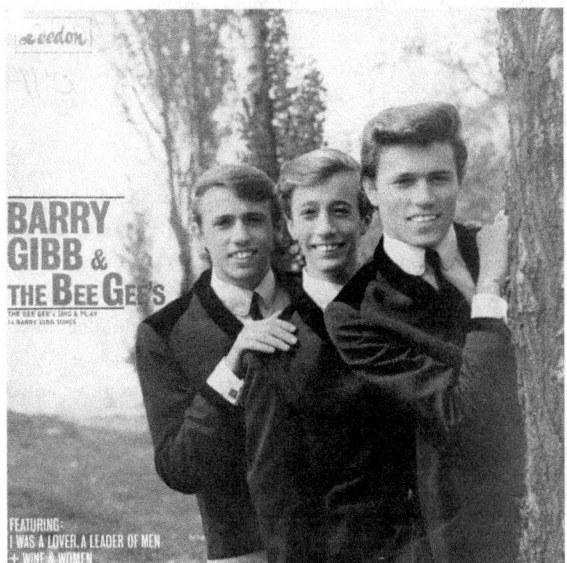

• Sunday, August 29, 1965
The Sydney Morning Herald reports that the Bee Gees had a car accident on their way home from Goulburn the other night. Luckily no one was hurt and now "Wine And Women" looks like it is on its way to "being their first record to make the charts."

• Wednesday, September 1, 1965
Maggie Makeig's Australian Beat column in Everybody's reports: "The Bee Gees have joined the Jacobsen outfit and they set off on September 4 for a Queensland tour with Col Joye and The Joy Boys, Sandy Scott and Little Pattie. The Bee Gees are doing nicely with 'Wine and Women' and the flip side 'Follow The Wind,' is the song Bee Gee Barry Gibb was asked to write for The Seekers. But the boys decided the number might collect too much dust before it finally came out, so they used it themselves."

1966 o 1966

o October 1965
With the success of "Wine And Women," the Bee Gees and Bill Shepherd are given studio time to work on new material. In addition to taping their next single, the Bee Gees put down three new Barry Gibb numbers: "I Don't Think It's Funny," "How Love Was True" and "To Be Or Not To Be." All of these will turn up next month on the Bee Gees' first Leedon album.

Meanwhile, Dennis And The Delawares issue a double-sided, Barry-penned release: "Bad Girl" c/w "They Say." Also this month, Noeleen Batley issues Barry's "Watching The Hours Go By," with background support from the brothers. This disc also carries Barry's first-ever credit as a record producer.

o November 1965
A quick follow-up single—"I Was A Lover, A Leader Of Men" (a virtual knock-off of "Wine And Women") coupled with the P.F. Sloan-styled "And The Children Laughing"—does little to boost the Bee Gees' popularity. However, it does hasten the release of their first-ever long-player: *The Bee Gee's [sic] Sing & Play 14 Barry Gibb Songs* (issued at the end of the month).

o Monday, November 22, 1965
The Sydney Morning Herald reports that the first single by Steve and the Board (featuring Colin Petersen on the drums)—"Giggle Eyed Goo" c/w "Rosalyn"—is issued today by the Spin label. Nat Kipner's son, Steve, is the leader of the band. Steve will later work extensively with Maurice when he forms Tin Tin (with Steve Groves) in 1969. Steve & The Board guitarist, Carl Keats (a.k.a. Carl Groszman), will also work with both Colin and Maurice at the end of the 1960's.

o December 1965
Lynne Fletcher issues a cover of Barry's "You Do Your Loving With Me" on Australian HMV.

o Wednesday, December 8, 1965
Everybody's reviews the Bee Gees' debut album: "Barry Gibb, long acknowledged as one of Australia's best songwriters, and his two brothers Maurice and Robin, make up the Bee Gees. As a trio they have hovered around the fringe of the top for a long time but never quite made it on record. Their first LP features tremendous arrangements, expert musicianship, a wealth of dubbing, and their latest single, 'I Was A Lover, A Leader Of Men.' It's a good sound marred by the fact that the lyrics are hard to understand. I prefer the tracks where the Bee Gees take solos and the message is clear."

o Saturday, December 18, 1965
In Australia, the Bee Gees are seen on television's *Brian Henderson's Bandstand* singing their recent singles "Wine And Women" and "I Was A Lover, A Leader Of Men."

1966

o March 1966
Having lost producer Bill Shepherd (who returns to his native UK, but will regroup with the brothers in March 1967), the trio's first release of '66 is the folkie lament, "Cherry Red," backed by the fuzz-laden "I Want Home." When this single flops, it also becomes their last release for Leedon. Hugh Gibb moves his boys to Nat Kipner's Spin label (which is still distributed by Festival). Kipner will introduce the Bee Gees to Ossie Byrne and his St. Clair Recording Studio (56 Queens Rd. Hurstville, Sydney). St. Clair is predominately used for audition tapes and demo discs, as well as advertising "special attention to original material workouts."

When the Bee Gees begin recording at St. Clair with Byrne they become true studio rats, barely leaving to make personal appearances.

Robin: "Ossie was a vital part of that team. He'd spend many hours of his time with us exploring those avenues we wanted to go down. He gave up all his studio time, and gave it to us. We were in there twenty-four-hours-a-day.

"We were trying ideas out, as opposed to making records. We were actually investigating styles. We were being influenced by what we were hearing in the UK and American charts. And we were taking not our style as a band, but more of our styles as songwriters. We were trying them out on different songs. So, in that way, that was invaluable to us."

o Sunday, March 20, 1966
The Sydney Morning Herald reports that former Aztec, Vince Maloney, has formed a new group, the Vince Maloney Sect.

● Monday, March 21, 1966
The Kommotion label issues the first disc by the Vince Maloney Sect: "She's A Yum Yum" c/w "No Good Without You."

● Saturday, March 26, 1966
In Sydney, the Vince Maloney Sect makes their concert debut.

● Monday, March 28, 1966
The Bee Gees fly to Melbourne to make the first of two appearances on Melbourne's highly successful teenage music program, *The Go!! Show*, hosted by Ian Turpie. Also appearing on this episode are The Strangers, Bobby & Laurie, The Five, Colin Cook, Two Much, Yvonne Barrett and Billy Adams.

● April 1966
Barry copyrights two new songs—"House On The Windy Hill" and "Listen To Your Heart"—though recordings of these have yet to surface. The Bee Gees will, however, begin stockpiling recordings around this time for future release such as Barry's "How Many Birds"; "Playdown"; "Second Hand People"; "Big Chance"; and "Born A Man."

Also around this time, Barry and Robin begin their songwriting collaboration with the songs "Tint Of Blue" and "Glass House." Meanwhile, Robin composes "I Don't Know Why I Bother With Myself" solo and Maurice contributes the Beatle-y "Where Are You." Most of these recordings turn up on the Bee Gees' second long player, *Spicks And Specks*, issued at year's end.

● Sunday, April 17, 1966
In Australia, the Bee Gees appear on Billy Thorpe's new television show: *It's All Happening*.

● Tuesday, April 19, 1966
In Australia, Vince Maloney and The Sect appear in Melbourne on a promotional tour for the television program, *Kommotion*.

● May 1966
In Australia, the Bee Gees' first release on Spin—the Righteous Brothers-like "Monday's Rain" with Robin singing lead in a low register, and the Beatlesque "All Of My Life"—is issued to only minor response. Meanwhile, the Richard Wright Group issue Barry's "Neither Rich Nor Poor" as one side of their Australian HMV single this month.

● Friday, May 13, 1966
The Bee Gees fly to Adelaide to appear on the city's premier teenage music program, *Action*, hosted by 'Big' Bob Francis. Also appearing on this installment are Silhouettes, The Sevens, Trevor Pridham, Sheridan Walshe, Tony Worsley, and Marty Rhone.

● Friday, June 24, 1966
Masters for an album called *Monday's Rain* are assembled today at St. Clair Recording Studio. The LP will be temporarily shelved when the single of "Monday's Rain" fails to excite record buyers. Other recordings in the can from this period include Barry's "Exit, Stage Right," "Like Nobody Else," "Top Hat," "Coalman" and "Morning Of My Life" (as well as Maurice's "All By Myself" and Robin's "Lum-De-Loo").

Also during this period, the brothers pen and record their first ever three-way collaborations: "The Storm," "Butterfly," "Terrible Way To Treat Your Baby," "I'll Know What To Do" and "Forever." Another recording from this era is a cover of "Lonely Winter," composed by Carl Keats nee Groszman of Steve and the Board. All of these tracks will mysteriously surface in 1970 on a two-album set titled *Inception/Nostalgia* (issued in Germany and France, and later in Japan).

● Sunday, June 12, 1966
In Australia, the Bee Gees appear once again on Billy Thorpe's *It's All Happening* television program (alongside such artists as Warren Williams, The Allusions, Marlene Atcheson, and Gigi Galon).

● July 1966
The Bee Gees are constantly recording at St. Clair, sometimes to create masters, often to create new demos, and occasionally just for fun. Another batch of recordings from this era includes covers of the Beatles' "If I Needed Someone," "Paperback Writer," "Ticket To Ride" and "You Won't See Me" as well as the Lovin' Spoonful's "Daydream." These tracks will also appear in 1970 on *Inception/Nostalgia*.

An altogether different set of covers—"The End"; "Hallelujah I Love Her So"; "I Love You Because"; "Somewhere"; "The Twelfth Of Never"; "You're The Reason I'm Living"; and

1966

"You're Nobody Till Somebody Loves You"—with the brothers taking on middle of the road classics and country also turn up on *Inception/Nostalgia*. However, it is harder to pin down the specific origins and timing of this group of recordings.

Barry recalled these oddities in 2006: "In fact we found some full orchestra tracks with things like 'Somewhere,' 'Twelfth Of Never' and we didn't even cut the track, we just sang on them. Robin went and did 'Somewhere,' I did a version of 'Somewhere' but that got lost. Then I did "Twelfth Of Never.' I think we were just learning how to make records. It was a little more than just writing and recording. It was, 'How do we make these things really come to life?'"

- Sunday, July 17, 1966
The Sydney Morning Herald reports that the Vince Maloney Sect has split.

- August 1966
The Bee Gees guest on M.P.D. Limited's single "Absence Makes The Heart Grow Fonder" c/w "I Am What I Am" (issued in both Australia and Germany).

- Wednesday, August 3, 1966
Bob Staines, Melbourne correspondent in *Everybody's* mentions his shock to read that Sydney radio stations are not playing the Bee Gees' new single "Monday's Rain." "'Not original enough,' they said. But a quick check in Melbourne also revealed only one radio station here (3KZ) was playing it."

- Saturday, August 13, 1966
Billboard magazine reports that Barry Gibb has received the Gold Award for best Australian composition in a ceremony held at Adelaide's Hotel Australia. The awards were selected by a panel consisting of 5KA management, executives and disc jockeys from all Australian record releases up to May 31st. An item on the award in *Billboard's* August 27th issue refers to Barry as Belinda Music Publishing's "leading contract writer."

- Monday, August 22, 1966
Barry Gibb marries Maureen Bates.

- September 1966
A second Spin single—the highly original "Spicks And Specks" and their first real foray into an orchestral pop style (though it features only a horn), "I Am The World"—gives the boys some much-needed exposure and will ultimately click as a hit.

- Thursday, September 1, 1966
The Bee Gees perform at Sydney Town Hall for members of the Young Australia Club (alongside such acts as Vince Maloney—now solo, the Throb, Dinah Lee, Christine Roberts, as well as Kevin Todd and the Soul Agents).

- Sunday, September 4, 1966
The Sydney Morning Herald reports that sixteen-year-old Annie Shelton has her first disc out this week featuring songs written by Maurice and Barry with help from Nat Kipner (though the single, "Talk To Me" and "I Miss You," will feature only Maurice, Nat and Ossie Byrne's names as writers). The paper also notes that, "Maurice Gibb with Nat Kipner wrote the new Mystics' single 'Don't You Go, I Need Your Love.'"

Both singles are issued by the Down Under label, whose two prior releases were similarly Gibb related. Bip Addison's Down Under 45 features "Hey" c/w "Young Man's Fancy" (both sides penned by Maurice with Nat Kipner). Meanwhile, Sandy Summers' release for the imprint included "Messin' Around" (written by Maurice with Nat Kipner), backed by Barry's "A Girl Needs To Love."

- Sunday, September 25, 1966
The Sydney Morning Herald reports that Vince Maloney's first solo single is now available: "I Need Your Lovin' Tonight" c/w "Mystery Train." Like the Sect single, it is issued via Kommotion. The single will fail commercially, but is produced by Nat Kipner and features the Bee Gees on vocal backgrounds providing an essential link to their joint work. Vince will become an integral part of the brothers' next musical stage in London during March 1967.

• October 1966

The Bee Gees guest on yet another release from the Down Under label, a record by April Byron: "He's A Thief" (written by Maurice with Nat Kipner) c/w "A Long Time Ago" (composed by Barry). April, a teenage singer who is said to look like Elizabeth Taylor, claims also to share Ms. Taylor's distant relation, the poet Lord Byron.

The Gibbs also lend their voices to Ray Brown And The Whispers' "Too Late To Come Home" single issued by Festival this month. Meanwhile, Maurice co-produces (with Tony Barber) a single by Denise Drysdale—"Sunshine Shadows" c/w "Rescue Me"—on the Phono Vox of Australia label.

• Wednesday, October 12, 1966

The Bee Gees appear on the Australian ABC television program *Be Our Guest* (alongside singer Ray Brown and dancer Anita Ardell).

• Friday, October 21, 1966

In Crowulla, Vince Melouney marries Dianne Mitchell. Following the nuptials, Vince will move to London.

• Saturday, October 29, 1966

In Australia, the Bee Gees appear on television's *Go!!* show alongside host Johnny Young (who will record with the Gibbs in 1967).

• November 1966

In Australia, Steve and the Board issue their own version of Barry's "Little Miss Rhythm And Blues" on their LP, *The Giggle Eyed Goo*. This year, their drummer Colin Petersen recorded three singles with the group, as well as participating in several Bee Gees sessions (as drummer). Colin will soon decide to move to England to get back into acting. Before he leaves the continent, he will visit the Gibbs and lay the ground work for a reunion in the New Year. His replacement in Steve and the Board will be Geoff Bridgford, another drummer who will work with the Bee Gees later in the decade.

• Sunday, November 6, 1966

In Australia, the Bee Gees appear again on Billy Thorpe's live television show *It's All Happening* performing live renditions of "Spicks And Specks" and The Rolling Stones' "Out Of Time." Also appearing in this episode are Sylvia Raye, Ian Turpie, Jeff St John & The Id, Bobby Day, Tony and Royce, The Kinetics, and Ross Coleman.

• Wednesday, November 9, 1966

Today's issue of *Everybody's* features Bob Staines' column In Touch With Melbourne in which Staines notes: "The Bee Gees just can't crack it in Melbourne. Their latest effort 'Spicks and Specks,' a brilliantly produced number, is not taking off the way it deserves in Melbourne. It scraped into the 3UZ Top 40 at 39, lasted one week only, then faded out. And yet it soared to the top in Sydney. Why? If you can pin point the trouble please write to me."

• Saturday, November 19, 1966

The trio appears in a specially filmed insert on *Brian Henderson's Bandstand* program in Australia performing "Spicks And Specks" (at Bankstown Airport in southwest Sydney). Also this month, the shelved *Monday's Rain* LP is rebranded as *Spicks And Specks* and sent into record shops (the only actual musical change is "Spicks And Specks" replacing "All Of My Life" as the side two opener).

• Friday, November 25, 1966

Hugh Gibb writes to Brian Epstein's NEMS enterprises management agency informing the company that the Bee Gees are planning a trip to London and are seeking representation.

• December 1966

Singer Ronnie Burns hits with a double-sided Bee Gees-penned and performed single—"Coalman" c/w "All The King's Horses"—on the Spin label. The Twilights cover Barry's "Long Life" on their eponymous EMI/Columbia label debut album. The Bee Gees provide vocal backgrounds on one side of a single by Vyt—"Why Do I Cry"—issued by Australian CBS and both sides of a Spin 45 by Marty Rhone: "She Is Mine" c/w "Village Tapestry."

• Sunday, December 11, 1966

The Sydney Morning Herald says the Bee Gees' hit "Spicks And Specks" was written ten minutes before the group were due to record. "We had been sitting around trying to think of good names for groups," says Barry. "We came up with 'the Spicks And Specks' and one of us said, 'Hey, that would be a good title for a song.' And even after we had written and recorded it, we didn't really like it. We didn't want to release it."

Now a Top 5 hit in Australia, "Spicks And Specks" has beckoned the group to return to England and try their luck in a more lucrative market. The paper says Barry has written more than two hundred songs, and that over one hundred of them have been taped by the Bee Gees (though only about fifty have seen release) and the rest are going to England with the boys. The article claims that Bobby Darin invited Barry to migrate to the States and write songs in partnership, but the eldest Gibb brother didn't want to be separated from his siblings and face the draft. His income from songwriting last year is pegged at $1,000.00 (Barry says much of this is from American cover versions, like Wayne Newton).

1966 • 1967

• **Wednesday, December 28, 1966**
Everybody's reports that Mike Furber's next single features two new Bee Gees compositions—"Where Are You" c/w "Second Hand People"—and will be issued on January 9th, 1967.

1967

• **Tuesday, January 3, 1967**
The Gibb family set sail aboard the SS Fairsky bound for England. On board, the Bee Gees perform regularly (as a part of their return passage fares) and spend much of their down-time writing songs for their next album.

• **Saturday, January 7, 1967**
According to an account by fellow Fairsky passenger Avril Miller in *Fabulous*, the Bee Gees' scheduled live performances begin this evening at 11:30pm in the ship's Grand Social Hall. Hugh Gibb serves as drummer to back up Barry, Robin and Maurice. Their set includes "Spicks And Specks."

• **Wednesday, January 11, 1967**
In *Everybody's*, Bob Staines writes about the talking at the start of Ronnie Burns' recent Gibb penned single, "Coalman": "One voice says 'take eleven' or 'eleven.' Festival in Melbourne were horrified when they heard the record and messages flashed to Sydney complaining they had got the wrong tape. It appears that the Bee Gees who wrote the music were mucking around with a mike in the studio while Ronnie was putting down the disc. But the mike was left on, hence its mumbles. Anyway, it was decided that the unscheduled noises sound OK, so they have been left in."

Another single left over from the Gibbs' final Australian days—Lori's "Who's Been Writing On The Wall Again" c/w "In Your World"—features two of Barry's songs with the Bee Gees on background vocals. It will creep out this month on Australian RCA; "Who's Been Writing On The Wall" had previously been an unsuccessful single for Jenny Bradley. Lori is actually Lori Balmer, perhaps the youngest artist to work with the Gibbs. In 1968, she will find herself in England and once again making music with the Bee Gees (see July 23, 1968).

• **February 1967**
In Australia, Spin issues a single—"Born A Man" c/w "Big Chance"—featuring two tracks from the Bee Gees' recent LP.

• **Sunday, February 5, 1967**
The *Sydney Morning Herald* reports that just before setting sail to the UK, the Gibbs discovered Jon Blanchford singing in Brisbane. This week, his first release as Jon is issued on Leedon: "Upstairs, Downstairs" c/w "Town Of Tuxley Toy Maker, Part One." Both sides are penned by the Gibbs, who also provide backing vocals on the disc. The paper mentions that radio airplay is so far strong, though Jon is concerned with getting banned for the use of the word "hell" in "Upstairs, Downstairs."

• **Tuesday, February 7, 1967**
The brothers Gibb disembark from the Fairsky at Southampton, England. The vessel came into port the previous evening. Barry later tells the *Los Angeles Times*: "We signed one week after we arrived in England with Robert Stigwood. He had heard tapes which we sent to him from Australia. Before we went to see him, we went to the organization that handles the Seekers (another Australian group). They threw us out and painted a very black picture. Said there were too many groups around and that it was impossible. So we thought, 'That's fine,' we were glad we were told that because it made us work. Within a week, Robert called and we signed with him for five years."

"We arrived flat broke," Robin told the author in 2006. "We were sleeping in an unfurnished house somewhere in Hendon, which is a suburb of North London. We had the spirits and hopes of young teenagers and my mother and father were actually pulling their hair out. Stigwood had been trying to contact us through Polydor; they found out we were in the country and somehow located us to this house in North London. And Robert came on the phone and said 'Now, look I've heard these tapes and I want to do business with you guys. Wherever you are, just come on in.'"

• **Friday, February 24, 1967**
Record Mirror notes this as the date when the Bee Gees officially sign a management, publishing and production agreement with svengali Robert Stigwood. In fact, their most recent Australian release, "Spicks And Specks" had already been picked up for release in Britain by Roland Rennie at Polydor, and is now issued. Instead of putting the boys into clubs to work, Stigwood wisely focuses the band's energy on songwriting and demoing new material in the studios of London. "It's impossible to overstate their international potential," he says of the inking, "both as performers and composers."

• **Saturday, February 25, 1967**
The *New Musical Express* runs an ad for the Bee Gees' first British release, "Spicks And Specks." Pictured are the brothers Gibb with drummer Colin Petersen—who *Record Mirror* will state officially joined the group on the day of the single's British release. In May, he will tell Bill Harry of *Record Mirror*: "I knew the boys in Australia and we had a discussion about joining them. I came on ahead to London as I'd originally intended to concentrate on a film career. But the film business is such a slow process that even though I gave myself four years to make it in films here, I decided on joining the Bee Gees instead."

"Colin was a good drummer," Barry told the author in 2006. "He was originally with a band called Steve and the Board. We were very close with him. He was a successful child actor in Australia. Colin came over to England of his own accord to try and make it as a film actor. It was very organic. We all sort of got sucked up into one place. We did a little showcase for Robert at the Saville Theatre as a band for the first time. We'd never been a band. In Australia, it was always clubs and hotels."

"We knew [Colin] was going to England ahead of us," said Robin in 2006. "He didn't come to England with us. But he did meet us at Waterloo Station when we arrived and he actually provided us with the house in Hendon. He looked for it and got it for us and we had somewhere to stay when we got there. But, then, there was really no link to that we'd actually be recording [with him]. It just kind of came together. We had to go to the studio, he was a drummer, he was there and we said, 'Look, come, we don't have a drummer.'"

"When I decided to come to Britain," Colin recalled in a 1969 Record Mirror interview, "I stopped off in Sydney to see the Gibbs. Barry asked me to be their drummer when they came over...Then I had a letter from Hugh Gibb and I sorted somewhere out for them to stay and stored their equipment in my flat."

• March 1967
In London, the Bee Gees (including Colin Petersen) demo material at Polydor Studios (including "One Minute Woman") and complete writing the song "New York Mining Disaster 1941" during an unexpected power outage. "It began in Hendon," said Barry in 2006, "in the semi-detached house that we'd rented after arriving off the ship. We were sitting in that little lounge in Hendon and the very first verse we had. So when the power went out at Polydor, and we were sitting on the stairs with the echo, what we did was we had nothing else to do but continue that idea. So we did that.

"We ran through a lot of stuff [at Polydor Studios]. I think we did about a week there, straight. Robert sort of dropped in every night and sort of would suggest things. Tell us what he didn't like and tell us what he did like. The songs [for Bee Gees' 1st] were formulated in that week from ideas before that on the ship. In other words, 'You've got to make an album, guys. Get on with it.' In those days, if you weren't the Beatles, you made an album in three weeks and that's basically what happened."

Meanwhile back in Australia, another female singer, Jenene, issues a Spin label single featuring Maurice and Nat Kipner's "So Long, Boy" one side, and Barry's "Don't Say No" on the flip. Both tracks feature the Bee Gees on background vocals and were produced by Nat Kipner before their departure. Jenene is Jenene Watson, currently a star on the Australian ABC's children's television program, Crackerjack.

• Saturday, March 4, 1967
The NME reviews "Spicks And Specks" calling it "a bit dated," but still thinking it "very good indeed." Robin is given special mention for his vocal on the flipside, "I Am The World." In the same issue, the paper's Pop-Liners column notes: "Robert Stigwood of Nems Enterprises has signed four-piece Australian group, the Bee Gees (currently working in Britain), to a five-year agency contract."

Also today, the Bee Gees visit I.B.C. Sound Recording Studios (35 Portland Place, London, W1) for the first time to tape backing vocals for a recording of their "Town Of Tuxley Toy Maker, Part One" by another of Robert Stigwood's charges, Billy J. Kramer (currently recording for Robert's Reaction label). IBC, as it will be referred to herein, will become the Bee Gees' home away from home for the next five years, and the venue that they use most consistently for this phase of their career in Britain.

• Tuesday, March 7, 1967
In London, the Bee Gees begin sessions for their first British album at IBC's Studio A with producer Ossie Byrne and engineers John Pantry and Damon Lyon-Shaw. The recording format for this, and most of the Bee Gees' first year of recording in London, will be ½" four-track tape running at 15 i.p.s. (inches per second) aligned to the N.A.B. (National Association of Broadcasters) frequency curve. The Bee Gees will be augmented from this first session on by guitarist Vince Melouney, who traveled to London at the end of 1966 and after a spell working at a Simca car dealership, is invited to play on the group's recordings by Maurice.

"I hung with [another Australian band, the Easybeats in Wembley, when I came over the England] for awhile and that's how I found out the Bee Gees were in town," Vince explained to the author in 2006. "One of the guys from [the Easybeats' record label, United Artists] was over at the Easybeats' place one day and said, 'Oh there's this Australian band called the Bee Gees have just arrived in town.' I happened to be there that day. Somehow or another, I was able to get a hold of their phone number. Maurice said, 'Oh, we've got a recording session. Why don't you come and play guitar on what we're putting down?' I said, 'Fine.' So he gave me the address. I had to go and borrow a guitar [from the Easybeats' Harry Vanda]. I caught the train into London and found IBC studios and that's the night we recorded 'New York Mining Disaster.'"

Indeed, this session kicks off with an early rendition of "New York Mining Disaster 1941." The first surviving pass (a short false start) is announced as "Take one again," perhaps indicating that some earlier takes were rolled over and the process was restarted to save tape (the original tracking sheet for this session has at least nine takes crossed out preceding the first surviving pass). Take two is complete with two guitars (Barry and Vince), bass (Maurice) and a simple kick drum pattern (Colin). Take three features overdubbed harpsichord (Maurice) and backing vocals from the brothers. The results are solid, but the group and Ossie Byrne endeavor to record further passes of the song.

Takes four through seven are incomplete, but take eight is another well-performed rendition (as is take ten). Nevertheless, the Bee Gees press on through to take thirteen, which receives overdubs of harpsichord, harmonium, kick drum and two sets of backing vocal harmonies. These results will be transferred to a second four-track tape (called a "reduction") for further overdubs and balancing at the end of today's session; the production will be completed on March 13th.

Next up is Barry and Robin's "I Can't See Nobody." A different tracking set-up is in place for take one of this song with two guitars (Barry and Vince), harpsichord (Maurice) and drums (Colin). Maurice switches back to bass for take two, which is complete. On take four, Robin adds a lead vocal, with Barry and Maurice providing vocal backgrounds and harmony. This take will not receive further production work, but in 2006 is mixed by the author for release as a bonus track on *Bee Gees' 1st*. Takes five and six are incomplete, and take seven is marked as the master. It will receive overdubs of backing vocals and harpsichord before being transferred to a second four-track tape for further production work on March 13th.

Another of Barry and Robin's creations, "Red Chair Fade Away," is actually taped over part of the tape echo return reel for Billy J. Kramer's "Town Of Tuxley Toy Maker, Part One."

The tracking set-up is similar to today's other recordings: guitar, bass and drums. Of particular note, right from the start Colin's drumming is crisp and impressive. Take four is the first complete performance; take five will be considered the master and receive overdubs of fuzz guitar and a strange woodwind sound—like a blown bottle—barely audible on the final production, but something of importance, since it is double-tracked. Robin's bizarre vocalizing heard on the end of the song (sounding like a farmland animal) is also present on the initial four-track recording. The results of today's work will be transferred to a second four-track tape for further production touches on March 13th.

The final song from this session, "Turn Of The Century," is another Barry and Robin-composed fantasy. "It was one of the first things that we had come up with on the ship coming from Australia," recalled Barry in 2006. "...Once again I think that the Beatles had changed everything, they changed lyric forms of pop songs...Most of their songs were very picturesque and lyrical. So we were influenced by that heavily." To conjure up the imagery, Maurice plays harpsichord, Barry and Vince add guitars and Colin holds down the drums.

"I remember the harpsichord very well," commented Maurice to Ken Sharp in 2001. "When we were coming over to England, we wrote the song 'Turn Of The Century.' In Australia you'd get all these records like 'Matthew And Son' by Cat Stevens and he had this very baroque harpsichord on it [Author's note: actually the sound of a tack piano]. Where could you get a six-hundred-year-old harpsichord in Australia? The country's only two-hundred-years-old, where are you gonna find a six-hundred year old harpsichord? So I used to put thumbtacks on the hammers of pianos to try and get the same sound, couldn't do it of course. I didn't realize they were plucked, not hit! (laughs)

"I said to Robert Stigwood, 'Is there any chance we can get a harpsichord for the session?' He said he'd see what he could do. I walked into the session and there was a two-tiered harpsichord and I freaked! I absolutely loved it. I played all the harpsichord on that album. That was my dream instrument at the time."

Take one is complete, but far sloppier than the rest of today's performances, hinting at either fatigue or unfamiliarity with the song. Takes two through four are incomplete and incorporate some rehearsal with Barry directing Maurice's chord changes. Take five is passable, but Ossie and the band work through to take seven, which is considered the master. It will receive lead and backing vocal overdubs (featuring some different lyrics than the final version). This version is mixed in 2006 by the author for release as a bonus track on *Bee Gees' 1st*. The final production will be completed at a second session on March 13th.

1967

• Wednesday, March 8, 1967

At IBC Studio A, the Bee Gees work on a second day of album sessions with producer Ossie Byrne and engineers Michael Claydon and Phillip Wade. The band will tape seven takes of brisk, guitar based arrangement of "House Of Lords." Barry plays electric guitar, Vince provides the melody hook on a second guitar, Maurice is on bass and Colin plays drums. The entire production is submixed to a single channel of a ½" four-track tape. The first take is complete, but takes two through six are fragmentary. The final performance, take seven will be considered the master from this session, and will be worked on at a further date (see March 15th).

The second song of this session is the novelty number, "Mr. Wallor's Wailing Wall." A part of the Gibbs' live presentation up to this point had included comedy material, and although none of these works would make it to their final discs (perhaps at the advice of Stigwood), the brothers would always tape left-of-center novelty tracks throughout their studio careers. "It was our infatuation with the Goons and that humor," Barry told me of this song. "'Mr. Wallor's Wailing Wall' was right up that alley. It's just silliness. It was, 'How absurd can our lyrics become and still have people say oh, I like that song?'"

The instrumental set-up for this track features Maurice on tack piano, Barry and Vince on guitars and Colin on drums. The first six instrumental passes are incomplete, as the band is unclear of the song's whimsical structure. According to taped comments from either Vince or Colin, Ossie Byrne is giving some form of musical direction to help with the proceedings. Take seven is deemed "good" from the control room, yet the band presses on through two further false starts, before completing the final performance, take ten. This last take is considered the master and will receive overdubs of bass (Maurice) and a lead vocal from Robin (with Barry on a very close double), as well as a track of background vocals. The production will continue on March 15th, with Barry even taping a lead vocal at one point.

• Thursday, March 9, 1967

At IBC Studio A, the group works once again with producer Ossie Byrne and engineers John Pantry and Damon Lyon-Shaw. The first track of this session is the Beatle-y "I Close My Eyes," composed by all three brothers. "Well, it's just a dreamy song, isn't it?," commented Barry in 2006. "It's a song probably about getting stoned. People did that, you know?"

The tracking set-up is similar to the other songs thus far recorded with two guitars (Barry and Vince), bass (Maurice) and drums (Colin). Takes one through six of this song will be incomplete, false starts. The final performance, take seven, will be the master and will receive overdubs of organ (Maurice) and vocals from the group. The lyrics at this stage are not complete and verse one will be repeated twice. This version is mixed in 2006 by the author for release as a bonus track on *Bee Gees' 1st*. The production will be completed with further reductions and overdubs on March 15th.

This session's second song is "One Minute Woman," credited to Barry and Robin. "I wrote 'One Minute Woman' on the ship coming over myself," explained Barry to me in 2006. "There's a little bit of ambiguity about that one, but it is my song. I think the real bottom line for this band was that we were always influenced by someone else. In fact, we would say to each other: 'Let's write the next Beatles single,' or 'Let's write the next Beach Boys single,' and see what happens. You'd place yourself in that other world as if you were that group. Something would happen because of that. In this case, it was Otis Redding. We were extremely influenced by the Stax musicians. That's where that came from. That's the kind of group this was, it was always drawing from other artists. Always, 'We love that record, let's do something like that, but let's see if we can do something better than that.' Which didn't work, but that's how you did it. Robert would often say, 'You may have been influenced by someone else doing this, but it comes out as the Bee Gees.'"

At its earliest stages in today's recordings, "One Minute Woman" bares little resemblance to a Stax production. An earlier demo (probably taped at Polydor and which exists only in acetate form) is even more pop-oriented, featuring bongos in place of drums and some different lyrics. Takes one through seven of the final studio version are incomplete, false starts. Take eight is a complete pass, but the results are still somewhat choppy. Today's final take, twelve, will receive vocal overdubs from Barry and Robin singing in unison, organ from Maurice and backing vocals from all three brothers. This version is mixed in 2006 by the author for release as a bonus track on *Bee Gees' 1st*. The production will take on a more intentionally soulful edge when new vocals are taped on March 15th.

Today's final song is the lyrically incomplete "All Around My Clock" (Barry will hum a melody over the organ break that is never filled). The first two performances are false starts, with the third take being considered the master. It will receive vocal overdubs with Barry and Robin alternating lead and sitar-like instrumental additions from Maurice. Another, shorter version of "All Around My Clock" survives in publishing files with an unknown European vocalist taking lead (not one of the Bee Gees). All of these vocals are erased when work continues on this track at a March 15th session. Still this track will remain seemingly unfinished. The only released version (mixed by the author in 2006 as a bonus track on *Bee Gees' 1st*) is derived purely from today's four-track without any later production touches.

• Saturday, March 11, 1967
Record Mirror notes that the Bee Gees have been added to the bill of the Fats Domino/Gerry & The Pacemakers Easter week show at London's Saville Theater. This will mark the Gibbs' first live performance in the UK since the 1950's! (see March 27th)

• Monday, March 13, 1967
After a weekend break, sessions resume at IBC. Today, overdubs will be added to last week's recording of "New York Mining Disaster 1941," the contents of which are carefully reduced to a single channel of a new, four-track reel. The empty tracks of the new master will incorporate the following augmentation: an orchestral arrangement of brass; strings and percussion from Bill Shepherd on one channel; and double-tracked lead and backing vocals on the remaining two tracks.

Although this production is now complete and imminently releasable, Robert Stigwood (who serves as executive producer on all of the Bee Gees' record releases through the 1970's) will encourage the group to tape a new version of "New York Mining Disaster" on March 15th. "That was really down to Robert Stigwood," explained Robin of the different versions attempted for this song, "because he really knew what he wanted to hear. We did the first version with full orchestra, you know, the wall of sound and everything, it was almost Phil Spector-ish. And it was big. Sounded wonderful and Robert heard it and said, 'No, no, no. Play it like you played it to me in the room.' Because we played the song originally to him [with] just the guitar and our voices. He said, 'I want that on the record. I don't want an arrangement behind you. I want it without the orchestra. I want to hear the human quality of this song, you know, just bare-bone, just guitar and voices with maybe a single cello.' And that was the atmosphere he wanted and that's what we ended up with." In 2006, today's completed first version will be mixed by the author for inclusion as a bonus track on *Bee Gees' 1st*.

A reduction mix for "I Can't See Nobody" is next completed in five takes. Once again, last week's efforts are condensed to a single channel of a new master tape and the empty tracks will be filled with the following augmentation: an orchestral arrangement of brass; strings and percussion from Bill Shepherd on one channel; and a lead vocal from Robin on another. The final production also incorporates double-tracked backing vocals which are added to the remaining open track and on Robin's lead vocal track on the choruses.

Meanwhile, the production of "Red Chair Fade Away" is completed with the work of another arranger, Phil Dennys, who provides a wild orchestration featuring brass, strings and tack piano (all taped on one channel). The remaining tracks feature double-tracked vocals from Barry and Robin and some Mellotron keyboard flute sounds (including some pitch bends straight out of the Beatles' recently released "Strawberry Fields Forever") from Maurice, which are doubled in places alongside the vocal tracks.

(Author's note: It is highly unlikely that Shepherd and Dennys worked side by side at today's session conducting their individual scores in an alternating pattern. However, the dating and information from the surviving tape boxes have been carefully transcribed here to give the closest and most accurate timeline possible. Suffice to say, with multi-track recordings, it is possible to add overdubs at any point without making date notations on the tape box or leaving aural evidence of specific changes. Nevertheless, the engineers at IBC were fairly meticulous and present a relatively full picture of the work involved in these productions in their notations on the tape boxes.)

Also on this busy day, the band will tape two new songs. First up the soulful and lyrically unusual "I've Got To Learn" is recorded in four takes. The tracking setup features Vince playing the lead guitar riff, Barry playing rhythm guitar, Maurice on bass and Colin on drums. All the instruments are recorded on a single channel of a ½" four-track tape. The first take is considerably faster than the final version and takes two and three are performed at a slower pace, but are incomplete. Take four is considered the master and receives overdubs of organ (Maurice) and a doubling of the lead riff (Vince) on one channel, tambourine on another and a lead vocal from Robin on the last (including some vocal ad libs from Barry at the tail end of the performance). Although this production is undoubtedly complete, "I've Got To Learn" will initially be passed over for release. In 2006, this track will be mixed by the author for inclusion as a bonus track on *Bee Gees' 1st*.

The final song taped today is Barry and Robin's medieval fantasy number, "Cucumber Castle." From the looks of the original recording worksheet, it is possible that numerous takes were initially made of this track and rolled over to save tape. When work resumes, take one is called anew and the song is completed in three passes. The backing track consists of Barry's opening rhythm guitar, Vince's guitar augmentation, fuzz bass guitar (Maurice) and drums (Colin). The master, take three, receives overdubs of guitar runs (Vince) and harmonium

(Maurice) on one track, and a vocal from Barry on another (leaving one track of the tape blank). In 2006, take three in this rough form will be mixed by the author for inclusion as a bonus track on *Bee Gees' 1st*. The production will be completed with further overdubs on March 15th.

● Wednesday, March 15, 1967

After a day's rest following Monday's marathon session, the Bee Gees reconvene at IBC Studio A to cut a new version of "New York Mining Disaster 1941" with producer Ossie Byrne and engineers John Pantry and Michael Claydon. The key difference in this remake is a piercing feedback guitar intro and outro that is extraordinarily creative, but ear-shatteringly unlistenable. The other instrumentation is thus far similar to the previous version with guitars (Barry and Vince), bass (Maurice) and kick drum (Colin). Ossie will ask for a "nice, loud count-off" from Barry, but since Vince performs the feedback intro, Ossie soon decides this is irrelevant to the production. The orchestral accompaniment will introduce some other dynamics into this rendition when it is added at a session tomorrow (see March 16th).

Other production work completed today includes overdubs on "Turn Of The Century," which receives orchestral augmentation from arranger Bill Shepherd in the shape of brass, strings and stirring percussion. The orchestral introduction of oboe and strings is added as a separate overdub on track four of the tape, which is otherwise occupied by backing vocals from the brothers for the remainder of the song. The remaining open track, three, is where Barry and Robin's dueling lead is added.

"I Close My Eyes" will get orchestral augmentation via a Phil Dennys arrangement. Phil is a popular session pianist who also does arrangements that are somewhat more experimental and less symphonic than those of Bill Shepherd (by comparison). For this production, the original backing track is reduced to one channel, leaving another solely for brass and flute, a third for strings, more flutes and brass, and finally all of the brothers' vocals on another. (It is possible that Dennys' work is completed at a session tomorrow—see March 16th).

"Cucumber Castle," meanwhile, has some Bill Shepherd-arranged strings, brass and percussion added to a single track, leaving a track for lead vocals from Barry (with harmonies from Robin) and final channel just for a simple Mellotron overdub from Maurice (which only begins during the song's second verse and is more of a bass part, using the keyboard's low organ sound, as well as a coda that is mixed out of the final production).

Although "House Of Lords" is transferred to today's new master reel, the only addition to the production appears to be an organ part. This particular version will remain incomplete and the song will be remade at another session (see April 5th). Also today, "Mr. Wallor's Wailing Wall" has all of its previous overdubs wiped, excepting the brothers' backing vocals. It will go through another stage of production on April 4th.

"One Minute Woman" has two tracks of entirely new lead and backing vocals added to the basic recordings from March 9th, as well as a sumptuous Phil Dennys brass and string arrangement (possibly recorded tomorrow). In particular, Barry's soulful lead vocal brings the production towards his initial vision of a Stax recording. Today's work is rounded off with "All Around My Clock," which is stripped of its lead vocal from March 9th, and reduced to a single channel of a new four-track tape. However, no further production work will occur on this song and it will remain unissued in this state.

● Thursday, March 16, 1967

Working with engineers John Pantry and Damon Lyon-Shaw, Phil Dennys adds a simpler orchestration to version two of "New York Mining Disaster." This is one of the few times the Bee Gees will stray from working with arranger Bill Shepherd (one of their former studio mentors in Australia). It is probable that Dennys is brought in at the suggestion of Stigwood, who has employed Phil on some of his other Reaction label productions. Other augmentation on the final take of this version (called "six," but actually the seventh attempted performance) is a track of backing vocals and another of lead vocal harmony from Barry and Robin.

Despite the added effort, the results of today's work will be rejected by Stigwood, and the song will be remade sans the guitar feedback on March 21st (but keeping most of Dennys' orchestral score). In 2006, version two of "New York Mining Disaster 1941" will be mixed by the author for inclusion as a bonus track on *Bee Gees' 1st* (an earlier, shorter mix of this recording, also by the author, briefly appears on advance copies of the reissue, but is replaced on the final product by a later mix with more studio chat).

● Tuesday, March 21, 1967

The Bee Gees return to IBC Studio A to tape a third version of "New York Mining Disaster 1941." Slated as "final remake," the first take will in fact become the version of "New York Mining Disaster 1941" issued as a single worldwide. It employs the same basic tracking setup of the previous versions with two electric guitars (Barry and Vince), bass (Maurice) and kick drum (Colin). At the end of the performance, Ossie Byrne remarks from the control room, "I think you've done it, gentlemen." Nevertheless, the band will work through two further complete takes of the song before deciding to return to the first pass for overdubbing.

The final master will be augmented by Phil Dennys' sparse woodwind and cello-led orchestral arrangement, a track of backing vocals and another of lead vocal harmony from Barry and Robin. The song will be mixed into mono within the next few days (along with "I Can't See Nobody") and be made available as a single by April 15th.

Also at today's session, the Gibbs alone tape a much simpler production: "Craise Finton Kirk Royal Academy Of Arts." The backing is a simple piano part from Maurice, with Robin taking the lead vocal (closely doubled and harmonized by in sections by Barry). "'Craise Finton Kirk' was done that way where we just thought, 'Well, why not just one instrument? Why does everything have to be a full band?'" recalled Barry in 2006. "We started being more selective about what instrument would play in the songs. It became more of a fascination for us."

Despite its simplicity, it appears that the brothers taped perhaps eight incomplete takes of the song before rolling the tape back to start fresh (the problem, Robin says, is the producer's handwritten lyric sheet, as he states, "I can't read Ossie's words". Barry tells Robin to "get a pen and print them," after which Ossie quips "write 'em out yourself then—don't try to blame me..."). The new take one of this song is complete, and though the Bee Gees will perform another three takes (with only the final take being complete), this first pass will later be mixed in 2006 by the author for release as a bonus track on *Bee Gees' 1st*. The final master, take four, is virtually indistinguishable and will remain as just Maurice's piano with some filtered lead vocals from Robin and Barry.

● Thursday, March 23, 1967
At IBC Studio A, the Bee Gees continue sessions in a simpler and altogether more rocking vein. "Please Read Me" will feature the basic Bee Gees line-up of two guitars, bass and drums. The original recording worksheet seems to indicate at least four takes were rolled over (or erased) prior to a newly called "take one." Indeed some tuning issues hamper the first several takes with Barry's open-tuned guitar, which leads the arrangement, clashing at times with Vince's simple guitar stabs. However, Maurice's melodic bass runs particularly lift this song's dynamics and are the signpost of things to come for the Bee Gees. Still, most of the initial takes of "Please Read Me" are fragmentary.

Take ten will be the first and finally complete pass of "Please Read Me," receiving overdubs of double-tracked Vince string bending, group backing vocals, tambourine to shore up the rhythm and some organ at the fade. These elements will then be reduced to two channels of a second four-track tape, where they are augmented by a track of lead vocals (sung in three-part harmony, with Barry on falsetto during the instrumental break) and a final vocal track for the last verse (again in three-part).

Historically, this final production features the first falsetto vocals of the Bee Gees on record, something of a stylistic trademark for the group in the next decade. "That was influenced by Brian Wilson," Barry explained in 2006. "That's the first time you'll probably hear any falsetto harmonies. We were doing that in a more Beatlesque fashion, but we were [inspired by Brian]." As for the lyrical meaning Barry says: "It's a visit to the psychiatrist, that's what it is. It is!"

Next up, a song called "Life" is briefly attempted. Take two features chord changes and drumming close in tempo and style to "Please Read Me," topped off by some heavily tremeloed guitar harmonics from Vince. This fairly complete instrumental rendition trails off with an unusual modulation and even more elaborate guitar harmonics. After completing take two, Ossie Byrne suggests the group have a listen, "to see what it sounds like." There is some discussion, so it is unknown if they take his advice. Two more performances are taped, the last being complete, though the recording worksheet notes this performance as "scrapped—no master." "Life" will remain an unissued curiosity, its lyrics unknown to this day.

A more up-tempo rocker, "In My Own Time," is the last item taped today. Take one is complete and features a more strident guitar part from Vince (ala the Beatles' "Taxman"); still, the results are solid with only Maurice looking for a groove to synch his bass in. Once completed, Ossie asks the group, "Can you do another one straight away?," adding, "That one speeded up a little bit." Before take two, Ossie says: "Watch the tempo, Colin." Vince and Maurice are more on point in this performance; nevertheless, this take is just a short false start.

Take three of "In My Own Time" will be considered the master and receive a double-tracked lead vocal overdub, as well as piano fills from Maurice and Vince's first-ever guitar solo on a Bee Gees record in the instrumental break. After this session, the brothers have the weekend to prepare for their first UK gig since they were boys in Manchester nine years previous.

● Monday–Saturday, March 27–April 1, 1967
Out of the studio at last, the Bee Gees make their UK stage debut at London's Saville Theatre this week (appearing nightly at 8:30pm and twice on Friday and Saturday at 6pm and 8:30pm). During this series of shows promoted by Brian Epstein (currently a business partner in NEMS with Robert Stigwood), they serve as openers for Fats Domino and Gerry & The Pacemakers.

According to an *NME* review published April 1st, the Bee Gees' set includes "Dizzy Miss Lizzy" and "Be-Bop-A-Lula." *Record Mirror* reviews the opening night, noting that the group does not perform their current single, "Spicks And Specks," and that the "rocker minority in the crowd spoiled their act completely." Vince later tells *Beat Instrumental*: "We were cutting the LP and rehearsing and were only together for two weeks before the show. We just about made it because we did rockers."

1967

● Tuesday, April 4, 1967
Back at IBC Studio A, the group returns to "Mr. Wallor's Wailing Wall," transferring their previous work to a new tape and adding a wailing vocal intro from Barry, plus banjo and brass. But they aren't done yet! The production will be completed on April 10th with a new set of lead vocals.

● Wednesday, April 5, 1967
Today, the Bee Gees revisit "House Of Lords" with a brand-new, baroque arrangement. Backed by harpsichord (on one track), as well as strings and flute (on another track), Robin will sing lead with all of today's takes (on a third track). The first performance is incomplete, possibly taped over by the comic spoken word play at the end of "Mr. Wallor's Wailing Wall," and several of the other takes are either miscalled or missing from the session tape.

Though several of the remaining renditions are solid and complete today, it is the final performance, called take seven (but in fact the last of only five surviving takes), that will receive an additional augmentation. Since there is only one open track on the four-track tape, this will be a double of the lead vocal from Robin plus harmonized choruses from all three brothers. Although the resulting master would fit nicely with the other tunes so far in the running for their upcoming album, "House Of Lords" is mysteriously never issued by the Bee Gees, despite its quality. In the meantime, Raymond Froggatt's band, the Monopoly, have recorded a cover version, poised for release on Polydor this month. It will not be a hit and the song will not be issued again until 2006, when "take seven" is mixed by the author for release as a bonus track on *Bee Gees' 1st*.

Robin: "Oh, yes— 'It must be good to live in the House of Lords.' That was one of the other early songs that we wrote I think on the ship coming over to England. And with all those harmonies; we did it in a Beatle-y way."

● Monday, April 10, 1967
At IBC studios, the Bee Gees complete their production of "Mr. Wallor's Wailing Wall" with a new set of lead vocals. Still the results will remain unissued until 2006, when "Mr. Wallor's Wailing Wall" will be mixed by the author for inclusion as a bonus track on *Bee Gees' 1st*.

● Tuesday, April 11, 1967
Robert Stigwood and Brian Epstein visit the group in session at IBC. For this occasion, the Gibbs spontaneously compose and record the haunting "Every Christian Lion Hearted Man Will Show You" in a single take. "It was one of the 'instant' songs," Barry stated in 2006, "and it came with Robert visiting the studio with Brian Epstein. IBC has a staircase that goes down into the studio. I remember us constructing it while they were there watching; with Maurice on the Mellotron and me on guitar. It was one of those things that just came up."

The first channel of the four-track (likely a reduction) features Barry's guitar, Maurice on Mellotron and separate organ overdub (playing bass notes and whole chords) and Colin's drums. Once again, Maurice does a fantastic pitch bend (as in "Red Chair Fade Away") to end the song. The second channel of the tape features picked bass, tambourine bathed in reverb, and at the close, Colin's final tom fills. Channel three and four feature all of the song's vocals, double-tracked.

"When I was in Rome, I visited the Coliseum," Barry later tells Bill Harry in *Record Mirror*. "I wrote a number about it on the last album, called 'Every Christian Lion Hearted Man Will Show You,' which would be suitable for one of these Roman Empire films. I liked visiting Rome because I am very interested in history—the only thing I was good at at school. I left school at thirteen. I don't even know what division means. I've had no education and I'm the first to admit it."

● Saturday, April 15, 1967
The *NME* reviews the Bee Gees' second British single, "New York Mining Disaster 1941." The paper writes: "Fascinating harmonies, underlined by cello, and a lyric that keeps you glued to the speaker."

● Monday, April 17, 1967
The band tapes their first live BBC radio session to be broadcast on the program *Saturday Club* (on April 22nd). Songs include "In My Own Time," "New York Mining Disaster 1941," "One Minute Woman" and "*Cucumber Castle*." The Bee Gees' BBC audition drew "rave notices" by

the panel. Additionally at this session, the brothers provide backing vocals for another group, the Gnomes Of Zurich, on their live rendition of "High Hopes."

Barry: "That's what made us a band is doing those types of shows like the BBC shows. Playing live as much as possible. And I think it came to being a good band at that point. [With] Vince and Colin in the first place it was an augmentation. It was almost like, 'Well, we're three brothers, but we need to look like a band.' The image was built that way by Robert and by our friendship with Vince and Colin. It looked good. It was the right way to go anyway. I think from those roots it became a good band."

- Friday, April 21, 1967

Back at IBC Studio A, the Bee Gees work on two new songs with Ossie Byrne and engineers Damon Lyon-Shaw and Philip Wade. First up, "To Love Somebody" is taped with very simple backing: Barry's guitar, Maurice on bass and Colin on drums. Vince's guitar augmentation begins during the song's second verse. Take one of "To Love Somebody" is nearly complete and quite close in dynamics to the final master. It peters out a bit at the tail and the band asks to do another take, but Ossie recommends they, "Come and listen to that much anyway." Takes two and three are incomplete, false starts, but take four is another full performance with a nice, laid-back feel. Since all the instruments are submixed to a single track of tape, this take also has some obvious elements that don't work—including Vince's guitar being too loud in spots. Take five doesn't appear to be taped at all or is just a discussion and take six is another incomplete, false start. Take seven is another full take, but lacks focus and the tape is stopped before the band finishes. Take eight will be the master and receive overdubs of Bill Shepherd's orchestral augmentation (strings, brass, tympani and harp) on two tracks and Barry's incredible lead vocal (which is surprisingly labeled as a "rough vocal," proving the Gibbs' rough takes are better than most other artists' final masters) mixed with Robin and Maurice's harmonizing on the choruses on the remaining channel.

Producer Ossie Byrne announces the next song at the session: "'Holiday,' the Bee Gees, back track only, take one." The entirety of this backing track is simply Maurice's shimmering organ part. All of the other overdubs made to this song will be built around his single performance. Take one is nearly complete, but falls apart towards the end. Take two sounds perfect, and is leadered off on the reel indicating it has potential for overdubs, but the brothers ultimately decide to press on. Take three sounds as if Colin may now be keeping time on the drums in the background, off mic. By the start of take four, it is also apparent that Barry and Robin have begun to sing along and there is some unrecorded rehearsal before a metronome is introduced for take four (which is incomplete) and take five (which is the master). The final take will initially receive overdubs of bass and double-tracked background vocals before being transferred to a second four-track during a reduction mix.

The final master for "Holiday" features Maurice's organ and bass combined to track one, Barry and Robin's alternating lead vocals on track two, Bill Shepherd's orchestral arrangement (of harp, percussion, strings and brass) on track three and the brothers' doubled-tracked backing vocals from the previous tape combined on the final channel. Now complete, "Holiday" will be featured on the Bee Gees' upcoming album and will eventually be pulled as a single for the U.S. market, becoming a hit there later this year.

- Saturday, April 22, 1967

Record Mirror publishes an article on the band, detailing their early successes and current activities. "We write about everything," says Robin. "Day-to-day events, personal experiences, stories. We used to write individually. But today each new number is a collaboration job. We've completed over a hundred songs."

- Wednesday, April 26, 1967

At IBC studios, the Bee Gees tape five takes of a newly-composed song, "Harry Braff." "'Harry Braff' we wrote one night during a visit to [the president of Polydor] Roland Rennie," Barry explained in 2006. "We had dinner with his family one night during these sessions. We were sitting on the floor, the three of us, after dinner at his house and we created that then. Then on our way back home to our own apartment in London, we stopped at Robert's and dragged him out of bed and made him listen to it. They were crazy times. It's nice to come up with things that give people pictures. We liked to have pictures. For about a week afterwards Robin walked around with a helmet with goggles on. He really did! And in those days you could. You could literally wear anything, 'cause the flower power thing had taken over and whatever you were wearing was just fine."

Take one of the song is announced as "Checkered Flag"; this pass is complete, and the performance is remarkable. Take two is much the same, the Bee Gees sounding more like a group than ever before. From take three onwards, Vince doesn't play his lead guitar with the group (perhaps holding off for a future overdub). Take five will be the master and the tape box indicates possible overdubs of fuzz guitar, organ and tympani. However, all that remains is a reduction, with one track of vocals (sung in three-part harmony) and a backing track with the added fuzz guitar (but seemingly no organ or tympani). Ultimately, the results are not quite what the Bee Gees are hoping for and "Harry Braff" will be re-recorded May 10th. In 2006, take five from today's session will be mixed in mono by the author for release as a bonus track on *Bee Gees' 1st*.

1967

- Saturday, April 29, 1967

"New York Mining Disaster 1941" enters the British singles chart today and will rise to #12 over the course of its ten-week run. *Record Mirror* says the band have signed a quarter-of-a-million-dollar record deal in the United States with Atlantic Records that will span the next five years. Their single will be issued in the States next week and a promotional tour of the U.S. will kick-off on June 2nd. Meanwhile, the band's album is planned for rush-release at the end of May.

Disc & Music Echo reports that: "New group the Bee Gees lashed out this week at widespread showbiz reports that their new single, 'New York Mining Disaster 1941,' had been written by Beatles John and Paul. Says 20-year-old Barry Gibb, whose name is on the record label as part-composer of the song with his brother, Robin: 'Complete rubbish! We've always written our own songs. I've been writing since I was ten—before Lennon and McCartney were even onstage. People can say what they like. If they don't believe us, they can ask the Beatles themselves.'

"Rumors started because the group had been signed to the Beatles management [NEMS] and because Lennon and McCartney have been known to write under different names for other artists...Bee Gees' denial comes on the eve of the boys signing a 80,000 [British Pounds] plus five-year record deal with Atlantic Records in America, the biggest ever for a new group."

- Saturday, May 6, 1967

The *NME* reports that Matt Monro and Cilla Black are considering covering Gibb brothers' material. Back in Australia, Nat Kipner uses five of the Bee Gees' backing tracks taped last year—"Exit, Stage Right," "Butterfly," "I'll Know What To Do," "Terrible Way To Treat Your Baby" and "Top Hat"—and adds Ronnie Burns vocals on top. The results will be issued on his Ronnie album this summer. Burns will also record his own version of Barry's "Morning Of My Life."

- Wednesday, May 10, 1967

At IBC Studio A, the Bee Gees work with engineers Michael Claydon and Damon Lyon-Shaw to tape a second version of "Harry Braff" for possible single release. The results are somewhat tamer and more refined than the April 26th version. Only one take is taped (again announced by an engineer as "Checkered Flag") using a single track of four-track tape and featuring two guitars, bass and drums. For reasons unknown, no further work is done on this rendition and the song will be remade July 30th. The Bee Gees' next release will be "To Love Somebody" c/w the recently recorded "Close Another Door" (taped at Ryemuse Studio in Mayfair on an unknown date during this period).

- Thursday, May 11, 1967

In Britain, the Bee Gees make their debut appearance on television's *Top Of The Pops* performing "New York Mining Disaster 1941." Also featured on tonight's programme is Lulu, who sings "The Boat That I Row" and meets Maurice Gibb for the first time.

- Saturday, May 13, 1967

In Britain, the Bee Gees perform in concert at the Maple Ballroom, Northampton. In today's issue of *Disc & Music Echo*, Maurice says: "We are NOT an Australian group and we do NOT like being compared to the Beatles." Barry adds: "We never wanted to go to Australia in the first place. But I was only 12 at the time and I couldn't very well complain."

"I didn't even know where Australia was," says Maurice. "The minute we got on the boat out to Australia, we knew we wanted to come home again as musicians. And we waited eight years for that day."

"The scene is so different [in Australia]," says Barry, "it is quite unbelievable. But the fans there are more enthusiastic; they so rarely see a big star, that when they do they really go mad."

- Sunday, May 14, 1967

In Britain, the Bee Gees are scheduled for gigs at two Nottingham area clubs tonight: the Britannia Rowing Club (sometimes known as the Brit Club) and the Beachcomber.

In Australia, The *Sydney Morning Herald* writes: "Meanwhile, the Bee Gees haven't been forgotten on the local scene. Maurice Gibb, one of the group is co-author with Nat Kipner of Barrington Davis' new record sides–'As Fast As I Can' and 'Raining Teardrops'–Barrington was born in Blackpool but he sings in Sydney.

- Tuesday, May 16, 1967

At IBC studio A, the Bee Gees work with engineers Mike Claydon and Damon Lyon-Shaw to a record a new take of "Spicks And Specks." The arrangement remains the same as the Australian recording, and the basic track consists of Maurice's piano, Barry's guitar and Colin on drums. Added to these are an overdubbed track of bass from Maurice and a single horn. The last track is left empty and the only vocal is some faint, off-mic singing from Barry to guide the band. At the end of the one and only take, Colin asks, "Is it long enough?," leaving one to wonder if this version is to be used as some sort of insert in a film or television appearance, perhaps for the brothers to sing live to this new backing track. Indeed the tape is left without any vocals, yet there is no documentation of the Bee Gees plugging this disc at this late date. Suffice to say, it is unlikely they have any far reaching plans for this particular rendition.

- Wednesday, May 17, 1967

The group flies to Holland to appear on television in Hilversum, after which they travel to Bremen, Germany to tape a spot for *Beat Club*.

• *Friday, May 19, 1967*
The Bee Gees are due in Holland for some television work.

• *Saturday, May 20, 1967*
Disc & Music Echo reports that Vince Melouney has officially joined the Bee Gees as guitarist. On German television, their first appearance on Radio Bremen's *Beat Club* is screened (a black and white lip-synched video tape performance of "New York Mining Disaster 1941"). Meanwhile, the *NME's* June Harris writes that Bee Gee fever is taking hold of the States: "...sales are expected to top 100,000 this week..." *Billboard* magazine states that sales are strong in Germany for the band's previous Polydor disc, "Spicks And Specks."

• *Monday, May 22, 1967*
In Britain, the Bee Gees appear live on BBC radio's *Monday Monday*.

• *Tuesday, May 23, 1967*
The Bee Gees head back to Germany for further television work in Frankfurt.

• *Thursday, May 25, 1967*
Back in Britain, the Bee Gees perform in concert at Liverpool University.

• *Friday, May 26, 1967*
In Scotland, the Bee Gees perform in concert at Galashiels' Town Hall.

• *Saturday, May 27, 1967*
In Britain, the Bee Gees perform in concert at Market Hall in Carlisle. The *NME* reports that the group will soon star in their own thirty-minute television spectacular financed by Deutsche Grammaphon and based around their *Bee Gees' 1st* album (which the paper says is nearing completion). Shooting is to commence on June 1st. The group are also said to be taping additional tracks for the album "to replace several items already recorded," though there is no actual evidence of this plan being carried through. The paper further says the Bee Gees will cut a new single next week, though this report too seems premature.

In the United States, the group scores their first chart entry with "New York Mining Disaster 1941" (amended by Atco with the subtitle: "Have You Seen My Wife, Mr. Jones"). Over the next fourteen weeks, the disc will peak at #7. *Billboard* magazine reports that, in less than two weeks, the disc sold almost 200,000 copies. Atco says the band will be over for a promotional trip in June.

• *Sunday, May 28, 1967*
In Britain, the Bee Gees perform in concert at Oldham Discotheque.

• *Monday, May 29, 1967*
In Britain, the group is heard once again on BBC radio's *Monday Monday*.

• *Friday, June 2, 1967*
The Bee Gees were due to travel to the US today for the first time, but their trip is delayed to accommodate filming of some promotional shorts. However, a planned album-length showcase of the group on film never materializes in this period (though clips of "New York Mining Disaster 1941," "I Can't See Nobody" and "To Love Somebody" will be distributed).

• *Monday, June 5, 1967*
At IBC Studio A, stereo masters for *Bee Gees' 1st* are assembled. The final album will feature fourteen Bee Gees originals.

• *Saturday, June 10, 1967*
Disc & Music Echo reports that the Tremeloes, Dave Berry and Unit 4+2 have all recently covered Gibb songs. *Record Mirror* notes that the Bee Gees recently completed a color insert film for the US television's *The Jackie Gleason Show*.

1967

- **Tuesday, June 13, 1967**
In Britain, the Bee Gees appear on ITV television's *As You Like It* (alongside Cilla Black, the Small Faces, the Spectrum and Billie Davis). At IBC Studio A, Robin and Maurice join singer Oscar (full name Paul Oscar Beuselinck, a recording artist for Stigwood's Reaction label) to tape a cover of "Holiday" arranged by Bill Shepherd and produced by Stigwood. The twins will overdub double-tracked background vocals on the final production (reduced to a single track for the final mix—the recording is only issued in mono). Oscar's release of "Holiday" in the UK later this September coincides with the success the song enjoys as a single in the States (see September 13th). Oscar's rendition, however, will not chart (though he will later appear alongside the Gibbs in their motion picture version of *Sgt. Pepper's Lonely Hearts Club Band*).

- **Saturday, June 17, 1967**
The Bee Gees' manager, Robert Stigwood, tells the *NME* from New York: "Everyone is clamoring for Bee Gees songs. At least fourteen artists including the Cyrkle, Sounds Incorporated, Dave Berry, Tremeloes, Oscar and Tony Rivers are considering songs by the group."

- **Friday, June 23, 1967**
In Britain, the Bee Gees appear in concert at Scraptoft Teachers Training College in Leicester. Also on the bill are Cat Stevens and Georgie Fame. In the shops today, Unit 4 + 2 have issued a single of an older Gibb composition, "Butterfly."

- **Saturday, June 24, 1967**
In Britain, the Bee Gees appear in concert at Manchester's New Century Hall. Meanwhile, *Disc & Music Echo* reports that Otis Redding will record the brothers' "End Of My Song" (a tune recently demoed alongside "Gilbert Green" and an item called "Indian Demo" at London's Central Sound). Also noted in the paper, Barry has recently flown to New York to meet with Bobby Darin (who is considering covering some Gibb material). The brothers also hope to write for Wilson Pickett. *Billboard* says the group's promotional trip to the United States will now kick-off on the country's Independence Day, July 4th.

(Author's note: The undated tape box for the Central Sound demo session features at least two complete performances of "Gilbert Green," recorded with Barry on twelve-string guitar, Maurice on piano and Colin on drums, all on a single track of ½" four-track tape. Only the second performance receives overdubs of Maurice on bass, lead vocals from Robin—with Barry's harmonies on another track and a track of background vocals. Gerry Marsden will soon tape a version of this song—see June 27th—but the Bee Gees' own rendition will remain unissued until 2006 when the author mixes this demo session tape as a bonus track for *Bee Gees' 1st*.

"End Of My Song" as listed as "Otis Redding Demo" on the tape box sticker and under the tape label the original inscription is "Ray Charles High Climber," a reference to the style of the tune and the lyric line: "I was a high climber." Only one take of this demo exists with the basic track of Barry on twelve-string guitar, Maurice on piano and Colin on drums all on a single channel. Barry's lead vocals and Maurice's bass appear on separate tracks as overdubs. The last item taped at this session, titled randomly "Indian Demo," is actually just a jam of Vince—who is noticeably absent from today's other recordings—Maurice on bass and Colin on drums. The results are rather like Cream and occupy a single track of tape. Nevertheless, they seem quite rehearsed and hint at what the rhythm section of the band sound like without Barry and Robin.)

- **Monday, June 26, 1967**
In Britain, the Bee Gees tape another radio session for *Saturday Club* (for broadcast July 1st) including "I Can't See Nobody," "To Love Somebody," "In My Own Time" and "Holiday."

- **Tuesday, June 27, 1967**
In Britain, Gerry Marsden tapes a version of Barry and Robin's fantasy, "Gilbert Green." The track is produced by Robert Stigwood and arranged by Bill Shepherd. Unfortunately, this release is not a hit, particularly because the Bee Gees have already composed a follow-up for Gerry to record (see August 2nd).

- **Friday, June 30, 1967**
A third British Bee Gees single is released: "To Love Somebody" backed with "Close Another Door."

- **Saturday, July 1, 1967**
In Britain, the Bee Gees are heard on BBC radio's *Saturday Club*. Also, the flipside of their first US single, "I Can't See Nobody," hits *Billboard*'s bubbling under charts at #128.

Barry: "It was written in a dressing room [in Australia] with girls getting changed. So the comment, 'I can't see nobody,' is pretty apt actually. You just have to change the way it's written! It was written with Robin and I sitting together in that dressing room having to share it with the girls who weren't wearing anything if that's how you want to visualize it.

"Our sister [Lesley] was a snake dancer; she used to dance with a snake. She used to do her shows with us as well [in Australia]. You know it's pretty bizarre, all of it actually. Being in the same dressing room with dancing girls, but when they changed you were still sitting there. Nobody bothered to say anything. Well, you know the fact that you are kids, it didn't cross their minds, but in our minds we weren't!"

● Sunday, July 2, 1967
The Bee Gees are due to travel to the USA to kick-off a promotional tour. According to *Billboard*, the group will spend their first three days in New York City visiting disc jockeys and seeing editors of magazines and newspapers.

● Friday, July 7, 1967
In Florida, the Bee Gees appear at a Miami Atco sales convention to meet with record distributors. *Billboard* reports it is the most successful gathering of this sort in the label's history, with orders being written for three million dollars in sales.

● Saturday, July 8, 1967
In Los Angeles, fellow Atco artists, Sonny & Cher, host a party for the Bee Gees. *Billboard* says the group is scheduled to spend three days in Hollywood, after which they will visit a number of midwestern cities, including Chicago, Detroit and Cleveland. Also today, *Disc & Music Echo* report that Manfred Mann bassist (and early Beatles acolyte) Klaus Voormann has designed a special sleeve for the Bee Gees' album, released next week.

Meanwhile, the *NME* reveals plans for a Bee Gees feature film to be called *Lord Kitchener's Little Drummer Boys*. The group is to compose the score and "several songs" for the film. "The story tells of five youngsters who enlist in the Army as boy musicians and subsequently become involved in a war. The screenplay is being written by Mike Pratt, who is particularly well-known for his TV scripts."

● Thursday, July 13, 1967
The group visits Detroit, Michigan on their promotional tour of the United States.

● Friday, July 14, 1967
Their debut international long player, *Bee Gees' 1st*, is scheduled for release (but will be delayed to accommodate Klaus Voormann's artwork—see July 22nd).

● Saturday, July 15, 1967
Today, the Bee Gees' second British-made 45—"To Love Somebody"—enters the chart for a single week at #50. Stateside, the release does much better, rising to #17 during a nine-week run. Perhaps the group's presence in the States is a contributing factor to its success in America and relative failure in Britain. Nonetheless, they will return to London tomorrow at the conclusion of their coast-to-coast promotional tour.

The group's Australian friend, Johnny Young, recently visited with the Gibbs in London and recorded a single for Polydor of "Craise Finton Kirk." Later in Australia, he discussed another possible reason for the relative failure of "To Love Somebody" with journalist Maggie Makeig: "'Craise Finton Kirk' got to number fourteen on the pirate charts and was selling 700 a day until the pirate stations closed down. Then it stopped dead. Nothing. Radio Caroline stayed open but every record on the air had to be bought; which cost about $500 a fortnight. You had to give them 10 days notice that you wanted to buy, and because everything happened so quickly, it was chaos. Anyone buying time was liable to go to jail, so buying time turned into real cloak-and-dagger stuff. There I was unlucky and so were the Bee Gees. 'To Love Somebody' did nothing in England because all exposure stopped. If the sales of 'Craise' had gone up to 1000 a day, I probably would have made the top 20."

● Sunday, July 16, 1967
The *Sydney Morning Herald* reports that Johnny Young's latest single, "Lady" (written by Barry Gibb) is being well received in the UK where the singer is on holiday. While in town, Young will tape a few more Gibb songs with the brothers' arranger Bill Shepherd (including a version of "Every Christian Lion Hearted Man," which will appear on his *Surprises!* album).

● Monday, July 17, 1967
The Bee Gees return to Central Sound Studio (9 Denmark Street, London, WC2), where they recently demoed three songs (see June 24th). Today their session begins with a soulful number called "Ring My Bell." The work set up is similar to that of IBC, with all the backing track (Barry and Vince's guitars, Maurice's piano and Colin's drums) taped to a single track of ½" four-track tape. The main difference is the sound quality, which is somewhat inferior to IBC and heavily compressed.

1967

Three takes will be made of "Ring My Bell," all of which are complete. The final pass will receive overdubs of bass from Maurice, a set of backing vocals from the brothers and a track of lead vocals with Barry on the verses and Robin on the bridge. The production will be enhanced with orchestration and revised lyrics (and bass guitar) on August 1st.

The second item taped today, "And The Sun Will Shine," is a ballad showcase for Robin, along the lines of "I Am The World." Take one features Barry on guitar, Maurice on piano, Colin on drums and possibly Vince on bass (recorded live to a separate track). Robin can be heard off-mic singing, but it isn't until take two that his vocals are captured properly. The first pass has several mistakes and for the second performance, the bass may be overdubbed by Maurice. Robin's lead vocal is on a separate track. This initial version is only meant as a demo, but will inevitably be the basis of the final master recording (albeit with some later overdubs). Still, the Bee Gees will attempt a new version on July 25th.

The final tune demoed today, "Day Time Girl," is a slow and dreamy piece. The song is tracked beginning with Maurice on piano, then Vince enters on guitar, followed by Barry strumming a twelve-string in open-tuning and Colin on drums. The first two passes are incomplete, take three being the final performance master. It will receive overdubs of bass from Maurice on a separate track and another track of lead vocals. Like "And The Sun Will Shine," this initial version is only meant as a demo, but will inevitably be the basis of the final master (which will encompass later overdubs, such as orchestration—they key factor in deciding to keep these demos as masters). The production will be revisited on July 30th.

- Thursday, July 20, 1967

The group is scheduled for a four-day Scandinavian jaunt for television and promotional appearances in Sweden, Norway and Denmark.

- Saturday, July 22, 1967

In the United States, Dick Clark's *American Bandstand* television show airs a promo film of the group performing "New York Mining Disaster 1941." *Record Mirror* reports that a delay in the production of the cover of *Bee Gees' 1st* has pushed the album's release until July 28th. Advance orders in the United States are over 100,000 for this long player. Sonny & Cher are said to be recording four Gibb numbers (though none are ever issued) and (perhaps erroneously) DJ David Jacobs is said to have recorded a version of "Gilbert Green."

- Monday, July 24, 1967

In Britain, the Bee Gees will be heard daily this week on BBC radio's *Swingalong*.

- Tuesday, July 25, 1967

The Bee Gees begin work at a relatively new location, Chappell Recording Studios (52 Maddox Street, London, W1), reopened in March of this year, and manned by a former IBC trainee, John Timperley. Robert Stigwood is named as the A&R person on the box, but it is possible that producer Ossie Byrne is still present. Today the Bee Gees will attempt a new recording of "And The Sun Will Shine" (demoed July 17th at Central Sound). At least two new takes will be taped today (with several more incomplete passes erased to save tape). The instrumental track will consist of Barry's twelve-string guitar, Colin's drums, Vince on electric six-string and possibly Maurice on a very-faintly recorded bass.

The second take will be augmented with overdubs of harpsichord, bass guitar, piano, more electric guitar and double-tracked backing vocals. The new backing track is fully-produced and stunning, yet the group will return to the Central Sound demo never adding a lead vocal to this fantastic recording. The demo version will, however, be augmented with orchestration at a session on August 1st (when the flaw that Bill Shepherd's orchestral charts are written to the Central Sound recordings, rather than the new Chappell takes is discovered).

Also recorded today is an early version of "The Earnest Of Being George," titled at this point, "Granny's Mr. Dog." However, this first version of the tune bears almost no resemblance to the later recording. The first pass is announced as "Take one again," hinting that some rehearsals or early takes were "rolled over" in an effort to save tape. The arrangement of "Granny" is considerably faster than the final "Earnest Of Being George" leaving no clue to the meter in which the lyrics will be sung. The instrumentation is two guitars, bass, maracas and drums. Vince in particular goes wild with electric guitar antics on take two. By take four, Maurice's bass has dropped out of the mix, and will soon be repatched to a separate channel (along with some drums) for take five. This performance will end in a cacophony of reverbed piano (obviously overdubbed on the bass track). "Granny's Mr. Dog" a.k.a. "The Earnest Of Being George" will be remade on September 7th.

- Saturday, July 29, 1967

Perhaps spurred by the single's US success, "To Love Somebody" re-enters the UK singles chart and over the next four weeks will rise to #41.

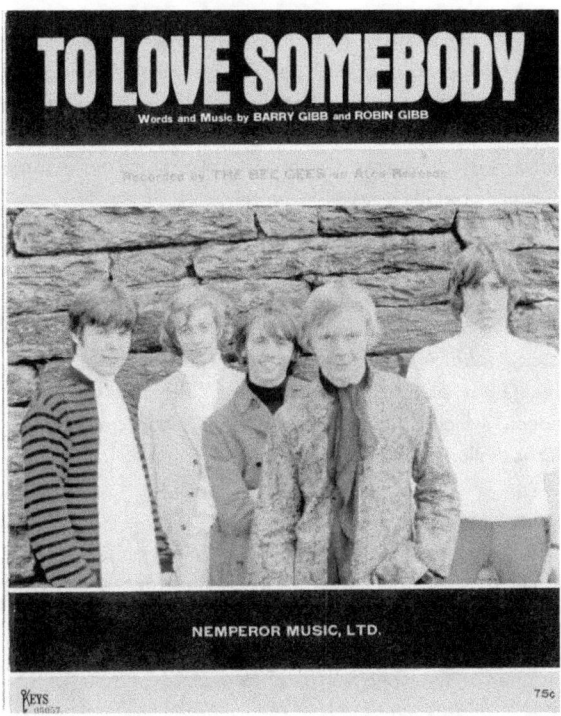

• Sunday, July 30, 1967
At Chappell Recording Studios, the Bee Gees resume work with producer Ossie Byrne and engineer John Timperley. First at this session the Bee Gees tackle a new track, "Birdie Told Me." Played lightly with Barry on electric twelve-string, Maurice on bass, Colin on bongos and Vince's on acoustic rhythm, the basic track is all recorded to a single channel of four-track tape. As many as early four takes seem to have been crossed out and rolled over to save tape; even in the new set of takes, the first three are incomplete, false starts. Take four will be the master and is augmented by two tracks of drum overdubs from Colin—alternating on the A and B sections of the song—and Vince's electric guitar solo (which shares one of the drum channels). Later at this session, "Birdie Told Me" will be subject to a reduction mix to make room for overdubs of Bill Shepherd arranged strings and woodwinds, as well as a lead vocal track from Barry (with harmony from Robin in sections) and then a full track of backing vocal harmonies from the brothers. The final verse is sung in harmony across both tracks.

The second item on today's agenda is a third version of "Harry Braff." The set-up for this recording is Maurice on piano, Barry and Vince on electric guitars and Colin on drums. The first five takes are incomplete and there seems to be a great deal of discussion between Barry and Ossie on how to perfect the song's intro. Several of the takes will not be recorded at all to save tape. Take six (slated as "take five") will be the master take and receives overdubs of acoustic twelve-string guitar and bass on one channel, and double-tracked lead and backing vocals spread across the remaining two tracks. "Harry Braff" will receive a final production touch later on August 1st.

The third song from this date, "All So Lonely," is an early version of a song later recorded as "Vince's Number." Only two takes will be made of this tune today, with Vince on acoustic twelve-string. The second pass will be augmented by overdubbed drums (Colin) and bass (Maurice), but no further work shall occur on this version of the song. It will be remade on August 31st as "Vince's Number." Though he does not recall it as such, it is very likely that Vince Melouney penned this track.

Also at this session, "Day Time Girl" is remade with same basic arrangement of the July 17th recording, except that this new version (taped in three short takes) incorporates a string quartet. However, since their charts were written to the Central Sound demo, they don't synch-up (especially during the speedy closing section). Someone in the studio comments, "This isn't the same back track that I heard." Looking for a solution, the Bee Gees will immediately return to the Central Sound demo and overdub the strings on that recording. This process is done by dubbing over the Central Sound tape to another machine at Chappell running at 30 ips, rather than 15 (as is the custom with all the sessions from Chappell in this era). Perhaps one of their four-track machines ran at 15 ips and the other at 30. The string arrangement synchs up perfectly and the production is complete.

• August 1967
In Britain, Esther and Abi Ofarim issue a double-sided Gibb penned single—"Morning Of My Life" c/w "Garden Of My Home"—the single is produced by Robert Stigwood and arranged by Phil Dennys. Also this month, Dave Berry issues the first cover of a Gibb song penned last year, "Forever" (on the Decca label).

Meanwhile in Australia, a group called The Kids (Michael Griffiths and Tony Borg) sings over the Bee Gees' 1966 backing tracks for "How Many Birds" and "Big Chance." The results are issued on the Spin label.

• Tuesday, August 1, 1967
A final day of work at Chappell produces Barry's "Barker Of The UFO." "My fascination with UFOs," Barry explained to the author in 2006, "which began then, has intensified over the years. I'm sort of a UFO freak, you know. It's easy to write because I loved the subject so much. So, it started when I was really young and just continued. There's no question that it's Beatlesque and also it's very much like 'Jumbo.' I hear those elements and I remember that song fondly. That's one of my favorites."

1967

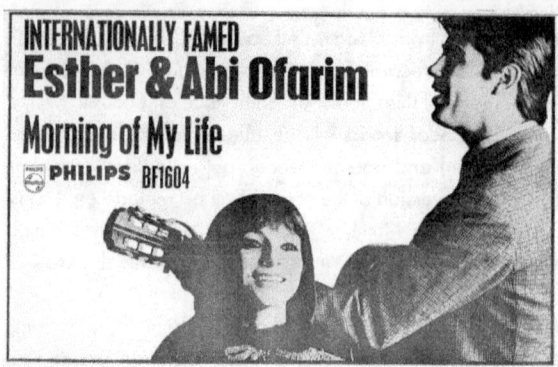

The production will be built up from one track of backwards percussion. Added to this will be a track of acoustic guitar and piano, another of Barry's lead vocal, a third with bass from Maurice and drum fills from Colin. This will then be "bounced" to a second machine where the tracks of vocal, bass, drums and backwards tape are combined to a single channel. To these, overdubs of are added of a harmony vocal from Barry, a separate backing vocal (also from Barry) and finally Bill Shepherd's orchestration (of brass, strings and percussion). The final production will initially be available only in mono. In 1990, Bill Inglot will mix the song to stereo for the first time for the *Tales From The Brothers Gibb* box set.

Also at this session, another of the Central Sound demos, "Ring My Bell," will be augmented with new tracks of lead vocals and backing vocals (each on individual tracks—Robin's vocal on the bridge is double-tracked across both channels). The final production touch will be a track of orchestration from Bill Shepherd and a new track of bass guitar from Maurice. Despite completing this excellent production (and even mixing it to mono at the time), "Ring My Bell" will remain unissued until 2006 (when the author makes a new stereo mix from the Chappell four-track to be included as a bonus track on a reissue of *Horizontal*).

Bill Shepherd will also add two tracks of orchestration (strings and woodwinds) to the July 17th recording of "And The Sun Will Shine" (requiring the original recording to be bounced twice to open up the necessary tracks). Shepherd will also augment July 30th's "Harry Braff" with wild brass and strings at today's session.

• Wednesday, August 2, 1967
In the United States, Associated Press syndicates an interview with the group conducted by Mary Campbell (likely carried out during the band's Stateside promo tour last month). "It's bad for us to write a song four days before a recording session," remarks Maurice. "We hate it by the time we get there. If we write something and rehearse it, we just write another song then and there. We all get new ideas."

"There were eighteen more tracks we threw out and they'll never be looked at again," says Barry of their recent album sessions. "They're on tape if another artist wants to go through them," adds Maurice. "I don't think an artist should use throwaways," counters Barry. "An artist should have songs written especially for him."

The group says that the song they have written for Gerry Marsden, "Gilbert Green," is about a composer of 125 years ago who dies in a fire, wondering whether his piano concerto is any good. After his death, the concerto becomes famous. The Gibbs plan a follow-up called "The End Of Gilbert Green" which is purely an instrumental piano concerto with orchestration by Bill Shepherd.

• Tuesday, August 8, 1967
In Britain, the Bee Gees appear on television's *Dee Time*. In the studio, mono mixes are made at Chappell of "Birdie Told Me," "Harry Braff," "Ring My Bell" and "And The Sun Will Shine." Today's reduction of "Harry Braff" will likely be included on the mono release of *Horizontal*.

• Wednesday, August 9, 1967
The Bee Gees return to IBC studios to work with producer Ossie Byrne. First they will record "You Know How You Give Yourself Away" (later retitled "Sir Geoffrey Saved The World"). Only two takes of the song will survive, though it is likely that several rehearsals were rolled over to save tape. The basic instrumental structure will consist of two electric guitars (Barry on six-string and Vince on twelve-string), piano (Maurice) and drums (Colin). Take two will be the basis of the master version, receiving overdubs of electric twelve-string guitar, bass and backing vocals spread across the remaining three channels (track one being the basic backing).

"Massachusetts (The Lights Went Out In)" is the second song taped at this session. The basic instrumental structure is again two guitars (Barry and Vince), piano (Maurice) and drums (Colin). Take one is complete and features more piano from Maurice not heard on the final production, including a hooky figure that is only on this first take. For take two, Maurice switches from piano to bass and provides an equally hooky, albeit different bass line. This take is nearly perfect, though it falls apart slightly at the tail end. Ossie remarks: "There was a bit of noise in the pause there where you try to count Colin in. I think we better..." Indeed a guitar scratch can be heard in this section and the band press on with another performance at Ossie's urging. Take three will be the final master and subject to overdubs of acoustic six-string guitar and a track of backing vocals.

The next stage of production will be a reduction and transfer to a new tape for "Sir Geoffrey Saved The World." The basic track, bass and twelve-string overdubs are reduced to a single channel, a lead vocal from Robin is added on channel two (with harmonies from Barry and Maurice on the choruses), orchestration (mallets, brass and strings) from Bill Shepherd occupies track three and the final channel contains the first set of backing vocal overdubs. An earlier set of lead vocal overdubs with the lyric "You Know How You Give Yourself Away" reportedly exists on an acetate, but these original lines were erased and do not feature on the master multi-track.

The production of "Massachusetts (The Lights Went Out In)" will be completed with a reduction mix that incorporates the initial backing tracks with the overdubbed acoustic guitar on channel one. This will be augmented by a new track of lead vocals from Robin (sung in harmony with Barry in places) and a track of orchestration (mallets, brass and strings) from Bill Shepherd (the initial track of backing vocals remains from the first stage multi-track).

"The songs were already written and then Bill would do the arrangements," Barry explained to the author of the orchestral arrangement process in the Bee Gees' productions. "I think the most outstanding is 'Massachusetts' as an arrangement. We never expected him to do that. Sometimes we would sing what we would [imagine] the strings doing. But in this case he did that himself and I thought it was great. 'Massachusetts' was the first number one in England."

As for the song's initial genesis, Barry says: "There's two different memories. Robin remembers us doing it in a boat going around New York and I remember us checking in at the St. Regis with Robert, going to the suite and while the bags were being brought in we were so high on being in New York that we were sitting on a couch in the St. Regis hotel and that's how 'Massachusetts' began. I think we were strumming basically the whole thing and then I think we went on a boat round New York. I don't know if we finished it but I think that's where the memories collide. Everybody wrote it. All three of us were there when the song was born, how's that?"

- Thursday, August 10, 1967
At Chappell Recording Studios, Ossie Byrne and engineer John Timperley work on mono mixes of "Birdie Told Me," "Harry Braff," "Ring My Bell" and "And The Sun Will Shine."

- Friday, August 11, 1967
The Bee Gees were due to travel to Hamburg, Germany today to perform some club work, but have decided to stay put to avoid immigration issues. Earlier this week, Australians Vince Melouney and Colin Petersen were informed they would have to leave Britain by September 17th.

- Saturday, August 12, 1967
Bee Gees' 1st becomes the group's first British albums chart entry. Over the next twenty-six weeks, it will peak at #8. Meanwhile, British Bee Gees fans stage a protest at the cottage of Prime Minister Harold Wilson to prevent the possible deportation of Vince and Colin.

- Tuesday, August 15, 1967
Deirdre Meehan chains and handcuffs herself to Buckingham Palace to protest the possible deportation of Vince and Colin. Meehan is eventually ordered to return home by police. In reality, Meehan is a secretary working for Robert Stigwood who directs her to pull off this noteworthy publicity stunt.

- Wednesday & Thursday, August 16 & 17, 1967
At IBC studios, mixing for the Bee Gees' next single and album is underway with engineers Mike Claydon and John Pantry (including the songs "Massachusetts (The Lights Went Out In)," "And The Sun Will Shine," "Sir Geoffrey Saved The World," "Birdie Told Me," "Barker Of The U.F.O.," "Daytime Girl" and "Harry Braff").

- Friday, August 18, 1967
Go!! publishes an interview with the group conducted by Debbi Smith in London. "Every track on our album is different—to us," says Robin. "Yet people are still yelling Beatles at us. There's one track on the LP called 'In My Own Time,' and the kids in Pasadena, California have asked us, 'Is Paul there?' It's a bit frustrating not getting credit for our own work, flattering but frustrating. We may both be under the same organization, NEMS, but it's two different groups, folks!"

As for the hippie movement, Colin remarks: "There are millions of people out there in Asia. Why don't the hippies go out and help them instead of sitting around and turning on all day? They may say they love everybody but they forget everything except themselves."

- Saturday, August 19, 1967
Fabulous reports that the Bee Gees now have a British fan club run by Julie Barrett. For five shillings, fans receive a personally autographed photo of the band, a Bee Gee-Bopper Badge and an introductory letter. Newsletters are planned for every two to three months, and a Christmas card is also in the offing.

- Saturday, August 26, 1967
In Britain, the Bee Gees are scheduled to appear in concert at the Festival Of The Flower Children held in the grounds of Woburn Abbey, Bedfordshire. Also scheduled for this show are the Small Faces, Eric Burdon & the Animals, the Jeff Beck Group, Denny Laine and the Alan Price Set. In the United States, Bee Gees' 1st debuts on the albums chart where it will remain for a full year (fifty-two weeks). It will peak at #7.

1967

● Sunday, August 27, 1967
In Britain, Robert Stigwood's associate at NEMS, Brian Epstein, is found dead at his home of an accidental overdose. Following Epstein's passing, Stigwood will wind down his involvement with NEMS.

● Thursday, August 31, 1967
At IBC studios, producer Ossie Byrne and engineers Mike Claydon and Pete Wade work with the Bee Gees on two recordings. The first of these, "Vince's Number," is actually a new version of "All So Lonely," taped in a rather tentative form on July 30th. As many as ten incomplete performances were likely erased at the start of this session to save tape. By the time take number one is called anew, the band is ready to put this song to bed. The basic track features Maurice on celeste, Vince on acoustic twelve-string guitar and Colin on drums. Take two will be the master recording, receiving overdubs of bass (Maurice), picked electric guitar (Vince) and a final track of lead vocals from Robin (with harmonies) singing the song's somewhat rambling lyrics. Despite this production being fully complete, the song will never surface on any Bee Gees release.

Next up, the Bee Gees tape "All My Christmases Came At Once," a song later given to the Majority (and issued under the title "All Our Christmases" in 1968). The tracking set-up features Maurice on piano, Barry on electric wah-wah guitar, Vince on acoustic twelve-string guitar and Colin on drums. The first eleven takes of this recording are incomplete, false starts. After take nine, Barry suggests that Colin overdub his drums after the backing track is completed. Colin worries that the track won't be in time. Robert Stigwood is present in the control room and says: "Don't worry about getting it as a track; if you want to do it as a demo, alright, I give in." Barry responds, "We'll just do it without the drums, then put the drums on." Colin says, "No, it's too difficult, man." Vince adds, "It's too difficult that way." Maurice quickly says, "Come on, we'll just do it quick. You can make a mistake."

The Bee Gees make a few more attempts at the song and after take eleven, another false start, Maurice says: "Keep going man! It's only a demo!" Barry feels that even for a demo, it needs to be better. Maurice reminds the group of the time: "It's a quarter past ten."

Take twelve will be the final performance and ultimately the master recording of the song. It will be augmented by overdubs of bass (Maurice) and a single channel of vocals (Robin on lead with Barry's harmonies). The song will be used in the film *The Mini-Affair* (see October 26th), but a Bee Gees' recording will not initially find release. In 2006, the author will make a stereo mix of the "demo" from today's IBC four-track. This mix will be featured as a bonus track on a reissue of *Horizontal*.

● September 1967
In Australia, Noeleen Batley issues another Barry Gibb original on her latest 45: "The Wishing Song."

● Monday, September 4, 1967
At IBC Studio A, producer Ossie Byrne and engineers John Pantry and Mike Claydon work with the Bee Gees on two recordings. The first of these, "Horizontal," is based around Maurice's pounding piano track (with the sustain pedal liberally engaged), electric guitar fills from Vince and backing harmonies from Barry and Robin sung live with each track. From the very outset, the production idea is in place that these elements will be tripled as overdubs (or as Barry puts it during the session: "Doubled, three-times"). After two false starts, take three will be the basis of the master recording, to which three identical performances of the same elements—piano, guitar and vocals—are added. An unused idea at the tail of the master is Barry and Robin's voices treated with reverb, counting quickly.

"We just wanted to find out what would happen if we put eight pianos together," Barry explained to the author in 2006 of "Horizontal's" production process. "And that's what we did. That's another way we used to do it. What we would do is get an incredible sound first that doesn't have a song and then write the song based on the influence of that sound."

The second stage of the production features the four performances combined to a single track of a new four-track tape. To these, overdubs of Mellotron, double-tracked vocals and bass in sections (sharing one of the vocal tracks) will be added. This incredible production will soon become the title and closing track of the Bee Gees' second British-made album, *Horizontal*.

The second song taped at this session is the lyrically obscure, "Lemons Never Forget." "'Lemons Never Forget,'" explained Maurice in 2001 to Ken Sharp, "that was our punch at [the Beatles' Apple]. We were the lemons and they were the apple. So it was a Beatles/Bee Gees thing (laughs)."

"'Lemons Never Forget' was a bit of a send up on Apple," Barry agreed in a 2006 interview with the author. "There was a lot of chaos at that point about the Beatles' Apple Company. It was all over the industry that Apple was in disarray and that the Beatles were breaking up. So it was a bit of a play off on that situation."

The track itself is built around a basic set-up of Maurice's piano, Colin's drums and electric guitar from Barry. This group will work through four takes, the last of these being the master. However, the Bee Gees will attempt further takes (at least two more) before Colin gives up and they roll back to take four. To this they will apply overdubs of bass (Maurice) and lead guitar (Vince) on one channel and double-tracked lead vocals from Barry (with harmonies from Maurice in sections).

Historically, today's session will mark Ossie Byrne's final day as producer of new recordings by the Bee Gees. Despite the fact that he will soon have helped the Bee Gees achieve their first number one, "Massachusetts (The Lights Went Out In)," there is the notion that the Bee Gees have outgrown his talents now that they are surrounded by other skilled engineers and inspirational figures in London. "Ossie gave us the freedom to create," said Maurice in a 2001 interview with Ken Sharp. "He gave us unlimited time...And then he came to England with us and of course in England everyone said, 'We have so many producers here, what the hell are we gonna do with you?' We told them he was part of our team. In the end he turned out very nasty. Robert unfortunately had to tell him he wasn't part of us anymore. He did 'Massachusetts' with us but we did all the work. Ossie was just sitting there."

• Thursday, September 7, 1967
At IBC, the Bee Gees tape a new version of "Granny's Mr. Dog" (first attempted July 25th). The arrangement has changed dramatically in the interim. The pace is about half the speed and melodically it might as well be a different composition. Nevertheless, it is announced "'Granny's Mr. Dog' new version" from the control room and the basic track consists of two guitars (Barry and Vince), drums (Colin) and heavily tremeloed piano (Maurice). The band will make nine takes of the song, the last of these being the master. The first overdub will be a track of bass (Maurice), guitar treated with tape delay (Vince) and percussion (likely Colin on bongo and maracas). The remaining two tracks of this first stage master will be taken up with Vince's double-tracked guitar solo (as well as some brief handclaps on one track, which will not be used in the final production).

A reduction mix to a new four-track tape combines the basic track with the bass, percussion and Vince's double-tracked guitar on a single channel. To this, another track of electric guitar from Vince (tripling his solo) and double-tracked lead vocals from Barry (with some fleeting ad-libs from Robin or Maurice saying things like "right" and "oh") are added to the three open channels.

• Wednesday, September 13, 1967
Due to overwhelming US popularity, a third single is pulled from *Bee Gees' 1st*: "Holiday." Over the next nine weeks the single will peak at #16. In Britain, the Bee Gees record a radio session for broadcast on BBC's *Easy Beat*. Performances include "Massachusetts (The Lights Went Out In)" and "To Love Somebody."

• Saturday, September 16, 1967
The *NME* reports that Vince and Colin's visas are extended through October, but deportation still looms.

• Friday, September 22, 1967
In Britain, Adam Faith issues a unique rendition of Barry and Robin's composition "Cowman, Milk Your Cow." The brothers provide vocal backgrounds for this disc.

• Saturday, September 23, 1967
In Britain, "Massachusetts (The Lights Went Out In)" enters the singles chart and over the next seventeen weeks will reach #1. "We've never been to Massachusetts, actually,"

Barry later tells the *Los Angeles Times*. "The song represents anybody who wants to go back to where he came from. 'Massachusetts' was about the simple fact that everybody wanted to go to San Francisco, and this upset us. The character in the song was going to San Francisco to join the hippies, to take LSD, but when he left, his girl back home seemed much more important." Robin adds: "What it means is that anyone who wants to turn to LSD and leave solid things behind is a maniac. Fantasy is fantasy and reality is reality, so which is it going to be?"

Also tonight, the Bee Gees appear on British television's *Dee Time*. In Germany, the brothers (sans Vince and Colin, who remain in Britain for fear of not being readmitted) are seen for a second time on Radio Bremen's *Beat Club* in a videotaped, black and white lip-synch of "To Love Somebody." Despite their fears of being deported, today's *NME* notes that Vince and Colin's visas have now been extended through November.

1967

● Sunday, September 24, 1967
In Britain, the Bee Gees are heard on the radio series *Easy Beat*.

● Thursday, September 28, 1967
In Britain, *Top Of The Pops* airs a Bee Gees performance of "Massachusetts (The Lights Went Out In)." In Germany, they appear on *Der goldene Schuß*.

● Saturday, September 30, 1967
The *NME* says the Bee Gees are to appear in their own Southern TV spectacular to be shot in October and screened the following month. Director Mike Mansfield is hoping to secure national broadcasting for the program (which is to include other artists who have recorded Gibb numbers like Lulu, Julie Rogers and Esther & Abi Ofarim) in Britain.

The paper also runs an interview with the group conducted by Norrie Drummond. Of their recent hit, "Massachusetts," Maurice says: "We worked out the basic melody in about five minutes when we were in New York. Robin and I began, then Barry started throwing in ideas. I'm not quite sure why we thought of 'Massachusetts' in the first place because we weren't even sure how to spell it."

Commenting on the relative chart failure of "To Love Somebody" in the UK, Robin says: "Everyone told us what a great record they thought it was. Other groups all raved about it but for some reason people in Britain just did not seem to like it."

"I think the reason it didn't do well here," offers Barry, "was because it's a soul number. Americans loved it but it just wasn't right for this country. Yet most people who have heard 'Massachusetts' tell us they prefer 'To Love Somebody.' 'To Love Somebody' was a good record, but 'Massachusetts'

is a commercial record." The paper notes that they are currently working on a song called "World."

Also today, on British radio the Bee Gees are scheduled to appear live on the long-running BBC *Saturday Club* program alongside Billy Fury, Truly Smith and Dave Dee, Dozy, Beaky, Mick & Tich.

● October 1967
In Britain, Los Bravos issue their cover of Barry's "Like Nobody Else." Although their singer is German, Bravos are actually a Spanish group and in their homeland they will release a variant version of this song, "Como Nadie Mas."

● Monday, October 2, 1967
In Britain, the Bee Gees are scheduled to appear on the newly-launched Radio 1 programme, *Let's Go* (hosted by Dave Symonds), throughout this week.

● Tuesday, October 3, 1967
At IBC Studio A, the Bee Gees record a number of new songs including two potential singles: "World" and "Words." These will be the group's first productions in London without Ossie Byrne present (though Byrne will remain in Britain as a producer and manager for other artists). The first song taped at this date will be "With The Sun In My Eyes." For the tracking, Barry will sing live to Maurice's organ in this simple and superb production. Four takes will be made, but only the last of these, take four, will complete. This final take is then treated to overdubs of orchestration (strings and harp) from Bill Shepherd and a second lead vocal attempt by Barry (featuring some different lyrics and used only in one spot of the final production to fix a "p" pop in the word "prove").

The second production at this session will be the intense composition, "World." Barry will tell Bill Harry of *Record Mirror*: "The world is full of trouble every day, and we wrote the song ['World'] because we were seeking a meaning behind life. Why was I born? Why am I living? That's the whole story of the new single! We produce our own discs, and we do most of our recordings in IBC studios. We don't write songs outside the studios...we usually go into the studio with nothing but an idea. Then we just sit down and think, and work something out. The technicians understand and give us time to write."

Given the preparation described, the backing track for "World" is taped in a single pass. The initial track consists of guitar (Barry), organ (Robin), bass (Maurice) and drums (Colin). To this, overdubs will be added of heavily compressed piano (Maurice), another track of bass (Maurice), as well as lead guitar shrieks and closing solo from Vince and more ghostly organ from Robin (who also does some off-mic vocalizing). These elements will be transferred and reduced to a second four-track tape wherein the instrumental backing is condensed to a single channel. To this, Barry will add a lead vocal. Nevertheless, this version will not be used for the final production and a second reduction will soon be made.

For the final production, the instrumental track is once again reduced to a single channel to which overdubs will be added of Barry and Robin alternating "World's" lead vocals (double-tracked across two-channels, with the closing chorus sung in three-part harmony with Maurice), and a final track of Bill Shepherd's orchestration. According to contemporary interviews, Shepherd's orchestration may be added at a considerably later date from this initial session. Also of note, it features one short movement not featured in the final production.

Following "World," the Bee Gees tape "Words" in four takes. The instrumental foundation for this track will be Barry and Vince (electric guitars), Maurice (piano) and Colin drums. For the first two takes all of the band will start together, playing throughout the verses. Beginning with take three, Barry plays the first verse solo, before Vince and Colin join in (Maurice will sit out the arrangement, waiting to overdub his piano part on a separate track), giving the song a more dramatic dynamic. Take four will be the master version and it is treated to overdubs of Maurice on piano (channel two) and bass (channel three), as well as a lead vocal track from Barry.

For the next stage of production, "Words" will be transferred and reduced to another four-track tape. Maurice's heavily compressed piano track will remain on a separate track, as will Barry's lead vocal. However, Maurice's bass is combined with the bass track to make room for Bill Shepherd's orchestration (strings, harp, brass and mallets) on the final track. The brothers remaining vocal harmonies will be overdubbed in a final stage of reduction—these only exist on the mono mix of the song, and have never been located in multi-track form.

Also attempted at this session will be seven takes of an unfinished production called "Maccleby's Secret." The basic track is unusually spread across two tracks of the ½" tape with an organ intro (possibly Robin), two guitars (Barry and Vince), bass (Maurice) and drums (Colin). The song itself is similar melodically at this point to the Bee Gees' 1968 composition, "Pity"; a rather jaunty number with a haunting organ intro. The arrangement is not simple by any means, with numerous stops and starts, and is surprisingly well rehearsed.

Following take three, the arrangement changes considerably and the production utilizes only a single channel of tape with Maurice playing tack piano instead of bass (Robin's organ will disappear entirely at this point). The song takes on an almost novelty feel reminiscent of "Craise Finton Kirk" or "Mr. Wallor's Wailing Wall." Take seven is considered the master and will receive an overdub of bass from Maurice on a separate channel. Nevertheless, the production will halt at this point and "Maccleby's Secret" remains just that.

- Thursday, October 5, 1967
In Britain, BBC television's *Top Of The Pops* airs a repeat of the Bee Gees performing "Massachusetts (The Lights Went Out In)."

- Friday, October 6, 1967
In Britain, the Bee Gees are scheduled to appear live on radio's *Joe Loss Show* from the Playhouse Theatre, Charing Cross, London.

- Saturday, October 7, 1967
Record Mirror reports that the Bee Gees' next single release, "World," will be rush-released on October 20th. The paper says the group may appear in an hour-long spectacular covering their career that is to be produced by Deutsche Grammaphon. The production, scheduled for November, will entail the group returning to Australia to shoot some scenes. Also tonight, British television's ATV programme, *Good Evening!* with host Jonathan King airs a film insert of the Bee Gees.

- Monday, October 9, 1967
The group returns to the BBC to tape another live radio session for the corporation's *Top Gear* program (to be broadcast October 15th). Songs include: "Mrs. Gillespie's Refrigerator" (recently covered by the Sands on a Stigwood produced 45, but initially unissued by the Bee Gees), "I Close My Eyes," "In My Own Time," "New York Mining Disaster 1941," "Massachusetts (The Lights Went Out In)," "To Love Somebody" and "Cucumber Castle."

- Friday, October 13, 1967
In Britain, the Bee Gees are scheduled to perform at one in a series of "Friday-night Love-Ins" at Benn Memorial Hall in Rugby, Warwickshire. Also tonight, the group appears on British television's *Crackerjack* to promote their forthcoming single, "World" (of which an actual release will be significantly delayed).

1967

• Saturday, October 14, 1967
Record Mirror says that the Bee Gees will appear in concert at London's Saville Theatre on November 19th backed by a thirty-piece orchestra. The paper also states, rather enigmatically, that during the planned performance of "World," "twenty-five extras" will appear "in a tableau." The band's upcoming television special (to be produced by Southern Television) will be named *Cucumber Castle* (after the song).

• Sunday, October 15, 1967
In Britain, the Bee Gees are heard on BBC radio's *Top Gear*.

• Monday, October 16, 1967
At IBC studios, mono mixes are produced of "World," "With The Sun In My Eyes," and "Words" (with a rough vocal take).

• Wednesday, October 18, 1967
In Britain, the Home Secretary has decided to allow Vince and Colin to stay in the country after all. Back in Australia, Johnny Young is interviewed in *Everybody's* about his recent work with the Bee Gees. "I stayed with the Bee Gees for two weeks when I arrived," says Young. "They played me two tracks off the album they were putting together. 'Craise Finton Kirk' seemed my kind of song, so at a cost of $162.50, with the help of the Bee Gees, I put it down. I paid for it myself." The results gave Young a flash of interest in Europe (including an appearance on Germany's *Beat Club*).

• Thursday, October 19, 1967
In Britain, the Bee Gees are seen once again performing "Massachusetts (The Lights Went Out In)" on television's *Top Of The Pops*.

• Friday, October 20, 1967
A new single—"World" coupled with "Sir Geoffrey Saved The World"—is scheduled for release today in Britain, but will be postponed until November 17th.

• Saturday, October 21, 1967
In Britain, the group guests on radio's *Pete's People*. *Record Mirror* publishes an interview with Maurice conducted by David Griffiths. "Vince and Colin make suggestions," he says of the group's creative process, "which we use on the recording sessions, but other than that I don't think they want to step in and join us in our writing efforts in case they spoil our style and method which is obviously getting results at the moment.

"We've written songs for years, had a stockpile of two hundred and we've still got about fifty we're hoping will be useable." He says their new single, "'World' is more complicated. We spent a day and a night and a day recording it. The first day was all writing, and we also spent a day on arranging. We may add strings and other instruments but right now we're not sure. We want to be more adventurous in our work but perhaps 'World' is distinctive enough without any session musicians added."

• Wednesday, October 25, 1967
At IBC Studio A, the productions of "World" and "Words" are worked on today, including some new mono mixdowns (none of which will see release).

• Thursday, October 26, 1967
In Britain, the Bee Gees are seen once again on BBC television's *Top Of The Pops* in a repeat performance of "Massachusetts (The Lights Went Out In)." The Bee Gees also visit Twickenham film studios today to view rushes of a motion picture called *Wonderwall*. They are currently considering providing the score for this film, and have already done some scoring work on another feature, *The Mini-Mob* (later retitled the *The Mini-Affair*) directed by Robert Amram and featuring the Majority and Georgie Fame each performing Gibb songs.

Barry: "We were going to do *Wonderwall* (that George Harrison ended up doing). We actually visited the set. I remember that very well. *The Mini-Mob* was a '60s spy thing, there were a whole bunch of those things out at that time. And I never saw it either."

• Saturday, October 28, 1967
In IBC's Studio A, engineers Mike Claydon and Damon Lyon-Shaw complete the mono single mix for "World" and turn their hands to mono mixes for "Sir Geoffrey Saved The World," "Birdie Told Me," "Harry Braff," "Horizontal" and "Lemons Never Forget" (most of these will go unused).

The *NME* reports that *Bee Gees' 1st* has now qualified for a gold sales award in the United States and that "Massachusetts (The Lights Went Out In)" made #1 in Holland. The band's *Cucumber Castle* television special is to go into rehearsal next week.

• Monday, October 30, 1967
Robert Stigwood leaves for the States to negotiate the Bee Gees' first concert tour of America, after which *Record Mirror* says he will travel to Australia to negotiate a tour down under. At IBC Studio A, engineers Mike Claydon and Damon Lyon-Shaw assemble stereo mixes for their next LP, *Horizontal*.

• Tuesday, October 31, 1967
The Times Of London reports that manager Robert Stigwood will leave the umbrella of NEMS to operate his own independent Robert Stigwood Organization (RSO) to handle the Bee Gees (among other artists).

• November 1967
Hullabaloo publishes the first installment of a three-part interview conducted by Bruce Gedman and Paul Nelson with the Bee Gees during their US promotional tour (earlier this year). The magazine asks if they have met the Beatles. "I met John and George down at the Speakeasy (a club in London)," says Maurice. "...I walked in and John Lennon said, 'Bee Gees!' like this. And I said, "Hi." Paul had just walked out then. He'd gone with Jane Asher somewhere. And I just sat and talked to John and he said, "I dig your act," and so forth, which I thought was very nice of him to say."

"They tried to come into one of our sessions once," recalls Barry. Robert Stigwood explains: "They wanted to come in on one of the boys' earlier sessions, but I asked them not to, because I didn't think it would be particularly good." Maurice interjects: "Just imagine! All of a sudden, you look up at the control room and you see this guy with glasses looking down at you!"

"It wouldn't have worked," says Barry. "It would be very hard if the Beatles walked into your session." When asked of the composers he most admirers, Barry offers: "Burt Bacharach. His chords are brilliant. The Beatles, naturally." As for future aspirations, Barry says: "Robin has written a couple of books that haven't been published. He hasn't taken them to anybody. We write a lot of poetry which goes into our songs."

• Wednesday, November 1, 1967
In Britain, the Bee Gees appear in concert at the Locarno, Stevenage.

• Thursday, November 2, 1967
In Britain, television's *Top Of The Pops* airs a further repeat performance of "Massachusetts (The Lights Went Out In)."

• Friday, November 3, 1967
In Britain, the Family Dogg (a group led by producer Steve Rowland) issue a cover of "The Storm," written by all three brothers.

• Saturday, November 4, 1967
The *NME* reports that the "newly-independent" RSO will commence producing the Bee Gees' feature film project, *Lord Kitchener's Little Drummer Boys*, which was held up previously by "work-permit problems." The paper goes on to write: "Stigwood will resign from NEMS at the end of November to launch his new company in collaboration with Germany's Deutsche Grammophon and Holland's Phillips Phonographic. The Bee Gees, the Foundations and the Cream are among the artists who will leave the NEMS banner and continue to be handled by Stigwood."

Record Mirror says that Barry Gibb traveled with Stigwood earlier this week to New York City for negotiations. The paper also publishes an interview with Barry conducted by Bill Harry: "On average, we write about six songs a week—and we put them down, not as demos, but as possible singles. Every song we write these days is an attempt at a single, and we cut them all in the recording studio. In fact, every track on our album has been an attempt at a single.

"In the last ten years, we've written hundreds, thousands of songs. I've been writing since I was nine. There are dozens of our numbers around here that'll never be used, although they could be good for somebody."

• Sunday, November 5, 1967
A London-bound train Robin is traveling on becomes derailed, killing 51 passengers. This tragic event will inspire the song "Really And Sincerely." In December, he will tell *Record Mirror's* Derek Boltwood of the tragedy: "...my first reaction was to think of God...I was quite safe and completely unharmed, so I felt it was my duty to try and help the injured passengers who were still trapped in the wreckage...But that train crash has effected me in a lot of ways...Being brought so close to death like that seems to have made me realize just how pointless it is to get too hung up on trifling little matters."

• Tuesday, November 7, 1967
At IBC Studio A, the group works with engineers John Pantry and Phillip Wade to record six takes of the future B-side "Sinking Ships." Maurice is in the control room for the initial tracking and asks, "Are you just going to call it, 'Sinking Ships'? To which Barry replies, "Yep." One of the engineers will then announce the song from the control as, "'Sinking Ships'—dedication to NEMS" (a reference to Robert Stigwood's former employers).

All of the instruments are initially recorded on a single track with Vince playing acoustic twelve-string, Barry on electric six-string and Colin on drums. After take one, Barry asks: "Maurice, you getting a big sound on the acoustic? Alright, lovely. I don't want mine featured; I want this featured." Colin asks for the engineers to stop the tape for a minute, after which his drums will appear on a separate track from take two on. Take two comes to a halt when Vince breaks a string (and Barry remarks that there is "No Dick" referring to their road manager, Dick Ashby). Takes two through five are rather chaotic arrangement-wise, and it is not until take six that the group pulls through a full performance.

Take six will become the basis of the master, receiving an overdub track of heavily-compressed piano from Maurice and another featuring his Mellotron and Vince's lead guitar parts. "Sinking Ships" will be subject to a further reduction and overdubs to complete the production (see below).

Also at this session, the Bee Gees tape three short takes (the first two of which are short false starts) of "When Things Go Wrong." This song is a bluesy, twelve-bar styled number with two guitars, drums and heavily reverbed organ (achieving almost an "ice rink" sound). The track is not particularly distinguished and it will be left incomplete and unissued.

On an undated reel the production of "Sinking Ships" is completed following today's session. The instrumental backing will combined with the previous overdubs of bass, Mellotron and lead guitar on one channel, leaving the other three open for double-tracked lead vocals from Barry and Robin, as well as a final channel for Bill Shepherd's orchestration (brass, strings and percussion). At first tipped as a single (see November 10, 1967), "Sinking Ships" will surface on January 26th as the flipside of "Words" in mono only. In 1990, Bill Inglot will remix the song for stereo when it is included on the *Tales From The Brothers Gibb* boxed set.

At the same undated session that finalizes "Sinking Ships," takes of an early version of "Chocolate Symphony" will be taped. These have a stronger lead guitar presence from Vince and the backing track will be topped off with overdubs, but never any vocals. The song will be remade on January 8, 1968.

• Friday, November 10, 1967
The Bee Gees (minus Robin who is still in shock from the train accident) tape an appearance for British ATV television's *Good Evening!* At the taping Barry tells the *NME*'s Keith Altham their next single is called "...'Sinking Ships,' all about life and death. It has a connection with disasters like plane crashes—this must sound a bit sick—but really it's not—you'd have to hear the record. We have to add strings to it yet." Altham also queries Barry on the possible release of the Gibb's older Australian recordings. "Someone sneaked a copy of our Australian album over to the States and they were playing things like 'Claustrophobia' over the air there. But these old discs bear so little relation to what we are doing now it would be ridiculous for anyone to issue them."

• Saturday, November 11, 1967
In Rotterdam, the Bee Gees headline a concert at the "hippy-happy" festival (supported by the Buffons and Daddy's Act) a "teenage fair" type of show. On Friday, the headliners were the Jimi Hendrix Experience and on Sunday it will be Pink Floyd. While in Holland, the Bee Gees are also to make some television appearances.

In the United States, "Massachusetts" (given a slightly revised title by Atco, "(The Lights Went Out In) Massachusetts") begins an eight-week chart run and will peak at #11. *Billboard* magazine reports that Robert Stigwood has begun the formation of a US branch of his RSO, with David Shaw named as the financial director of the new company. Stigwood says the newly formed RSO will get involved in film and television production on an international level. Their first project in this field will be *Lord Kitchener's Little Drummer Boys*, "...to be shot on location in Kenya early next year."

In Britain, *Record Mirror* reports that the Bee Gees will appear at the Los Angeles Forum on January 27th for two shows (at a fee of $30,000 for both). This show will not take place and the band will not appear at the Forum until December 1976! At that time they will record a live performance issued under the more-than-appropriate title, *Here At Last*.

• Monday, November 13, 1967
In Europe, an album assembly with twelve of the Bee Gees' Australian tracks is mastered under the title, *Second Hand People*. It will be remastered in fake stereo in February 1968 and retitled *Rare, Precious & Beautiful*.

• Friday, November 17, 1967
In Britain, on the day their new single, "World," is issued, the Bee Gees are scheduled to take part in a midnight show at Lewisham Concert Hall. The proceeds will benefit the Mayor of Lewisham's train disaster appeal (after the tragic Hither Green rail accident involving Robin on November 5th). Earlier in the evening, they will switch on the Christmas lights on London's Carnaby Street alongside Faye Dunaway (after which there will be dancing to music, and free soft drinks and cigarettes). Because of their late arrival in Carnaby Street, they may not appear at the Lewisham concert.

• Saturday, November 18, 1967
In South West London, the Bee Gees perform in concert (with support from Tony Rivers & The Castaways and The Bunch) at St. Mary's College, Twickenham. Also today, the *NME* reports that the Bee Gees will star in an hour-long Christmas television special, *How On Earth*.

• Sunday, November 19, 1967
In Britain, the Bee Gees perform two shows at London's Saville Theatre (where they made their UK stage debut earlier this year). Maurice tells the *NME* in advance that, "...we're having a thirty piece orchestra and a hundred extras to enact scenes from mythological and historical events."

In any event, the *NME* says the second set this evening includes "New York Mining Disaster 1941," "Every Christian Lion Hearted Man," a bit of "You Keep Me Hangin' On" (with some Vanilla Fudge-type guitar work from Vince), a cover of "Hi Heel Sneakers" (with Barry on lead vocals), "Words," "Gilbert Green," "To Love Somebody," Cream's "Strange Brew," "Massachusetts (The Lights Went Out In)" and "World." Tonight's shows are opened by the Bonzo Dog Doo-Dah Band, the Flowerpot Men and Tony Rivers & The Castaways. In the audience for at least one of the sets is Paul McCartney with girlfriend Jane and her brother Peter Asher.

1967

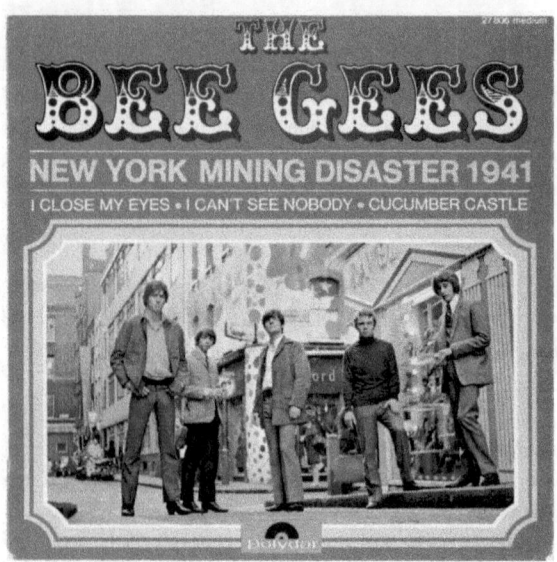

● Monday, November 20, 1967
The Bee Gees are scheduled for a three-day trip to Paris, France (for television work). The group will be videotaped in color for French television lip-synching "Massachusetts (The Lights Went Out In)" and "Sir Geoffrey Saved The World."

● Thursday, November 23, 1967
The group visits Bremen, Germany to tape another segment for *Beat Club* airing on Saturday.

● Saturday, November 25, 1967
In Germany, the group is seen once again on Radio Bremen's *Beat Club*. This television program features videotaped performances in black and white of the group lip-synching to "Massachusetts (The Lights Went Out In)" and Johnny Young performing his cover of "Craise Finton Kirk." In Britain, their latest single, "World," enters the charts and over the next sixteen weeks will peak at #9.

● Tuesday, November 28, 1967
At IBC Studio A, the group works with engineers Mike Claydon and Damon Lyon-Shaw on three new recordings. First up is "Out Of Line," for which the basic track will be spread across two tracks. These feature Vince (electric guitar) and Colin (drums) in one channel and Barry (electric guitar) in the other. This rendition of "Out Of Line" will be highlighted by Vince playing a guitar figure that is dropped from the final arrangement. Overall, these performances sound quite different melodically and rhythmically to the final product. Take ten will receive an overdub of heavily compressed piano from Maurice, but this version of the song will go no further. "Out Of Line" will be remade at tomorrow's session.

The second song that will be taped at this session is an early version of Robin's "Really And Sincerely." "I was in a train crash at the time," Robin said of the inspiration behind this track in a 2006 interview with the author, "and it's kind of a song after that. [Molly Hullis] who was not my wife at the time, we were living together, was in the crash with me. It was kind of about our relationship at the time, so it had a personal tone to it. It was also about the time we nearly got killed. So I suppose it really was an emotional time."

Take one from this session is incomplete and suffers from technical problems; take two will be considered the master. The instrumental set-up for this track is Maurice on piano (on one channel), Barry (electric guitar) and Colin (drums) on another. To this, separate overdub tracks of Maurice on Mellotron and bass will be added. All of these instrumental elements will be copied to a new four-track and reduced to a single channel. To this, Robin will add a lead vocal track, but nothing further is done with this version when it is decided to remake the song at tomorrow's session. In 2006, this second stage four-track will be mixed the author to mono for inclusion as a bonus track on *Horizontal*.

The final song worked on at today's session is an early version of "Swan Song." It shares a similar instrumental structure to "Really And Sincerely," beginning with Maurice's piano, and augmented by Vince (playing guitar harmonics in the intro), Barry on guitar (and off-mic vocals) and Colin (drums). The instrumental track is once again spread across to channels with Vince and Colin in one channel and Barry and Maurice in a second.

Before take four, the engineer suggests that Vince leave off his harmonics for now (and save them for an overdub). Take six will the master from today's session and is subject to overdubs of guitar harmonics (Vince) and more piano (Maurice) in one channel, as well as bass (Maurice) in the remaining channel. "Swan Song" will then be transferred to a new four-track tape, with all of the above elements reduced to a single channel. To these, overdubs will be added of lead vocals from Barry and Robin, as well as a track of backing vocals from the duo. However, the lead vocal performances will be incomplete and remain so when it is decided to remake "Swan Song" at tomorrow's session.

● Wednesday, November 29, 1967
A second day at IBC Studio A working with engineers John Pantry and E. S. produces two takes of a second unissued version of "Swan Song." The basic instrumental track is made up of Barry on acoustic guitar and Colin on drums. Take one is a complete performance, but it will be will be take two that is used as the basis of today's master. To this, overdubs will be added of guitar harmonics and lead from Vince, as well as piano on one track. The two remaining tracks will consist of more double-tracked lead guitar from Vince, one channel of which is shared with a bass guitar track from Maurice (and during the last verse, a bit more piano from him as well). Towards the end of today's session, the basic band tracks of guitars, piano, bass and drums will be reduced to a single of a new four-track tape. To these overdubs will eventually be added of Barry's lead vocal, backing vocals from Barry and Robin and orchestration from Bill Shepherd (strings, brass and percussion). Despite completing another full production, it will be decided to remake "Swan Song" again on December 13th. In 2006, the author will make a stereo mix from today's four-track of "Swan Song" for use as a bonus track on a reissue of *Horizontal*.

"Out Of Line" will also be remade during this session, beginning with the basic tracking line-up of Barry on acoustic twelve-string and Colin on drums. Overdubs will follow of piano (Maurice) sharing one channel of Vince's double-tracked lead guitar part, and on another separate channel, a track of bass from Maurice. Later during this session, "Out Of Line" will be transferred to a new four-track tape and all of the instrumental elements of the backing track will be reduced to a single channel leaving the other channels open for overdubs. These will be filled with three tracks of vocals: double-tracked lead vocals from Robin (mostly sung in three-part harmony with his brothers) and a separate track of backing vocals (also sung in three-part harmony by the brothers). In 2006, the author will make a stereo mix from today's four-track of "Out Of Line" for use as a bonus track on a reissue of *Horizontal*.

Also at this session, a new song, "The Change Is Made" (announced by an engineer as "The Change Has Come") will be recorded, twice. "I remember that was done at 2 o'clock in the morning," remembered Robin in a 2006 interview with the author. "It started out as a writing session which Barry evolved. It's like a semi-soul song, what they called a soul song in those days."

The initial tracking line-up will be Barry on acoustic guitar, Vince on electric and Colin on drums in one-channel. On track two, Maurice will play Mellotron (using the flute sound) live along with the band track. After take two, Maurice will change the Mellotron set-up from the flute sound to a patch of brass mixed with strings (three violins). The band will tape five takes of the song, the last of these being marked as master "for moment." Indeed, the Bee Gees will decide to remake the song later in this session.

Focus will now turn to a second and final version of Robin's "Really And Sincerely." The first few takes will begin with Barry playing acoustic twelve-string and Maurice using the accordion patch on the Mellotron. However, these will merely be short false starts; the final take (labeled as "two," but in fact the third attempt) will have Maurice's Mellotron erased by a bass track and augmented by overdubs of Robin's lead vocal (on one track) and a unique antique keyboard mixed with orchestra (strings, brass and mallets) on the final channel. "It was a piano accordion that I bought in Paris," Robin said in 2006 of the keyboard he played on the final production, "a one-hundred-year-old piano accordion which I still have. Particularly the chorus was written on that in Paris on that piano accordion on the first night I bought it." The completed production will soon be mixed for inclusion on *Horizontal*.

This particularly productive session will continue with a remake of "The Change Is Made" (still labeled as "The Change Has Come"). The tracking line-up will remain as Barry on acoustic guitar, Vince on electric and Colin on drums in one-channel. On track two, Maurice will once again play Mellotron. Following the completion of just one take, Maurice will overdub a track of bass guitar and this will be the basis of the final master. The four-track will then be copied and simultaneously reduced to a new tape (combining guitars, bass, drums and Mellotron to a single-channel). The engineer again announces the song title as "The Change Has Come" and Barry finally corrects him before taping his lead vocal, stating: "Change Is Made" (though for the final round of the lyric, he will sing "Change Has Come" and says at the end, "I'll leave that anyway"). Other overdubs to this track will include lead guitar from Vince on one channel and a separate track of Bill Shepherd's orchestration (strings, brass and tympani). The completed production will soon be mixed for inclusion on *Horizontal*.

1967

• Thursday, November 30, 1967
In Britain, television's *Top Of The Pops* features the Bee Gees performing their latest single, "World." The audio from this performance (essentially the same as the commercially released master) will be used for BBC World Service radio shows with some fake applause added.

• December 1967
In Australia, some of the group's earlier recordings are issued on an album called *Turn Around, Look At Us*. The LP features a current photo of the Gibb brothers and its press release misleadingly states the album was "recorded just before they left for England."

• Friday, December 1, 1967
At IBC Studio A, the Bee Gees work with engineers John Pantry and "E. S." [complete name unknown] to record two yuletide masters for the upcoming ATV television special, *How On Earth*. The Gibb original "Thank You" will be captured in four takes. The basic track will consist of Barry on acoustic twelve-string guitar, Vince on electric six-string and Colin on drums on a single channel. A second channel features Maurice playing organ live with the others. Take four will be subject to overdubs of Maurice playing bass and piano (on separate tracks). All of these instrumental elements will be transferred and reduced to a single track of another four-track tape. Later in this session, three tracks of vocals will be overdubbed (including a lead from Robin and backing vocals from all three brothers).

The second item taped today is simply labeled as "Medley" (and will consist of excerpts from the songs "Mary's Boy Child," "Silent Night" and "The First Noel"). The basic track will again consist of Barry on acoustic twelve-string guitar, Vince on electric six-string, Colin on drums and a second track of Maurice playing organ. The band will work through five takes of this concoction, the last of which will be the basis of the master. To this, overdubs will be added of guitar and bass on one track and one chord of organ for a few seconds on another. Following these overdubs, all of the instrumental work will be transferred to a single-channel of a new four-track tape. To this, double-tracked lead vocals from the brothers will be added (sung solo by Robin at first and then switching to three-part harmony). The completed productions will be used in the special taping on December 14th (broadcast December 24th). In 2006, the author will mix both songs from today's session tape into stereo for inclusion as bonus tracks on a reissue of *Horizontal*.

Prior to today's session, Derek Boltwood interviews Robin for *Record Mirror*. At the conclusion of the talk (which runs in the paper's December 16th edition), Maurice and Barry arrive to collect their brother for the session. "Come on Robin," says Barry, "we've got to write a Christmas carol this afternoon, and we're a half-an-hour late already." To which Robin replies, "Don't worry about that, I wrote one last night."

• Saturday, December 2, 1967
The 8 features an interview with Robin conducted by Nick Logan. "We get ideas for songs everywhere and anywhere," says Robin. "It's a telepathy type of thing with us, sort of written in the mind...It's pretty scary at times and it's not confined to music. Barry and I can be walking along a street together when we just start singing the same song in the same key at the same time.

"It can be frightening but we never talk about it to each other in case we put a mental block on it. But we are very grateful for it; we wouldn't like it to go...Ninety percent of it is mental telepathy. 'Massachusetts' is an example. I had this line in my mind all day; 'The lights all went out in Massachusetts.' Later that night I mentioned to Barry and he said: 'Yes, I know. I've already got the tune for it.' So we wrote the rest of the words together and Maurice did the arrangement."

• Monday, December 4, 1967
The Bee Gees are scheduled to begin filming an oft-delayed television project for Southern-TV called *Cucumber Castle*. Set at a castle near Maidstone, the hour-long show is slated to include a parody of the Beatles' recent *Our World* "All You Need Is Love" telecast. The Bee Gees' plans include reuniting a similarly star-studded audience like the one attending the Beatles' session. Nevertheless, the project will never reach fruition in this form and it will be more than a year before they are actually engaged in shooting this production.

• Saturday, December 9, 1967
The *NME* reports the Bee Gees will issue a soundtrack album from their *Cucumber Castle* film (currently set to start filming on January 3rd) early next year.

• Wednesday, December 13, 1967
At IBC Studio A, the group works with engineers John Pantry and Phillip Wade to tape a third and final version of "Swan Song." The initial track features two guitars (Barry and Vince) and drums (Colin). The first few takes suffer from guitar tuning issues. Beginning with take four, Maurice will play piano throughout the song. However, at this point all the instruments are still confined to one channel of the ½" four-track tape.

The arrangement will change again for take five; the basic track at this point is just acoustic twelve-string guitar and drums. For take six, an electric six-string guitar is added to the mix (but Maurice's piano is still missing). Take eight will be complete and initially marked as a possible master (receiving an overdub of piano from Maurice—though his performance will not be completed). For the remaining takes, Maurice will be heard playing piano on a separate track. Take seventeen will be the final master and will duly receive overdubs of backing vocals from Barry and Robin, as well as a track of orchestration from Bill Shepherd (brass, strings and mallets). The basic track and piano will be combined onto one channel of a new four-track tape; the orchestral overdubs will also be transferred to this new mix and combined with Barry and Robin's backing vocals. After these elements have been satisfactorily balanced, a new track of acoustic guitar and bass will be overdubbed. The final production touch will be Barry's lead vocal; "Swan Song" (once tipped as a single—see December 23rd) will be issued on next year's *Idea* album.

• Thursday, December 14, 1967
In Britain, television's *Top Of The Pops* airs a repeat of the Bee Gees' performance of "World." Also today, the group tapes their spot for television's *How On Earth* (see December 1st) at Liverpool Cathedral (for telecast December 24th).

• Friday, December 15, 1967
At IBC Studio A, mono and stereo masters are assembled for the Bee Gees' forthcoming *Horizontal* album.

• Saturday, December 23, 1967
The *NME* reports that the next Bee Gees single will not feature "Swan Song" (as originally planned), but will instead couple "Words" with "Sinking Ships."

• Sunday, December 24, 1967
In Australia, Barry and Robin Gibb are due back in Sydney today (accompanied by Robert Stigwood) for the first time since they set sail at the top of the year. They will spend Christmas down under. In Britain, their spot on *How On Earth* is telecast.

• Tuesday, December 26, 1967
In Britain, the Bee Gees are seen in Part Two (Part One aired on Christmas day) of a special year-end edition of television's *Top Of The Pops* performing "Massachusetts (The Lights Went Out In)" and in interview inserts about this year's trends. Robin offers a pound to anyone who can stand up and explain to him "I Am The Walrus" by The Beatles (whose *Magical Mystery Tour* film debuts later this evening, also on BBC-1), while Maurice declares that Angus McBrandy (the Scottish folk-singer) will be the biggest thing in the next ten years.

• Thursday, December 28, 1967
In Britain, television's *Top Of The Pops* airs yet another repeat of the Bee Gees' performance of "World."

• Friday, December 29, 1967
Barry and Robin Gibb leave Australia for a few days in Turkey. At Sydney airport, Barry tells *The Sydney Morning Herald* of their upcoming feature film: "It will be a comedy drama about the Boer war," he says. "It will be made in color and in the cast will be Goon Man himself, Spike Milligan."

• Saturday, December 30, 1967
In Germany, the Bee Gees are seen in a pre-taped, lip-synch performance of "World" on television's *Beat Club*.

Producer Ossie Byrne announces the next song at the session: "'Holiday,' the Bee Gees, back track only, take one." The entirety of this backing track is simply Maurice's shimmering organ part. All of the other overdubs made to this song will be built around his single performance. Take one is nearly complete, but falls apart towards the end. Take two sounds perfect, and is leadered off on the reel indicating it has potential for overdubs, but the brothers ultimately decide to press on. Take three sounds as if Colin may now be keeping time on the drums in the background, off mic. By the start of take four, it is also apparent that Barry and Robin have begun to sing along and there is some unrecorded rehearsal before a metronome is introduced for take four (which is incomplete) and take five (which is the master). The final take will initially receive overdubs of bass and double-tracked background vocals before being transferred to a second four-track during a reduction mix.

The final master for "Holiday" features Maurice's organ and bass combined to track one, Barry and Robin's alternating lead vocals on track two, Bill Shepherd's orchestral arrangement (of harp, percussion, strings and brass) on track three and the brothers' doubled-tracked backing vocals from the previous tape combined on the final channel. Now complete, "Holiday" will be featured on the Bee Gees' upcoming album and will eventually be pulled as a single for the U.S. market, becoming a hit there later this year.

1968

● **Monday, January 1, 1968**
According to the *Daily Mirror*, Barry and Robin land in the hospital in Istanbul suffering from exhaustion. Robert Stigwood says the duo was placed under sedation after a lengthy flight from Sydney, Australia.

"It was supposed to be a holiday but there were people waiting for us to arrive," Barry tells the *NME* upon their return, "press and television people wanting us all the time. Not that we mind interviews. It's great that somebody is taking an interest in you.

"Robert advised we should go to hospital for a check up. They told us we were suffering from mental and physical exhaustion. So we decided to rest up. There wasn't much we could do."

● **Wednesday, January 3, 1968**
Filming on the Bee Gees' *Cucumber Castle* special is delayed due to Robin and Barry's health. They are due back in London tonight.

● **Thursday, January 4, 1968**
The Los Angeles Times reports that local radio station KRLA gave out guitarist Vince Melouney's phone number, causing a deluge of calls. "The first I knew about it was when KRLA disc jockey, Bob Dayton, called me to say he had just given my number out over the air during his show," says Melouney. "After that the calls came non-stop. I didn't get a wink of sleep all night. I'm told the international exchange out there was blocked by kids wanting my number."

● **Saturday, January 6, 1968**
In Britain, the Bee Gees are seen on television's *Once More With Felix* show (hosted by folk songstress Julie Felix). According to an early report in *Record Mirror*, the group is scheduled to perform "World" and "Birdie Told Me."

● **Monday & Tuesday, January 8 & 9, 1968**
At IBC Studio A, the Bee Gees will begin the year with a number of new tracks, including "The Singer Sang His Song." The basic tracking set-up for this number is a channel of Maurice (piano) and Colin (drums) and another of Barry (acoustic guitar and off-mic vocals). The atmosphere is light, as the band joke through four false starts before making the master, take five. For this final pass, Maurice's piano is placed on a separate track (leaving Colin on channel one and Barry on channel two). In addition to these three tracks, augmentation of bass and reverbed lead guitar will be overdubbed and combined on the final open channel.

Later, all of the basic instrumental tracks will be reduced to a single channel of a new four-track tape. Vince will then make a further overdub of lead guitar harmony that will be blended in a track of backing vocals by all three brothers. The final set of overdubs on "The Singer Sang His Song" will be Robin's lead vocal track (sung in harmony with his brothers in sections) and a track of Bill Shepherd-conducted orchestration. "The Singer Sang His Song" will be mixed in mono for single release February 16th. In 1990, the song will be mixed in stereo by Bill Inglot for the *Tales From The Brothers Gibb* box set.

Next up, a second version of "Chocolate Symphony" (first recorded circa November 7, 1967) will be taped. The basic tracking set-up for this version is Barry (acoustic guitar), Vince (electric guitar) and Colin (drums), all recorded to a single channel of four-track tape. The first six takes will be incomplete and subject to a great deal of discussion regarding the arrangement. Take seven will be the first complete pass of the song and Maurice even attempts overdubbing piano to this take, but the instrument is out of tune with the basic track, so he will stop after only a minute or so. The performances will be fragmentary until take thirteen, which is considered the master. To this, Maurice will add overdubs of piano and bass (each on a separate track).

For the final reduction (and master) of "Chocolate Symphony," all of the instruments thus far taped will be combined to a single channel of a new four-track tape. To this, overdubs will be added of backing vocals (Barry, Robin and Maurice), lead vocals from Barry (with Robin and Maurice on the choruses) and lastly orchestration courtesy of Bill Shepherd. Though the track is undoubtedly the equal of the Bee Gees' other work from this era, "Chocolate Symphony" will remain in the can (and despite its commerciality, it will not even be covered by another artist). In 2006, the author will mix the final four-track to stereo for inclusion as a bonus track on the Reprise reissue of *Idea*.

The third song that will be taped at this lengthy recording date is the haunting "Down To Earth." The first five takes—featuring Barry (on acoustic twelve-string), Vince (electric six-string) and Colin (drums)—will be incomplete. Take six will be a full pass and considered the master, receiving overdubs from Maurice of piano and bass. Eventually, all of these elements will be combined to a single channel of a new four-track tape. To these overdubs will be added of Robin's lead vocal, with double-tracked choruses sung in three-part-harmony with Barry and Maurice. The final track will be utilized for orchestration conducted by Bill Shepherd (featuring solo saxophone in places, which is unique for a Shepherd score).

1968

• **Wednesday, January 10, 1968**
A third day at IBC's Studio A finds the Bee Gees at work with engineers Mike Claydon, Phillip Wade and Damon Lyon-Shaw. The first item taped at this session will be the mysterious instrumental, "Gena's Theme." "It was actually written for a film," Robin recalled in a 2006 with the author, "but I've forgotten what that film was going to be. There was another along with that that Sounds Incorporated did, 'The Square Cup.' It was in the same period as that was written; I remember writing it with Barry and Maurice." "The Square Cup" will be demoed at some point in this era (with just guitar and the brothers wordlessly singing the melody line), but a Sounds Incorporated rendition is unknown and certainly unissued. Another rendition of "The Square Cup" will surface next year on a German Polydor single by Orchester Max Greger.

"Gena's Theme" will be tracked with the line-up of Barry (acoustic guitar), Vince (electric guitar), Maurice (organ) and Colin (drums). After take two Barry mentions something being "for The Shadows" (perhaps this song was offered to the venerable instrumental outfit). Someone in the studio will ask, "Is this for an album?" To which Barry will reply, "I don't know; they want us to put it down." A voice from the control room quickly interrupts: "We've got less than two hours." Following five incomplete passes, take six will be the final performance and the basis for the master. To this overdubs will be added of bass, acoustic twelve-string guitar and a final track of mandolin, marimba, flute, harp and strings. This four-track will be transferred to a 1" eight-track tape for further production in June (see June 25th). An edited version of the instrumental will later be issued on the German-only LP, *Eine Runde Polydor*. A longer, period mono mix will be included as a bonus track on the 2006 reissue of *Idea*.

"Jumbo" will be the next song tackled at this date. "The song is about is an elephant obviously—an imaginary elephant for a child," Barry will explain in a 2006 interview with the author. "It's really a lullaby. It's a spirited little thing. I don't think it's over special. I just think it's one of those things that struck me as something you would sing to a child."

In March 1968, Barry will tell Bob Farmer in *Disc*: "We thought up the song around the idea that every child has an imaginary pet. In the song, 'Jumbo,' is the imaginary elephant who trails around with the child. I know that when I was small I used to daydream about having a lion as a pet."

Six brief false starts will be taped of "Jumbo" with the basic line-up of Colin on drums (in one channel) and Barry on acoustic twelve-string guitar alongside Vince on electric six-string (both balanced on a second channel). Take seven will be the master take and is treated to overdub tracks of Mellotron and two guitars, as well as another of bass.

Following this augmentation, all of the basic instrumental elements will be combined to a single channel of a new four-track tape. A further set overdubs will then be added of Barry's double-tracked lead vocal and lead guitar licks from Vince. Next month, "Jumbo" will be mixed to mono for single release on March 22nd. In 1990, both stages of the four-track masters will be resynched for the first stereo mix of the song by Bill Inglot (included on the *Tales From The Brothers Gibb* box set).

The final song tried at this session will be "Bridges Crossing Rivers." The initial tracking line-up will consist of Barry (acoustic guitar and off-mic vocal), Vince (electric guitar) and Colin (drums) on one channel and, in a separate channel, Maurice (bass). Beginning with take two, Maurice's bass is added to the first channel instrumentation (leaving three open channels for future overdubs). Vince's guitar part will give these early takes an almost Spanish feel. The final master will be take seven and this is later augmented by overdubs of organ (the same as used on "Holiday") and yet another track of bass. Nonetheless, this particular production of "Bridges Crossing Rivers" will go no further; the Bee Gees will tape a new version in June (though an exact recording date is unknown—see June 25th). "Just another trial song that sort of fell by the wayside," Barry will remember of "Bridges Crossing Rivers" in a 2006 interview with the author. "Not bad you know, but it was lacking something. We would always say, 'It needs something. It's not right. Let's leave it. Keep moving. Keep moving.'"

● Thursday, January 11, 1968
In Britain, the Bee Gees are seen in a repeat performance of "World" on television's *Top Of The Pops*.

● Saturday, January 13, 1968
The *NME* runs an interview with the Bee Gees conducted by Nick Logan. Barry says of their upcoming motion picture: "It will be a comedy film but it will also have death and drama and tragedy. We want to make people laugh and cry. People love to cry."

"We'll be writing the basic script, the skeleton of it. Then we'll hand it over to an experienced scenario writer. If we don't like the finished film we won't release it. That was where the Beatles went wrong."

● Monday, January 15, 1968
At IBC Studio A, the Bee Gees work with engineers Michael Claydon and Damon Lyon-Shaw to record "She Is Russia," a mid-tempo, acoustic-based number. The basic tracking line-up for this tune will be Barry (acoustic guitar), Vince (electric guitar) and Colin (drums) all balanced on one channel. Take three of the song will be complete and is leadered (indicating this as a potential master), but no overdubs will made to this performance. The band will play through five more fragmentary performances before taping the final pass, take nine. This take drags and doesn't improve on the earlier performances (which is perhaps why take three was considered a possible master). Whatever the case, the song will be shelved and never revisited.

● Tuesday, January 16, 1968
In Hanover, Germany, the group visits a Polydor convention where they are awarded a seven-foot-high gold disc (and five individual solid gold miniatures) for sales of "Massachusetts (The Lights Went Out In)."

● Thursday, January 18, 1968
At a Polydor reception in London, the Bee Gees receive a gold disc (presented by actress Juliet Prowse) for sales of "Massachusetts (The Lights Went Out In)". According to *Record Mirror*, the home secretary who had granted a reprieve to Vince and Colin, Mr. Roy Jenkins, had been asked to present the award, but he was unable to do so.

● Saturday, January 20, 1968
In the United States, "Words" becomes the Bee Gees' latest singles chart entry. Over the next eleven weeks, it will peak at #15. This single will be issued in Britain next week (see January 26th).

● Sunday, January 21, 1968
The Bee Gees fly to Los Angeles for television and press work, as well as their first-ever Stateside concert. This evening they will attend a benefit premiere of Richard Lester's film *How I Won The War* (starring John Lennon) at the Fine Arts Theatre. The event is sponsored by radio station KRLA to benefit the L.A. Free Clinic on Fairfax Avenue (on November 25, 1972 the group will perform a benefit in support of the same facility).

In the local press, Barry will tell the *Los Angeles Times* of their current activities: "We've done a half-hour concerto, which we're about halfway through with. It's the type of thing that the great geniuses like Beethoven used to do. Half-an-hour. People don't listen for half-an-hour. Basically we did it for a change. There isn't even a name on it yet. It's a challenge to ourselves, to see if people will say, 'That's nice,' or not. If not, we'll try something else. There are a hundred things we've done that have not yet been done by pop groups. No one will hear them but us for the next six months, until they come out.

"We haven't used any sound effects. We're against sound effects, we're against Flower Power, we're against LSD, we're not in any trend or trying to push any trend. As soon as you got a trend, you have to die with that trend."

1968

● Friday, January 26, 1968
In Los Angeles, the Bee Gees tape an appearance for American CBS television's *Smothers Brothers Comedy Hour* (to be aired on February 4th). In Britain, they are seen in a pre-taped segment on *All Systems Freeman* and the same date as their single "Words" c/w "Sinking Ships" is issued.

● Saturday, January 27, 1968
In Anaheim, California, the Bee Gees make their American concert debut with two "near-sell-out" shows (6 & 9:30pm) at the Convention Center. Openers include their Atco label mates Vanilla Fudge, as well as Spanky & Our Gang. In the audience for this historic event are members of the Mama's And The Papa's, the Monkees, the Turtles, Buffalo Springfield and the Smothers Brothers. According to the *Los Angeles Times*, the Bee Gees' set includes: "New York Mining Disaster 1941," "Every Christian Lion Hearted Man Will Show You," "The Earnest Of Being George," "And The Sun Will Shine," "Words," "Gilbert Green," "Turn Of The Century," "To Love Somebody," "Holiday," "In My Own Time," "I Can't See Nobody," "Massachusetts" and "World."

"What really knocked us out," Barry will tell Judith Gershman in *Teenset*, "is that when we came on stage for the second concert, the orchestra applauded us. That doesn't happen at home."

The show is promoted by former DJ, Bob Eubanks, and his business partner Steve Wolf, who jointly paid the band $15,000 to appear. Out of this, the group paid for a thirty-piece orchestra to "achieve their recording sound," says Eubanks.

● Saturday, February 3, 1968
In Britain, "Words" enters the singles chart and over the next ten weeks will peak at #8. *Record Mirror* publishes an account of a recent encounter with the group at Robert Stigwood's "jungle pad" (no doubt occurring this past January, based on their hectic itinerary). Discussing the Beatles' album, *Sgt. Pepper's Lonely Hearts Club Band*, Robin says: "I expect The Beatles supervised most of the artwork themselves. They're taking too much of other people's business in their own hands. I sat down prepared to enjoy [*Magical Mystery Tour*] and it was all right for a while and then I got bored and gave up."

"It was badly directed and edited," adds Barry, "you can't direct yourself properly. You're not in a position to judge how things are going." Maurice offers: "I liked it." Robin continues, "But it was so dated—that sort of thing had all been done in *Help!* Look at the 'I Am The Walrus' scene. Flower Power went out months ago. They're behind in their own trends."

As for their own film plans, Barry remarks: "We're about to make two. The first is *Cucumber Castle*, an hour's show based on the Knights of the Round Table. We've just finished writing the script." When asked if this put them in the same category as the Beatles directing themselves, Barry countered: "We are, after all, song-writers. We're expecting to be slammed. But if it doesn't work out, it won't be released. Anyway, two top professional comedy writers—Galton and Simpson—have read it and said it's very funny." The direction and camera work will be left to the professionals, concludes Maurice. The interview, which was conducted by Dave Griffiths, disintegrates when Robin and Vince face off in a discussion of fans and the blues guitarists Vince admires. Barry and Maurice wander off and Colin begins shouting at Robin, much to the amusement of the *Record Mirror* writer and cartoonist (sent along to sketch a picture of the boys).

● Sunday, February 4, 1968
The group appears in taped color lip-synch performances of "Words" and "And The Sun Will Shine" on U.S. television's *Smothers Brothers Comedy Hour.*

● Tuesday, February 6, 1968
The Bee Gees return to London from Los Angeles.

● Thursday, February 8, 1968
The Bee Gees set off for six Scandinavian concerts backed by a twenty-five piece orchestra. On British television, the Bee Gees will be seen once again in a repeat performance of "Words" on *Top Of The Pops.*

● Saturday, February 10, 1968
In the United States, *Horizontal* debuts on the albums chart; over the next twenty-two weeks, it will peak at #12.

● Tuesday, February 13, 1968
The band tapes another live radio session for BBC radio's *Top Gear* (to be broadcast February 18th). Songs include: "Birdie Told Me," "With The Sun In My Eyes," "The Earnest Of Being George" and "And The Sun Will Shine."

○ Wednesday, February 14, 1968
In IBC Studio A, the Bee Gees tape a new song called "In The Summer Of His Years." The basic track will be taped with Barry on electric six-string guitar, Maurice playing piano and Colin on drums (all taped to a single channel of four-track tape). Take two will be complete and the band plays it back for review before they decide to tape another performance. Take three is also complete, but Vince will say from the control room that they, "have to do it again" because of the ending. Beginning with take four, Maurice's piano is moved to a separate channel of the four-track.

Take seven will be the master take of the song and is soon treated to overdubs of Maurice's Mellotron for the first half of the song and for the second half, organ (returning to Mellotron for the fade of the song). Both keyboard parts will be dubbed to a single channel of the ½" tape, while the remaining open track will be devoted to a mixture of bass (Maurice) and lead guitar licks (Vince).

All of the instrumental elements from the previous four-track will eventually be reduced to a single channel of a new second-stage master. Vince's guitar parts and Maurice's bass will not be very audible in the new mix, so Maurice redoes his bass part on one of the open tracks. The remaining channels will be allocated to the brothers' backing vocals and Bill Shepherd's orchestral arrangement (flute, harp, mallets, strings and brass). The Bee Gees will undertake a third stage of production on this track during a February 21st session.

"I remember we dedicated that song to Brian Epstein," Robin recalled in a 2006 interview with the author, "the Beatles' manager, who had died in August of '67. We were on a boat in Monte Carlo Harbor and Robert's assistant came down the gang plank and said, 'We've got bad news. I've just been on the phone to London. They've found Brian, he's dead.' We were absolutely shocked. It was a dreadful, dreadful night getting back to London because we had to sail up the coast and try and get the plane back. Robert had to get back to London immediately, because he was [Epstein's business] partner. That's what I remember about that and of course that sowed the seeds of 'In The Summer Of His Years,' so we wrote that about Brian. There was a mixture of who we were going to sing about, because we liked to sing tributes to people."

○ Thursday, February 15, 1968
A second day at IBC Studios will produce the song "I've Decided To Join The Airforce." The basic tracking set-up will consist of Barry and Vince on electric guitars and Colin on drums (all balanced on one channel of ½" four-track tape). Following nine takes, the tape goes quiet and takes ten through twelve appear to have been erased. Recordings resume for take thirteen, the master, which will be treated to overdubs of Maurice's Mellotron and bass, as well as guitar fills from Vince.

This performance will be transferred to a new four-track where the basic track will be combined with the overdubs of bass and Mellotron to a single channel. Vince's guitar track will be redone for this second stage of production. Also added will be a track of Bill Shepherd-arranged orchestration and lead vocals from Robin (with harmony in sections from Barry).

"I've Decided To Join The Airforce" will reach a third stage of production on February 21st. A jokey entry written on today's session tape box—"Mellotroniaminy"—is nothing more than an engineer's fantasy. There is actually no other material taped at today's session.

○ Friday, February 16, 1968
At IBC Studio A, mono masters will be prepared for the Bee Gees' next single: "Jumbo" c/w "The Singer Sang His Song."

○ Saturday, February 17, 1968
Record Mirror reports that the Bee Gees are now set to headline a twenty-five city US tour, kicking off on July 26th at the Hollywood Bowl. The jaunt, expected to gross a million dollars, was set up by Stigwood, who returned from Los Angeles last week with news of the dates. "As far as I know," he says, "this will be the first time in America a group will have appeared live, before an audience, with an orchestra to back them." The band's television special, *Cucumber Castle*, has been delayed owing to exhaustion. Their film, *Lord Kitchener's Little Drummer Boys*, is now set to shoot in May in Kenya.

○ Wednesday, February 21, 1968
In IBC Studio A, the Bee Gees work with engineers John Pantry and Damon Lyon-Shaw to complete the productions of "In The Summer Of His Years" and "I Have Decided To Join The Airforce."

"Summer" will be transferred to yet another reel of four-track tape and have the bass from the second stage combined with the elements of the first stage four-track on one channel. To this, a lead vocal from Robin (with harmony from Barry in places) will be overdubbed. The second stage tracks of backing vocals and orchestration remain unchanged (and on separate channels). The completed production will appear on the Bee Gees' third London-made album, *Idea*.

The third and final stage of production on "I've Decided To Join The Airforce" will see the tune bounced to a new four-track tape. On this, Vince's guitar will be combined with the basic tracks and a second track of vocals will be added on a separate channel; Bill Shepherd's orchestration will occupy the remaining channel. The completed production will be included on *Idea*. At the close of this session, engineer John Pantry will make mono rough mixes of both titles.

1968

- Saturday, February 24, 1968
In Britain, the Bee Gees' LP *Horizontal* enters the albums chart. Over the next fifteen weeks, it will peak at #16. On British radio, the group will be heard on BBC's *Saturday Club*.

- Tuesday, February 27, 1968
The group embarks on a German tour (with Procol Harum as openers) that *Record Mirror* will characterize as "thirteen dates in thirteen days." The opening gig is scheduled for today in Hamburg's Musikhalle (for "two sell-out shows" according to the *NME*). Today the Bee Gees will also hold a fan reception (autograph session) at a national newspaper office.

- Wednesday, February 28, 1968
In Germany, the Bee Gees' tour is scheduled for Stadthalle in Bremen. The *NME* will later report: "At Bremen they filled the 6,300 seater auditorium, the first time ever for a pop presentation."

- Thursday, February 29, 1968
In Germany, the Bee Gees' tour is scheduled for Niedersachsenhalle in Hannover. Meanwhile back in Britain, the Bee Gees will be seen once again in a pre-taped clip of "Words" on television's *Top Of The Pops*.

- Friday, March 1, 1968
In Germany, the Bee Gees' tour is scheduled for Liederhalle in Stuttgart.

- Saturday, March 2, 1968
In Germany, the Bee Gees perform in concert at Kongress-saal in Munich. Procol Harum will serve as openers for this gig.

Robert Stigwood tells the *NME*: "The Bee Gees' film has been delayed because of script troubles. We hope now to begin shooting the movie on location in Kenya in May." The *Cucumber Castle* television special has also been delayed until after the feature film's completion.

- Sunday, March 3, 1968
In Germany, the Bee Gees' tour is scheduled for Meistersingerhalle in Nuremberg.

- Monday, March 4, 1968
In Germany, the Bee Gees' tour is scheduled for Jahrhunderthalle in Frankfurt. Meanwhile in the United States, the Bee Gees appear in a special film clip of their song "Lemons Never Forget" on NBC television's *Rowan & Martin's Laugh-In* (filmed on location in Los Angeles during their January '68 trip).

- Tuesday, March 5, 1968
In Germany, the Bee Gees' tour is scheduled for Halle Munsterland in Munster. Barry will tell Bob Farmer in *Disc*: "...At Munster in Germany we had to spend the night at an army barracks because we couldn't get past the fans outside the hotel we were supposed to be staying at."

- Wednesday, March 6, 1968
In Germany, the Bee Gees' tour is scheduled for Messehalle in Cologne.

- Thursday, March 7, 1968
In Germany, the Bee Gees' tour is scheduled for Sportpalast in Berlin.

- Friday, March 8, 1968
In Germany, the Bee Gees' tour is scheduled for Stadthalle in Baunschweig.

- Saturday, March 9, 1968
In Germany, the Bee Gees return to Essen to take part in a Radio Luxembourg ceremony. After this event, the band will travel to the United States to make an appearance on television's *Ed Sullivan Show*. Meanwhile, *Disc* reports that Maurice and Lulu's romance is over.

- Tuesday, March 12, 1968
At IBC Studio A, engineer Mike Claydon will prepare mono mixes of the backing tracks for "Words" and "The Singer Sang His Song." These are likely to be employed for the band's television work where they can sing live over the original recordings without competing with their own voices.

- Sunday, March 17, 1968
In Britain, the Bee Gees will be heard on BBC radio's *Top Gear*. In the US, they will be seen on CBS television's legendary *Ed Sullivan Show* performing "Words."

1968

• Friday, March 22, 1968
In Britain, the Bee Gees' latest single—"Jumbo" c/w "The Singer Sang His Song"—will be issued today. At IBC Studio A, Barry, Maurice, Vince and Colin demo a new song: "By The Light Of A Burning Candle." The basic track is comprised of Barry and Vince (electric guitars) and Colin (drums)—Maurice will remain in the control room to produce the session. Beginning with take two, Barry will switch to an acoustic guitar. However, after playing back the results of take three, Barry will return to the electric for take four. Take eight will be the final performance at this session and considered the master.

Take eight will receive overdubs of Maurice on piano and bass, as well as a lead vocal track from the Bee Gees' protégés Marbles—Trevor Gordon and Graham Bonnet. At this stage, Trevor sings lead on the song with Graham on harmony. The song will soon be remade alongside another Gibb song, "Only One Woman," for Marbles' first single in August. The production of these discs will be credited to Barry and Maurice (along with orchestration directed by Bill Shepherd). Though many of the Bee Gees' penned tracks will be misses for other artists, Marbles' disc will be a Top 5 UK hit in September. "We went to school together in Australia," Barry will tell the NME in February 1969, "and we made a pact that if we made it first we would help them and if they made it first, vice versa."

Following this session, IBC Studio A will go through a period of remodeling and (according to Beat Instrumental) will be closed during daytime working hours in April. When the studio "reopens," it will be outfitted with a 1" eight-track machine imported from America. With minor exceptions, most of the Bee Gees output will be recorded in this format from June 1968 through to 1971 (by which time the advent of 2" sixteen-track is inescapable).

• Tuesday, March 26, 1968
In Britain, Barry will appear on Radio 1's Pop Inn.

• Wednesday, March 27, 1968
The group opens their first-ever UK tour with an elaborate, forty-minute show at London's Royal Albert Hall. Tonight's bill includes the debut concert of Grapefruit and support from the Foundations, as well as co-headliners Dave Dee, Dozy, Beaky, Mick & Tich. Tony Hall serves as compere. The Bee Gees will dominate the entire second half of the evening with a fifty-minute set.

Their show begins with a symphonic overture before the opener "New York Mining Disaster 1941." Tonight's set also includes "Jumbo," "I Can't See Nobody," "Holiday," "To Love Somebody," "Really And Sincerely," "With The Sun In My Eyes," "Birdie Told Me," a "Harry Braff" medley (incorporating elements of "I Close My Eyes," "The Singer Sang His Song" and "Horizontal"), "Words," "World" and the debut of "I Have Decided To Join The Airforce." Barry introduces the song, according to Record Mirror's Derek Boltwood, with the following monologue: "This is the 50th anniversary of the Royal Air Force. So we wrote a number called 'I've Decided To Join The Airforce,' and we got the R.A.F. Band to join in the number." Boltwood says the show is a "...victory hurrah for good pop music," and features backing from a sixty-piece orchestra, a mixed choir of forty (the Ambrosian singers), as well as the R.A.F. apprentices marching band.

Following the performance, screenwriter Johnny Speight meets with Stigwood and the band and accepts the task of scripting their proposed film, Lord Kitchener's Little Drummer Boys. The plot is detailed as "the pressganging of boys to join the army as bandsmen during the Boer War." Record Mirror will report that the band is scheduled to write and perform six new songs in the feature, which is budgeted at 500,000 pounds and produced by Associated London Films. Filming is due to start in October in Kenya, but a director has yet to be chosen. "This will be decided after I have written the screenplay," remarks Speight.

• Friday, March 29, 1968
In Britain, the Bee Gees' tour continues at the Town Hall in Leeds.

• Saturday, March 30, 1968
The Bee Gees' UK tour travels to the ABC in Chester and their single—"Jumbo" c/w "The Singer Sang His Song"—enters the British singles chart. During the next seven weeks, it will peak at a mild #25.

Barry tells Bob Farmer of their new 45 in today's edition of *Disc*: "We're moving away gradually from the big, dramatic ballad scene. Our new single, 'Jumbo,' is not a ballad. But the B-side, 'The Singer Sang His Song,' which was, at first, to have been the A-side, was too much like our other singles. Something had to be done and 'Jumbo' is certainly a change for us."

Of the group's camaraderie, Barry says: "We all get along fine now, although in the earlier days things were a little difficult between us brothers and Vince Melouney and Colin Petersen. They felt like outsiders and it didn't help that they never worked with us on writing songs. But that's in the past and we're all together now."

• Sunday, March 31, 1968
The Bee Gees appear in concert at Manchester's Palace Theatre. Bob Farmer of *Disc* will report: "...two Sunday houses were half empty. The fans who have turned up, however, have screamed their heads off."

In the press, Johnny Speight says of possible casting for *Lord Kitchener's Little Drummer Boys*: "I want a top comic to play Lord Kitchener, because it strikes me he was a buffoon. It will be hard to make the Bee Gees cockneys, but there will be bad language."

• Monday, April 1, 1968
As their tour hits Leicester's De Montfort Hall, the group is seen on U.S. television's *Rowan & Martin's Laugh-In* for a second time.

• Thursday, April 4, 1968
In Britain, the Bee Gees perform at the Regal Theatre in Cambridge. Barry tells Bob Farmer in *Disc* that following this gig: "We brought Beaky [of Dave Dee, Dozy, Beaky, Mick & Tich] back to London from the show in Cambridge in our car the other night and we played Monopoly all the way."

• Friday, April 5, 1968
In Britain, the Bee Gees perform at the Adelphi in Slough.

• Saturday, April 6, 1968
In Britain, the group is scheduled to perform at Sheffield's City Hall. The *NME* reports that screenwriter Johnny Speight (currently at work on the script for the Bee Gees' film which is now delayed until October), will offer the group some other roles in the meantime. Speight, the creator of the series *Till Death Do Us Part* (later adapted in America as All In The Family), had a television play *If There Weren't Any Blacks, You'd Have To Invent Them* halted two years ago by the BBC and Rediffusion as "too offensive." Speight feels that things have changed and despite the incendiary title, the premise of the work is to expose racism via satire. With fresh offers for the program, Speight tells the paper: "If a deal was finalized, the Bee Gees would have major roles in the production." This teleplay will be produced later this year (and again in 1974), but without any Bee Gees involvement.

In the United States, "Jumbo" enters the singles chart and over the next six weeks will peak at #57.

In Germany, the group is seen in a pre-taped, lip-synch performance of "Harry Braff" on *Beat Club*.

• Sunday, April 7, 1968
In Britain, the Bee Gees are scheduled to perform at Birmingham's Hippodrome.

• Wednesday, April 10, 1968
In Britain, the Bee Gees are scheduled to perform at the ABC Theatre in Carlisle.

• Thursday, April 11, 1968
In Britain, the Bee Gees are scheduled to perform at Green's Playhouse in Glasgow, Scotland.

• Friday, April 12, 1968
In Britain, the Bee Gees are scheduled to perform at the ABC Theatre in Edinburgh.

1968

- Saturday, April 13, 1968

In Britain, the Bee Gees are scheduled to perform at the ABC Theatre in Stockton. *Disc* reports that following last week's gig in Slough Barry told the paper's Bob Farmer: "Our one hope is that we make a good showing in our first film, *Lord Kitchener's Little Drummer Boys*. If we pass the test of this film, we'll be able to make more movies, either together or in individual parts. We'll carry on making records, of course—in fact, we have in the can some entirely new material right away from our big, emotional ballad kick..." The band are said to be busy composing songs for the score of screenwriter Johnny Speight's *Till Death Do Us Part* feature film ("Ballads and Alf Garnett might not seem to go together, but surprisingly they fit in most suitably," says Barry). A casting, meanwhile, is imminent on their own feature, "...We're hoping to line up one top comedian," says Barry.

- Sunday, April 14, 1968

In Britain, the Bee Gees are scheduled to perform at Liverpool's Empire Theatre.

- Wednesday, April 17, 1968

In Britain, the Bee Gees are scheduled to perform at Portsmouth's Guildhall.

- Thursday, April 18, 1968

On their day off, the Bee Gees tape a live radio session for *Saturday Club* (including "The Singer Sang His Song" and "Jumbo") for broadcast May 4th. This will be their last live radio session for two years.

- Friday, April 19, 1968

In Britain, the Bee Gees are scheduled to appear at the Gaumont Theatre in Hanley.

- Saturday, April 20, 1968

In Britain, the Bee Gees are scheduled to appear at the Odeon Theatre in Bolton.

- Sunday, April 21, 1968

In Britain, the Bee Gees are scheduled to perform at the ABC Theatre in Hull. As of this date, openers Dave Dee, Dozy, Beaky, Mick and Tich will be temporarily replaced by the Foundations on the tour through April 27th.

- Monday, April 22, 1968

In Britain, the Bee Gees are scheduled to appear in concert at the ABC in Lincoln.

- Wednesday, April 24, 1968

After a night off, the Bee Gees' British tour is scheduled for a stop at the Odeon Theatre in Salisbury.

- Thursday, April 25, 1968

In Britain, the Bee Gees are scheduled to perform at the Odeon Theatre in Romford.

- Friday, April 26, 1968

In Britain, the Bee Gees are scheduled to perform at the Odeon Theatre in Exeter.

- Saturday, April 27, 1968

In Britain, the Bee Gees are scheduled to appear at the Odeon Theatre in Cardiff. The *NME* reports that the Bee Gees will take over television's *Time For Blackburn* for an entire episode next month. They are expected to do the same in September when they are guests on America's *Hollywood Palace* (though this bit of publicity will not actually come to pass). In the United States, "The Singer Sang His Song" hits *Billboard's* bubbling under charts at #116. In Germany, the group is seen once again on television's *Beat Club* in a pre-taped, lip-synch performance of "Harry Braff."

Disc runs an article by Bob Farmer taking Stigwood's hype machine to task, specifically the Beatles/Bee Gees comparisons.

The svengali readily defends labeling the group as "most significant musical talent" in a featured interview. "But they are," Stigwood insists, "These boys arrived in England last year, sent me tapes of their early records which I played and thought very Beatlish. I might have gone no farther with them because of this until it was pointed out to me that the boys were barely sixteen-years-old when these songs had been written. So it figured if boys of that age could turn out material of that caliber they must have immense talent. Hence the label I gave them."

The Bee Gees' current tour and single are also given a spin by Stigwood: "The picture is not as gloomy as people are making out. It is making a profit and they are playing to seventy percent houses. But I accept full responsibility for the fact that it isn't a sell-out tour. I did over-estimate their drawing power in Britain...As for record sales, 'Jumbo' was aimed at the American market. I now realize it was a mistake to release it as an A-side in Britain because the public still want big, emotional ballads from the boys."

• Sunday, April 28, 1968
In Britain, the Bee Gees are scheduled to appear at the Granada Theatre, Tooting.

• Monday, April 29, 1968
The group flies to Munich, Germany to receive the Golden Otto Award from *Bravo* magazine. The event is open to the public and fans can call in and speak with the Bee Gees.

• Wednesday, May 1, 1968
The Bee Gees open a brief Irish tour in Cork at the Savoy. Meanwhile back at London's IBC Studio A, engineer Phillip Wade mixes instrumental versions of "The Singer Sang His Song," "Birdie Told Me," "To Love Somebody," "World," "With The Sun In My Eyes" and "Massachusetts (The Lights Went Out In)" to be used for the group to sing over in future television appearances.

• Thursday, May 2, 1968
The Bee Gees appear in concert at the Adelphi in Dublin, Ireland.

• Friday, May 3, 1968
The Bee Gees' tour closes at the ABC Theatre in Belfast, Ireland. Barry tells the *NME*: "It was a successful tour. I can't say we made a lot of money out of it because we didn't, but it was a fantastic experience for us. We learnt a heck of a lot."

• Saturday, May 4, 1968
Disc reports that the band is due to star in a television spectacular called *Frankie Howerd Meets The Bee Gees* (with comedian Frankie Howerd to be aired in August). Also in this issue, manager Robert Stigwood appeals to the band's fans to stop gathering outside his offices: "Our landlords are very worried about the fans, and have asked to keep the street clear." On BBC radio, the group is heard on *Saturday Club*.

• Sunday, May 5, 1968
In Britain, the Bee Gees are scheduled to appear on ABC television's *Eamonn Andrews Show*.

• Wednesday, May 8, 1968
In Britain, the Bee Gees travel to Southern-TV's Southampton studios to tape a special episode of *Time For Blackburn!*. In this program, the group are said to star, with the namesake host, Tony Blackburn, acting as their guest. They plan to perform numbers from *Horizontal* as well as some comedy type bits. The format is being masterminded by producer Mike Mansfield and manager Robert Stigwood. This is one of many film and television projects that Mansfield will undertake with the Bee Gees; since late 1967, Mansfield has been attached to their *Cucumber Castle* television special.

• Saturday, May 11, 1968
On British television, the group will be seen on *Time For Blackburn!* (taped on May 8th) in an episode also featuring former Manfred Mann lead vocalist, Paul Jones.

The *NME* reports that the Bee Gees' special with Frankie Howerd will be screened as a part of Thames Television's opening night on July 30th (though it will ultimately be delayed). The group's other television plans include a French-German co-production, to be filmed from July 8th through the 22nd and directed by Jean Christophe Averti (production on this will be pushed until later in the year; it will become the *Idea* special).

Earlier this week, the Bee Gees were to be filmed in the recording studio for a two-part television documentary, *The Years Of The Joker*. Created by German director Michael Pfleghar, this three-hour program is to be shot worldwide and include prominent figures from many walks of life; the Bee Gees will represent the "pop world." Scenes are scheduled to include the Bee Gees in concert at the Hollywood Bowl (but these will certainly not be shot, since the gig is later cancelled). Pfleghar is a prolific filmmaker in this period, but it is unlikely this epic is ever completed; professional recording studio footage of the band has yet to surface.

The Gibb brothers have also been signed to write the music for a thirteen-week series titled *Pippi Longstocking* (to be sponsored by the Swedish Government). Though the program ultimately goes on without any Bee Gees involvement, the brothers very likely do compose songs for this venture with a variety of titles rumored, but none actually confirmed.

• Sunday, May 12, 1968
In Britain, Robin attends the *NME* Poll Winners concert and will accept the award for "Best New Group" (on behalf of the Bee Gees) from Roger Moore at Wembley's Empire Pool.

- Saturday, May 18, 1968

The *NME* announces that the group is officially on holiday until they resume recording sessions in June. Robin later tells the paper of these travels: "After 'Jumbo' we went on holiday to different parts of the globe and met up again unfortunately in different parts of the globe." Barry picks up the story saying: "Strangely none of us knew where the others were going. I went to Los Angeles and got a bit fed up with the scene there. A few people I knew there I found to be phoney and I wasn't enjoying myself. So I came home and then went to Rome and when I got to the airport Robin was standing there. And it was a strange thing because I had just decided to go there on the spur of the moment. It was very weird considering that I could have gone anywhere. I thought Robin was in India but apparently he got fed up with it and decided to go to Rome as well. It's the telepathy thing again. It crops up all the time."

- June 1968

In the United States, the Jubilee label issues an album by the Sounds Of Modification featuring the Gibb-penned song, "You."

- Saturday, June 1, 1968

In Nassau, Colin Petersen marries Joanne Newfield, Brian Epstein's former assistant. Vince serves as best man (his wife, Diane, will be the couple's bridesmaid).

- Saturday, June 8, 1968

The *NME* reports that a proposed tour of Japan has been pushed back to September. In Britain, the group (back from their holidays) will be seen once again on Southern-TV's *Time For Blackburn!*

- Wednesday, June 12, 1968

Breaking in IBC's newly-installed eight-track recorder, the Bee Gees tape a batch of new tunes. The first of these, "Kitty Can," is sung in harmony by Barry and Maurice (prefacing much of their work on next year's *Cucumber Castle*). The song will be taped in a single take with just two acoustic guitars. To these tracks overdubs of drums and handclaps, bass, Mellotron and vocals will be added. The Mellotron overdub will later be erased to make room for Bill Shepherd's orchestration for the song. However, very little of Shepherd's work will be utilized in the final mixes of "Kitty Can." The monaural mix will be shorter owing to the fact that it runs at a faster pitch than the equivalent stereo dubdown (a varispeed oscillator is in place for this and all of IBC's early eight-track sessions to compensate for voltage issues with their new American-made machine). An alternate period stereo rough mix featuring Shepherd's score (and harpsichord) will be featured as a bonus track on the 2006 reissue of *Idea*.

Another one take wonder will be "I.O.I.O.," a rhythmic tribal number built around a catchy chorus line. Today's rendition will feature only the chanted chorus (and no verse lyrics) to a back drop of acoustic twelve-string, bass and three sets of drum tracks. On October 8, 1969, Barry and Maurice will remake "I.O.I.O." for eventual single release in 1970.

Significantly more time will be spent on "Let There Be Love." "'Let There Be Love' was written next to St. Paul's Cathedral in a penthouse apartment that we rented when we first arrived in England. With me and my then girlfriend [Lynda] who is my wife now. That song was written in that penthouse round about midnight. We'd just fallen in love and it was that type of mood I was in that night."

As many as nine takes of the track will later be "rolled over" (to conserve tape). Now that the Bee Gees have the luxury of eight tracks to experiment with, the path of their productions is less clearly detailed in the tapes that will survive. What is known is that "Let There Be Love" will begin with a basis of guitars (Barry and Vince), piano (Maurice) and drums (Colin). To this, Maurice will overdub bass and Mellotron. Over the next month or two, the vocals (which initially feature Barry exclusively), will be worked with, reviewed and erased, resulting in Robin singing the final verse. Also, Maurice's Mellotron will be replaced (and erased) by a track of Bill Shepherd orchestration. A period rough mix featuring Barry's first lead vocals and Maurice's Mellotron will be included as a bonus track on the 2006 reissue of *Idea*. Another, still unissued period mix reveals that there is significantly more to Bill Shepherd's score than used on the final production (as well as bringing to light that the vocals on this track are probably the last items altered in the production).

Also at this session, two instrumental jams will be committed to tape. "Stepping Out" is a bluesy number taped in two takes and featuring lead guitar from Vince, bass from Maurice and Colin on drums. The same line-up will next lay down "No Name," which is at first a cover of Cream's "Sunshine Of Your Love" and by take three develops into a twelve-bar blues improvisation. The track title, "No Name," will pop up again in a few sessions, but this is only an engineer's shorthand for an untitled composition; the two songs are unrelated. All of the tracks will be unissued.

- Thursday, June 13, 1968

At IBC Studio A, Robin demos a number of his recent songs, accompanying himself on guitar. Tunes committed to tape include "Indian Gin & Whisky Dry," "The Band Will Meet Mr. Justice," "Heaven In My Hands," "The People's Public Poke Song," "The Girl To Share Each Day," "My Love Life Expired," "Heaven In My Hands" and "Come Some Christmas Eve Or Halloween." Only "Indian Gin & Whisky Dry" and "Come Some Christmas Eve Or Halloween" will be remade with the Bee Gees. Also today, rough mixes are prepared of "Let There Be Love."

1968

- **Friday, June 14, 1968**

At IBC Studio A, the group will tape Barry's wistful "Kilburn Towers." The basic track will consist of Barry and Vince (acoustic guitars), Maurice (Mellotron) and Colin (drums). Beginning with take three, Colin will switch to bongos for a lighter feel and Maurice will introduce the song's wonderful Mellotron opening. This rendition will be a full performance, but after playing it back, the group will decide to press on with a few further takes. Take six will be played at a more relaxed tempo and closer to the final arrangement, albeit incomplete. The final, full performance of the song will be take eight, which is eventually topped off by double-tracked lead vocals from Barry, as well as tracks of percussion overdubs and Bill Shepherd-arranged strings.

Also at this session, the group will tape Vince's "Such A Shame," a rare non-Gibb written song in the Bee Gees' post-1967 catalog. "It's all about that it was such a shame that everything was falling apart," recalled Vince in a 2006 interview with the author, "that's what the song's about. It mentions Stigwood in the lyrics. In fact, I made a big mistake on that song to be honest with you. Barry loved it, wanted to sing it and I said, 'No, I want to sing it!' I wish I had let Barry sing it now."

"Such A Shame" will be tracked in three takes with Maurice and Vince on guitars (acoustic and electric) and Colin (drums). Following the completion of take three—the master—Maurice will overdub bass, piano and organ parts; Vince will add more guitar and harmonica. The production will be completed with two vocal tracks from Vince (and some harmonies from Maurice).

- **Monday, June 17, 1968**

At IBC Studio A, the group works with engineers Phillip Wade and Damon Lyon-Shaw to tape Robin's "Indian Gin & Whisky Dry" (first demoed June 13th). The song will be captured in a single take on eight-track tape featuring two tracks of vocals, plus two guitars (Barry and Vince), Maurice on bass and Mellotron and Colin on drums. The final open track will be utilized for Vince's detuned guitar introduction.

"I really enjoyed doing that," Vince recalled in a 2006 interview with the author. "We detuned a guitar on that and tried to get Indian. Not exactly like a sitar, but leaning in that direction. Robin sang that, that was good; experimenting a bit. We started to experiment in *Horizontal* away from everything they'd previously done. Not that there was anything wrong with what they'd previously done—it was terrific. They just started to experiment more with sounds, arrangements and then it came to a screaming halt after *Idea*."

"That was actually written when I was in India," recalled Robin in 2006. "I came up with the idea in New Delhi. I actually saw the title on a menu in a restaurant in India and sort of took the title from that and then finished it up together with Barry and everyone in London when I got back."

- **Tuesday, June 18, 1968**

At IBC Studio A, the band works with engineers Philip Wade and John Pantry on "When The Swallows Fly." The initial tracking set-up will consist of Maurice on piano (recorded in stereo on two tracks of a 1" eight-track tape), Vince and Barry on electric guitars and Colin on drums. Take one will be complete and fairly close to the final arrangement; nevertheless, the band will press on through three further takes before they are satisfied. Take four will be the master and duly receives overdubs of bass and lead voice (with backing harmonies on the choruses). The production will eventually be completed by additional percussion (including tambourine) and a track of Bill Shepherd-arranged orchestration.

"['When The Swallows Fly'] was written in Munich I think," recalled Robin in a 2006 interview with the author. "It was about the same time as 'Swan Song' was written. It was an IBC song. It was one of my favorites. I think Barry's vocal on that is fantastic." When the final mixes are prepared of "When The Swallows Fly," the stereo version will run slightly longer than the monaural mix.

Also at this session, the band will tackle a track listed on the tape box simply as "No Name." Barry will lead the tracking for this tune on six-string electric, joined by Vince on acoustic, Maurice on chugging swamp bass and Colin on drums. Take one of this number will be complete, but it is notated as being "scrapped." A new take one is announced following this and is taken at a much slower tempo. In fact, it sounds like a totally different song. In between takes, Barry will sing some lyrics indicating this song is fairly structured and nearly complete at the time of recording. Take four will be the final attempt at the number. Although it is complete, the production of "No Name" will go no further. Despite some unique chord changes, like so many of the Bee Gees' copious song ideas, it will be left behind in favor of newer creations.

• **Thursday, June 20, 1968**
At IBC Studio A, the Bee Gees will work on the title track to the forthcoming LP, "Idea." "['Idea'] was Jagger influenced," Barry recalled in a 2006 interview with the author. "In those days, of course, everything was either the Stones or the Beatles and everybody wanted to be in that sort of zone. So I think that it was certainly influenced by that. 'The Earnest Of Being George' was influenced by them. Sometimes Vince Melouney, because he was a rocker at heart, would influence us. I remember Vince on 'Idea' the [sings guitar lick]. It was wanting to do something with more aggression; with more energy. That's my greatest memory of it is looking for something that was a little more angry, a little more aggressive and that just came out in the studio."

Take one opens with Maurice's piano discord (recorded in stereo), before pounding into the verse with Colin on drums and Barry on acoustic guitar. Before take three, Barry suggests that Maurice let the opening piano discord ring out more before starting into the intro (Barry will eventually join in on this note with a simultaneous downbeat on his acoustic guitar). Maurice will also slow the tempo a bit, helping the song find a groove. Nevertheless, the first five passes of "Idea" will be incomplete false starts—though every take sounds promising. Take six will be the first full performance of the song, sounding very close to the final production. Still, the Bee Gees will go for a further performance beyond this which will result in the master, take seven.

The final production of "Idea" will be treated to overdubs of Vince's lead guitar line, Maurice's bass, two tracks of vocals and some added tambourine. The 1" eight-track runs slower in pitch to the final mixes owing to some voltage conversion issues with IBC's American-made eight-track machine. The tape box notes "Machine used to get 15 i.p.s.," hinting that a vari-speed oscillator was most likely in use for most of the mixing. The mono and stereo mixes of this track will differ wildly, with clapping and whistling only heard on the mono track (which also switches quite audibly to a different guitar and vocal track via an edit at 1:38). A shorter alternate mix from the period (first issued as a bonus track on the 2006 reissue of *Idea*) features more of this secondary vocal.

Also at this session, "Come Some Christmas Eve Or Halloween" (first demoed June 13th) is taped with Robin on organ and Maurice on acoustic guitar. Following a couple of false starts, take three will be the master performance and is eventually treated to overdubs of Mellotron and Robin's vocals. The song will initially be left in the can; in 2006 it will be mixed by the author from the 1" eight-track for inclusion as a bonus track on Reprise's reissue of *Idea*. The same mix will turn up on Robin's *My Favorite Christmas Carols* project (also issued in 2006).

The final number recorded at this date is the soon-to-be-classic, "I Started A Joke." "The melody was actually heard on the engines of a Viscount Turboprop airplane going over Essen in Germany," Robin will recall in a 2006 interview with the author. "I don't know whether you've heard the droning of an engine? It's a hypnotic thing. If you just go for a two-hour-flight, you hear this tone. Sometimes you'd hear it in church bells; you can hear hidden melody. It was the same in an engine, and it was this melody. I think me and Barry that night in the hotel in Essen, we got back between ten and twelve, we finished up the lyrics and we had the song.

"What we were trying to put across with that record, it's almost spiritual, yet it's very self-analytical. I think it's a very original piece of work because first of all it's like a person saying, 'I've got regrets, but I can only blame myself for something going wrong.' But it's not about someone setting themselves up as being a great person. It could almost mean that he stepped out of the picture and let people get on with their lives. A lot of people have their own interpretation of this song. I'm very proud of the song."

The first take will be started simply with Vince picking on an electric six-string guitar, followed by Colin on drums, Barry on acoustic twelve-string and Maurice plucking out a wonderful bass line (on the final take, this will give the track its majestic opening). Take one will be a short false start. Take two will be a complete performance and take three, the final master. The production will eventually be topped off by Bill Shepherd's rich orchestration (overdubbed across two channels), as well as two tracks of vocals (featuring an incomparable lead from Robin and backing vocals from Barry and Maurice). By year's end, "I Started A Joke" will be riding high in the US singles chart (see December 14th).

• **Friday, June 21, 1968**
At IBC Studio A, the band will record Barry's "Maypole Mews" (possibly inspired by a street name in Leeds). The tracking will be led by Barry on acoustic guitar and Colin on drums. Beginning with take two, Vince will join the arrangement playing a melody line on electric guitar; Maurice will augment this with a part on the Mellotron. The foursome will struggle through ten takes of the song before completing the final master, take eleven. This take will be augmented by an overdubbed bass part from Maurice; however, the production will go no further. In February 1969, Barry's pal David Garrick will issue a version of "Maypole Mews" on the Pye label. Nevertheless, the arrangement heard on Garrick's disc (produced by John Schroeder and arranged by Johnny Arthey) will differ radically from the renditions performed at today's session by the Bee Gees.

Also today, the band will tackle a song called "Men Of Men." The tracking set-up consists of Barry on acoustic guitar, Maurice on organ and Colin on drums. The group will tape five incomplete false starts, before completing the master,

take six. This recording will be augmented with overdubs of Mellotron, piano, orchestration from Bill Shepherd and a vocal recitation by Barry. The lyrics are in poetic medieval-style verse and the production, which is heretofore unissued, foreshadows the big ballad style of *Cucumber Castle*.

• Tuesday, June 25, 1968
At IBC Studio A, engineer Damon-Lyon Shaw will compile a 1" eight-track reel of the Bee Gees' recent productions including "Idea," "Come Some Christmas Eve Or Halloween," "I Started A Joke," "Maypole Mews," "Men Of Men" and "Gena's Theme." Another 1" reel simply dated "June 1968" from this period contains the compiled masters of "Kitty Can," "I.O.I.O.," "Let There Be Love," "Bridges Crossing Rivers," "Completely Unoriginal," "Kilburn Towers," "Such A Shame," "Indian Gin & Whisky Dry" and "When The Swallows Fly."

Given the flexibility of adding (and erasing) elements from the eight-track tapes, exact recording dates are unknown for the overdubs on "Gena's Theme," and the start and completion of "Bridges Crossing Rivers" and "Completely Unoriginal." The last two of these will be mixed in 2006 by the author for use as a bonus track on the Reprise reissue of *Idea*. Dates for IBC's eight-track session reels for the rest of the year are uncharacteristically absent.

• Wednesday–Friday, June 26–28, 1968
In IBC Studio A, the group works with engineer John Pantry on mono mixing selections for their next album, *Idea* (including "Let There Be Love," "When The Swallows Fly," "Indian Gin & Whisky Dry," "Kitty Can," "Idea," "I Started A Joke," "I Have Decided To Join The Airforce," "Down To Earth," "Gena's Theme" and "Swan Song"). Also during these sessions, Marbles' debut single, "Only One Woman," is mixed for release.

• Saturday, June 29, 1968
The *NME* (who picture the group in session from earlier this week) states the Bee Gees won't begin shooting their feature film until November. In Britain, the group will be seen yet again on Southern TV's *Time For Blackburn!* (in an episode also featuring Bobby Vee, Barry Ryan & Gulliver's People).

• Monday, July 1, 1968
At IBC Studios, mono and stereo mixing is in progress for the *Idea* album.

• Saturday, July 6, 1968
Billboard magazine reports that the group will kick-off a United States concert tour on August 1st in Sacramento, California. Support acts are proposed to include Spanky & Our Gang, as well as Kenny Rogers & The First Edition. The band's booking agents are hoping for guarantees as high as $25,000 with four west coast dates already booked (including Los Angeles, San Francisco and San Diego).

• Friday, July 12, 1968
At IBC, the group will tape two new songs: "I've Gotta Get A Message To You" and "I Laugh In Your Face." "Now that was a memorable night," Barry will recall in a 2006 interview with the author. "['I've Gotta Get A Message To You'] we wrote together, all three of us. I think that night I know for a fact we didn't sing the choruses in harmony. Robert called us back to the studio at 11 o'clock at night and said, 'I want the choruses in harmony, I don't want them in just melody. I want three-part harmony on the choruses.' So we went in and attempted that 'round about midnight. Everyone drove back to the studio and that's what we did. So, it was a very memorable night." Although both songs will be mixed to mono at this session for single release, "Kitty Can" will be featured as the flipside to "Message." "I Laugh In Your Face" will be included on the Bee Gees' next long player, *Odessa* (and today's mono mix will surface in 2009 on the Reprise reissue of that album).

• Saturday, July 20, 1968
Disc and *NME* report that the next Bee Gees single will be "I've Gotta Get A Message To You" instead of the previously slated "Idea." The single is to be issued in Britain on August 2nd (and slightly earlier in the US). "Idea" will appear on their forthcoming album of the same name scheduled for UK release on September 1st.

In the meantime, the Bee Gees will film some promos for "I've Gotta Get A Message To You" with director Peter Goldmann (who last year worked with the Beatles on their landmark clips for "Penny Lane" and "Strawberry Fields Forever"). These are to be used for television shows such as *Top Of The Pops*, *How It Is* and *Time For Blackburn!* since the Bee Gees plan to be in America when the single is issued. They are scheduled to appear on NBC's *The Tonight Show* July 31st, preceding the kick-off of their first US tour. The *NME* further notes that a proposed tour of Japan has been pushed back to February 1969.

• Tuesday, July 23, 1968
The Bee Gees work in the studio with young Lori Balmer, an Australian vocalist who had previously recorded with the brothers in 1966 (see January 11, 1967). The rather brilliant results will be issued on Polydor in November: "Treacle Brown" c/w "Four Faces West."

● Thursday, July 25, 1968
In Britain, the Bee Gees are seen on BBC television's *Top Of The Pops* plugging "I've Gotta Get A Message To You."

● Friday, July 26, 1968
Robin Gibb is diagnosed with nervous exhaustion, causing the cancellation of most of the Bee Gees' American tour and television appearances (due to start in Phoenix, Arizona on August 1st). In 1979's *Bee Gees—The Authorized Biography*, Robin's wife Molly will tell David Leaf: "There was no 'nervous exhaustion.' It was just a thing Robin did for the group, a way out of the tour."

● Wednesday, July 31, 1968
The Bee Gees' appearance on US television's *The Tonight Show* is cancelled.

● Thursday, August 1, 1968
A concert scheduled for the Coliseum in Phoenix, Arizona is cancelled.

● Friday, August 2, 1968
A concert scheduled for Los Angeles' Hollywood Bowl is cancelled.

● Saturday, August 3, 1968
A concert scheduled for San Francisco's Cow Palace is cancelled.

● Sunday, August 4, 1968
A concert scheduled in San Diego's Sports Arena is cancelled.

● Saturday, August 10, 1968
Sufficiently rested, the Bee Gees open their American tour at New York's Forest Hills Tennis Stadium (receiving thirteen curtain calls). "I've Gotta Get A Message To You" enters *Billboard*'s Hot 100 Bound listings at #101 and will ultimately rise to #8. In Britain, the single also enters the charts today and will rise to #1 during its fifteen-week chart run. Barry tells the *NME*: "It's not about death, although a lot of people will think it is." Robin confirms, "It's about a person who is about to die. He's going to his death because he's committed murder. But it doesn't mention the circumstances of his death or how he's going to die. It just tells that he is talking to a preacher and he wants to get a message to his girl or wife that he is sorta sorry and wants to apologize. He's killed a man who's been carrying on with his wife and he wants to get a message to her before he dies."

● Tuesday, August 13, 1968
On a break from their US concert tour, the group begins a series of recording sessions for their next album at Atlantic Studios in New York City. Today, production will commence on "Whisper Whisper." This song will be broken into two sections (that are eventually edited together to create a two-movement composition). Part one (the first two-and-a-half minutes of the number) will be tracked in five takes with Barry on acoustic guitar and off-mic vocals, Maurice on piano and Vince on electric guitar. The first two performances will be false starts; take three will be a full take of "part one" featuring a lead guitar part from Vince not heard on the final production. After a further false start, take four, Vince will switch to a more subtle accompaniment for take five. This performance will later receive an overdub of organ during the Atlantic sessions. Eventually drums, keyboards, bass, orchestration and vocals will be added at sessions in London.

Part two of "Whisper Whisper" will initially be led by Vince alone on acoustic guitar (with a strange wobble effect apparent on all the performances). The first four takes will be false starts, with take five being the final master and only full performance. This will eventually be augmented with calliope, bass, drums, vocals and additional guitar, but this version of "part two" will ultimately be scrapped in favor of a new recording made at a session tomorrow. Today's master will be mixed by the author in 2006 for inclusion on the 2009 reissue of *Odessa*.

○ Wednesday, August 14, 1968
In the United States, a concert scheduled for Rhode Island Arena in Providence is cancelled.

○ Thursday, August 15, 1968
In Britain, television's *Top Of The Pops* airs a repeat of The Bee Gees performing "I've Gotta Get A Message To You." In the US, a concert scheduled for Boston's Music Hall is cancelled (leaving the state of Massachusetts without a "thank you" for their inspiration). Instead, the Bee Gees' Atlantic Sessions continue with another uniquely American-inspired tune, "Marley Purt Drive."

Announced by the engineer as "Marley Purt Drive Area Code 213," the song is set unusually in the Los Angeles area (where the telephone prefix was once 213) and the nearby suburb of Pasadena (where the protagonist hopes to escape his orphanage by going for a Sunday drive on either the 134 or 210 freeway). The song will be tracked with Barry and Vince on acoustic guitars and Colin on drums. From the first take, the arrangement and song sounds quite similar to the finished product. The Band's recently issued *Music From Big Pink* and their single "The Weight" (which is just about to chart in the States) seem to be of considerable influence, especially in Colin's drumming. All of today's performances will be strong enough for release, and seemingly the only reason why the band work through six takes will be Colin' confusion on when to come back in for the final verse (from his drum break).

Take six will eventually be overdubbed with bass, keyboards (electric piano and organ), banjo (from Bill Keith of the Jim Kweskin Jug Band) and a brief burst of steel guitar. A vocal track from Barry (with harmonies from Maurice on the choruses) will also be added during the Atlantic sessions; however, this track will be supplanted by a new performance in London (with slightly revised lyrics). Bill Shepherd will also conduct orchestration for the song's ending (added at a later IBC session). In 2006, the author will make a mix of the Atlantic multi-track reflecting the song in its early production stage for the Reprise reissue of *Odessa*.

○ Friday, August 16, 1968
At Atlantic Studios, the group work with engineer Adrian Barber on a section for the production of "Whisper Whisper" labeled as "part three." Kicked off by a solo drum break from Colin, he will be joined in the tracking by Maurice on bass and Vince on acoustic guitar. Take one will be an incomplete false start; take two will be nearly complete, save for the ending (which is worked out before take three). Take four is a good performance, and afterwards, Colin suggests that they listen to it back. Take five will also be very close to the final master, however, it will not be until take thirteen that the group will be fully satisfied with the results (and even then, the master will be a composite of two takes). This final performance will be augmented by overdubs of Maurice on electric and acoustic pianos and Barry on vocals (with Maurice on harmonies). The production will be completed later this year in London by a Bill Shepherd brass chart and deft editing of "part one" and "part three." Also at this session, Barry and Maurice will tape two takes of a short piano demo of "First Of May." In 2006, the author will mix this performance for inclusion on the Reprise reissue of *Odessa*.

○ Saturday, August 17, 1968
A concert scheduled for the Bridgeport Music Festival in Connecticut is likely cancelled.

○ Monday, August 19, 1968
At Atlantic Studios, the band will tape two distinct arrangements of a song called "Pity." The initial version has a slow organ intro and builds into a fast paced performance of organ and piano. Seven takes will be made of this arrangement with the final performance being augmented by two overdubs of drums, vibes and lead vocals from Barry. In 2006, an edited version of this performance is mixed by the author for inclusion on the Reprise reissue of *Odessa*.

A second longer, slower and more deliberate arrangement of the song will be taped next. Again, the basic tracking will be simply piano and organ playing together for six takes. The final performance will be augmented by overdubs of Vince on electric guitar (playing only in sections) and background vocals from the brothers (mostly on the choruses) repeating the song's title, "Pity," ad infinitum. This menacing production—marked "no good"—will be left incomplete (and unissued) without any further embellishments.

Also at this session, Maurice will sketch out a solo piano demo of "Seven Seas Symphony" (with some background drumming). This performance was mixed by the author in 2006 for inclusion on the Reprise reissue of *Odessa*.

○ Tuesday, August 20, 1968
At Atlantic Studios, the Bee Gees' sessions continue with a song that is initially announced as "Untitled" but later named "Give Your Best." Captured in a single take, the track will feature the joyful fiddle of Tex Logan and banjo by Bill Keith (incidentally, Hugh Gibb will capture these session players in performance on his home movie camera). The instrumental track will be driven by Barry's acoustic guitar and filled out with electric guitar from Vince (playing intermittently), bass and drums. Barry will also lay down a guide vocal at this session with a first draft of the song's lyrics. Later this year, these will be revised at a session in London (including the addition of Robin's spoken introduction—"It's a square dance, Mr. Marshall..."). In 2006, the author will make a mix featuring the first draft lyrics for inclusion on the Reprise reissue of *Odessa*.

Also at this session, the Bee Gees will tackle the also initially untitled "Sound Of Love." This tune will be built on the simple accompaniment of piano, drums and bass. Barry will add an incomplete, rough vocal to the master; this will be replaced in London with a new vocal and a finished set of lyrics (topped off by an expansive Bill Shepherd orchestral arrangement). In 2008, the author will construct a mix of the track using as much of the original Atlantic vocal performance as is salvageable (supplanted in places by the finished London vocal) for use as a bonus track on the Reprise reissue of *Odessa*.

In Britain, Thames TV will air the sixty-five minute television special, *Frankie Howerd Meets The Bee Gees*. Colin tells the *NME* the show is, "...full of comedy skits and I think is far more important to us than being on *Top Of The Pops* every week."

○ Wednesday, August 21, 1968
Completing their Atlantic sessions, the Bee Gees record a nascent version of "Edison" with different lyrics and the title "Barbara Came To Stay." Completed in four takes, this will be the only track from the Atlantic sessions that has the distinct flavor of Robin's participation. The track is built around guitar, bass, vibes, piano, drums and some "scratch" vocals from the brothers (with Barry on lead). Later this year, "Barbara" will be transformed into "Edison" at undated sessions in London. In 2006, the author will mix the basic Atlantic version for inclusion as a bonus track on the Reprise reissue of *Odessa*.

○ Thursday, August 22, 1968
In Britain, television's *Top Of The Pops* airs a further repeat of the Bee Gees performing "I've Gotta Get A Message To You."

○ Friday, August 23, 1968
A concert scheduled for Minneapolis' Arena is cancelled.

○ Saturday, August 24, 1968
A concert scheduled for Detroit's Olympic Stadium is cancelled. Robin tells Nick Logan in the *NME*: "We've been working very hard on our new album and we've just finished it." The paper further notes that despite numerous cancellations, the Bee Gees have just received an offer of upwards towards $100,000 to perform two more concerts in New York City (from the promoter of their Forest Hills Stadium gig, Leonard Ruskin).

1968

A rare still from Frankie Howerd Meets The Bee Gees

- Sunday, August 25, 1968
A concert scheduled for Chicago's Opera House is likely cancelled.

- Monday & Tuesday, August 26 & 27, 1968
Manager Robert Stigwood tells *Disc & Music Echo's* Bob Farmer that Robin's health has once again become an issue and the rest of the group's US tour has been cancelled. Despite this statement, Hugh Gibb shoots silent footage of the band performing at the Ohio State Fair in Columbus, where the Bee Gees are scheduled to appear four times over two days on a bill featuring Roger Miller and comedian George Kirby. 100,000 people attend the fair on Monday, despite extreme heat, for the free entertainment. These could be the Bee Gees' last live performances in the United States until February 1971.

- Thursday, August 29, 1968
A concert scheduled for Saratoga Performing Arts Centre in New York is likely cancelled. In Britain, *Top Of The Pops* airs yet another repeat of the Bee Gees performing "I've Gotta Get A Message To You."

- Saturday, August 31, 1968
A concert scheduled for JFK Stadium in Philadelphia is cancelled. Meanwhile, *Idea* hits the US albums chart and over the next twenty-seven weeks will peak at #17. The *NME* reports that the group's follow-up album, "...will incorporate many of the tracks they have been recording in America...The LP will be called *The American Opera* and will consist largely of recordings the Bee Gees completed in New York..." Now in Los Angeles, the Bee Gees spend the weekend on holiday, water-skiing off the California coast.

- Sunday, September 1, 1968
The final show of the Bee Gees' US concert tour, scheduled for Columbia Maryland Music Pavilion, is cancelled. "What we were told was that the people loved to listen to the music," Vince said in 2006 of this haphazard first US jaunt, "but they didn't really want to come and see us! I don't know whether that was the truth. We were huge in Germany and some of the other European countries. We toured quite a lot over there."

- Monday, September 2, 1968
In Britain, *Idea* is officially issued (following an early Stateside release and sporting a different cover). In Los Angeles, the Bee Gees begin rehearsals for their appearance on ABC television's *Hollywood Palace*, to be broadcast in November.

- Wednesday, September 4, 1968
In Los Angeles, Robin and Maurice tape an appearance as celebrity contestants on television's *The Dating Game*. Maurice will win a date and a trip to Johannesburg, South Africa. Backstage, Maurice tells writer Ann Moses their recent sessions at Atlantic produced, "a load of rubbish." The trouble was, according to Maurice, they couldn't get the same sound as they were used to in London.

- Thursday, September 5, 1968
In Los Angeles, Barry and Robin visit radio station KRLA and are on-air for a full hour giving weather reports and conjuring various tomfoolery. In Britain, television's *Top Of The Pops* airs yet another repeat of the Bee Gees performing "I've Gotta Get A Message To You."

- Sunday, September 8, 1968
The Bee Gees return to Britain from New York City. Barry announces he will be splitting from the group at some future date to pursue an acting career.

- Monday, September 9, 1968
The group begins pre-production on their *Idea* European television special in Brussels with guests Julie Driscoll and the Brian Auger Trinity.

- Tuesday, September 10, 1968
Speaking with *Disc* from Brussels, manager Robert Stigwood denies that Barry will leave the group to pursue an acting career. Apparently Barry was recently deluged by film offers when he visited Los Angeles.

- Thursday, September 12, 1968
The Bee Gees briefly return to London (from Brussels) on a break from shooting their *Idea* special.

- Saturday, September 28, 1968

In Britain, *Idea* enters the albums charts and over the next eighteen weeks will reach a high of #4 (their best album placing to date). Meanwhile, Barry (in Brussels where shooting has resumed on the *Idea* special) tells *Disc* that he will indeed leave the group. "I have said that I shall be leaving the Bee Gees, and I stand by that," states Barry. "I don't know what all the confusion is about, for I have never said anything different. I shall be fulfilling all the existing commitments with the group, which will take up about the next two years. But the group scene is not an everlasting thing and in the pop business you can only go so far. I know that both Maurice and Robin share my ambition to break into films, but we will still do occasional concerts and TV shows together."

In the meantime, Barry tells *Melody Maker*, "When we get back from Belgium, we have three or four days off and then start a German tour. After that we start on our film. We will spend two months in Africa—mainly in Johannesburg—and then a month at Elstree."

- Thursday, October 3, 1968

At IBC Studio B, the Bee Gees tape "Nobody's Someone" with engineer Phillip Wade. The first three takes of the song will be short false starts, with just Barry playing acoustic guitar. For take four, Barry changes the tuning of his guitar, which seems to have the desired effect since this produces the final master of the song. The final production of the track will incorporate overdubs of Maurice (on bass) and Colin (on drums which play only during the final verse and chorus), as well as a full orchestral score from Bill Shepherd (including mallets and strings) recorded in stereo.

Despite the obvious quality of "Nobody's Someone," it will be initially unissued. Attempts will be made to mix the track on three separate occasions—1968, 1969 and 1972—perhaps hinting at three potential releases. Nevertheless, the song will be recorded a second time (though it is unknown if this alternate version predates or postdates today's recording) with just Barry's voice and a different orchestral score. The purpose of this alternate recording may be to demo a prospective cover version of the song. As it happens, in 1997 the author will be the first artist to release a cover version of this song (on an EP titled *Million Dollar Movie*). He will also later mix the Bee Gees' October 1968 version, which finally surfaces on the 2009 reissue of *Odessa*.

Sharing the same session reel as "Nobody's Someone" is the completed master for Robin's "Black Diamond." The song started life recently as a demo with Robin playing alone on the Mellotron. He taped three takes with this instrument before switching to the piano for another four takes. On the last of these performances Robin added overdubs of vocal and Mellotron accompaniment. Joining him on this demo are Maurice on acoustic guitar and Colin on drums. Despite the rough quality of the rather lengthy performance, "Black Diamond" is undoubtedly a wonderful composition displaying Robin's gift for melancholy fantasy. In 2008, the author will construct an edited version of this demo for release on the Reprise reissue of *Odessa*.

Following the completion of his first two demos, Robin taped a further piano sketch of "Black Diamond" accompanied by a cellist. However, it will be today's master version that fully reveals this song's potent imagery. Taped in three takes with just Barry on acoustic guitar (which is later double-tracked), the song will be topped off with Robin's lead voice (also double-tracked—with backing vocals from Barry and Maurice), Colin (on drums), Maurice (on bass and piano recorded in stereo), as well as Bill Shepherd's orchestral score (also recorded in stereo and, like many of this period's tracks, more extensive than heard on the final LP mix). The stunning final results will be heard on *Odessa*.

- Saturday, October 5, 1968

On the day that Barry serves as best man for the wedding of his friend, singer P.P. Arnold, *Disc* announces that the Gibb brothers will write a lavish West End stage musical. Meanwhile, Vince Melouney hopes to delve into record production, while Colin Petersen is currently dabbling in songwriting. Although the track he tendered for *Idea*, "Everything That Came From Mother Goose," was rejected, Manfred Mann are interested in covering his work (which is in the mold of their singles "The Mighty Quinn" and "My Name Is Jack"). Colin later tells *Disc*: "I write, but my songs are very Dylanish and country-inspired. Very odd lyrics in fact. Some turn out very ambiguous. 'Everything That Came From Mother Goose' is the best we've done and Manfred's Klaus Voormann is knocked out with it."

- Sunday, October 6, 1968

In Europe, the Bee Gees open a tour in Amsterdam.

- Monday, October 7, 1968

The Bee Gees are in Hilversum for television work.

- Friday, October 11, 1968

The Bee Gees are in Copenhagen for television work.

- Saturday, October 12, 1968

In Stockholm, the Bee Gees are scheduled to perform in concert. Meanwhile, *Disc* reports that manager Robert Stigwood has ordered Robin to get his hair cut. "I have no intention of getting my hair cut," says Robin. "I like it the way it is. After all, even Jesus had long hair."

In *Record Mirror*, Barry says he is still planning to go into films and leave "the group scene." "I'm glad that the Marbles are breaking through. But they're a duo, something different. When I first found them, I felt sure they had something unusual to offer. Otherwise the group scene is much too overcrowded."

Of the subject matter of the Bee Gees' latest disc, "I've Gotta Get A Message To You," Barry comments: "I am very definitely against capital punishment...The nominating of the moment that a man's life is going to be taken. The long wait. It's terrible and much more cold-blooded than the average murder. I just don't see how executions can be justified."

• Sunday, October 13, 1968
The Bee Gees are back in Copenhagen to perform in concert.

• Tuesday & Wednesday, October 15 & 16, 1968
The group does television work in Vienna. According to *Billboard*, they are due to return in November for a concert.

• Thursday, October 17, 1968
The Bee Gees return from Vienna to London in the hopes of doing some recording before their lengthy German tour. The *NME* reports that Barry's poor health halts these efforts. Nevertheless, the brothers manage to tape several undated tracks during the month of October with engineers Phillip Wade and Andy Knight (at IBC Studio A). These include Maurice's first solo composition since leaving Australia, a tune he tells the engineer is: "Tentative title, 'How Can You Tell.'" This song (later retitled "Suddenly") will be tracked in just two takes with Maurice solo on acoustic guitar. His basic track will augmented by solo vocals (later sweetened by Barry and Robin), bass, Mellotron and piano. The production will be filled out by Colin on drums and much later Bill Shepherd's orchestral arrangement (recorded in stereo and again more extensive than heard on the final album mixes). In the process of completing the production, a new vocal from Maurice will be taped over his Mellotron track on the 1" master. A rough mix from October 27th featuring Maurice's first vocal track and Mellotron (but sans Barry, Robin or Bill) will be included on the 2009 reissue of *Odessa*.

On the same session reel as "Suddenly," Barry's gorgeous "You'll Never See My Face Again" will be taped in three takes by just Barry and Maurice (on acoustic guitars). Once the basic track is completed, the production will be augmented by Maurice's chugging bass and soaring Mellotron lines. A rough mix from October 27th can be heard on the Reprise reissue of *Odessa* and shows the track in its first stage of production. A Bill Shepherd score (recorded in stereo) and two further tracks of vocal harmonies will be added to the track in November.

Another track on this reel, "With All Nations (International Anthem)," will later be described by Barry in *Melody Maker* as, "like an international anthem, for the whole world." This first version of the song features Bill Shepherd's orchestra spread across five tracks, leaving the brothers three open channels to sing their short pledge of allegiance to freedom, love and peace. Despite the purity of their message, their lyrics will later be dropped and the song remade at the end of the album sessions.

The last item from this period will become the title track to their album and is perhaps the most ambitious composition the Bee Gees will ever commit to tape. "'Odessa' is about a man on an iceberg after a shipwreck and his wife has run away with a vicar...it is very weird," Barry will later remark to *Melody Maker*'s Chris Welch. "It takes eight minutes to listen to, but kids won't have time if it's put out on a single. 'Hey Jude' was a different matter because it was repetitive."

This first version, titled "Odessa On The White Sea," will be very close to the final master in arrangement, but in the end will be a very elaborate blueprint. It features Maurice playing a flamenco-styled acoustic guitar described on the tape box as being a Lute. In fact, several other tracks from this era have this designation attributed to Maurice's guitar, but it may be a misnomer. Paul Buckmaster provides live cello accompaniment to Maurice's performances. Captured in just two takes, Barry recites details of the Dutch ship Onstrauss setting up this epic tale. Take two will be augmented by overdubs of Maurice on Mellotron and bass, Robin on lead vocals (with support from Barry in sections) and a full Bill Shepherd orchestral arrangement (recorded in stereo). At the tail end of take two, someone in the studio will remark that the results are "pretty good—pretty splendid." And they are. Nevertheless, a full scale remake of "Odessa" will be taped in short order. In 2009, an original rough mix (from November 24th) of this early take will be included as a bonus track on *Odessa*.

This final version of "Odessa" is taped four takes—though it is hard to know exactly when, since the master is confusingly compiled with some earlier recordings. Nevertheless the structure remains: Maurice again plucks out the intro (though his guitar sounds more like a steel string acoustic than a nylon) playing as before to Paul Buckmaster's cello. Barry will be in the control to offer direction, but Maurice and Paul seem to have their parts well rehearsed. At this stage the master has a recitation from Maurice detailing the British ship Veronica's status: "En route from Amsterdam, [Veronica] was lost at sea. There were no recorded survivors and the ship was struck off the British royal register." This part will be omitted from the final mixes, since it is mostly replaced by the same information sung in three-part harmony. The final production will feature extensive vocal work from all three brothers, bass and piano overdubs from Maurice, as well as Bill Shepherd's perfect orchestration (recorded in stereo).

• Saturday, October 19, 1968
Disc & Music Echo reports that Stigwood has given up on his fight to clip Robin's hair. His efforts have now turned to stopping Cream (another of his RSO artists) from breaking up—he will sadly fail on both fronts.

• Sunday, October 20, 1968
In London, Barry frightens off a prowler in his home with a revolver from his weapons collection. Police question the eldest Gibb brother for two hours after the incident.

• Friday, October 25, 1968
In London, the Bee Gees visit a new location for recording: Trident Studios (Trident House, St. Anne's Court, Wardour Street, London, W1). Here they will tape demos of two new songs—"Lamplight" and "Melody Fair." The first of these will be tracked with Barry (acoustic guitar), Robin (who joins Barry on off-mic vocals), Maurice (piano) and Colin (drums). The arrangement will be quite close to the final master; nevertheless, most of today's early performances are fragmentary as Barry and Robin sketch out "Lamplight's" structure. Following take five, Maurice will get frustrated by the halting nature of the proceedings and mock screams, "It's only a demo!" Barry says, "Well, let's not make it a band demo." The tape is stopped and performances resume with take six and the band will at last make it through most of the song. Take seven comes even closer to a complete performance, with only the ending falling apart.

Take eight will be halted when a plate of vegetables falls on the piano. Prior to take nine Maurice announces: "This is the last time I'm doing it." Barry responds: "So, make sure you know the end." "I knew it," Maurice offers, "after you started doing it but you've changed it round again for the second time." Barry: "I didn't change; I didn't know what was happening." Maurice: "'Cause I couldn't see you." Barry: "Well, if you'd have seen me, I still couldn't have told you." Despite the fact that their vocals are not being properly recorded, Barry and Robin discuss adjusting their positions in proximity to lyric sheet and the mic that's on Barry's acoustic guitar. Colin quickly reminds them: "We're not doing a record. It's a bloody demo!"

Take nine will be a full performance which quickly receives overdubs of bass from Maurice and vocals from Robin (with Barry and Maurice on the intro and choruses). In 2006, the author will mix this performance from the 1" eight-track session tape for inclusion as a bonus track on the Reprise reissue of *Odessa*. A new master version of the song will be taped in the next few days at IBC.

The second song demoed, "Melody Fair" will be captured in a single take and features the same instrumental line-up of "Lamplight": Barry (acoustic guitar), Maurice (piano) and Colin (drums). However, the demo version is considerably different than the final master. It is faster in tempo and features several lyrical and melodic departures (particularly the ending). Following completion of the basic track, Maurice will overdub bass and Barry will sing the lead vocal (harmonized by Robin and Maurice). In 2006, the author will mix and edit this performance from the 1" eight-track session tape for inclusion as a bonus track on the Reprise reissue of *Odessa*.

• Saturday, October 26, 1968
The *NME* reports that the Bee Gees have topped a poll in Italy's *Giovanni* magazine. On the strength of this, the group is planning a visit on November 20th. The paper says their recent trip to Vienna included concert appearances. The Bee Gees had planned to spend this week cutting a new single, but Barry's illness has slowed them down—in actuality they demoed and recorded several new numbers. *Lord Kitchener's Little Drummer Boys* is now set to start shooting December 9th.

• Sunday, October 27, 1968
At IBC Studio A, the band will prepare rough mono mixes of their recent productions including "Melody Fair," "Lamplight," "Suddenly" and "You'll Never See My Face Again." These all reflect the masters prior to the addition of Bill Shepherd's orchestral sweetening.

"Lamplight," which was likely recorded in the last twenty-four hours, is tracked with Barry and Maurice on acoustic guitars and Colin on drums. The first six takes will be fragmentary false starts as Barry and Maurice coordinate their parts (and deal with a broken string on Maurice's guitar). Take seven will be the master, receiving overdubs of piano, bass, and vocals from the brothers (Robin will sing lead on the verses). The production of this version will go no further, as it is decided to record the song for a third time next month. A rough mono mix of version two will appear as a bonus track on the 2009 reissue *Odessa*.

Another master from the last day, "Melody Fair," will be tracked with just Barry and Maurice on acoustic guitars. The mood in the studio is particularly light as the two clown around in Scottish accents and Barry tosses off a bit of Roger Miller's recent UK Top 20 single "Little Green Apples." Take one is considerably slower than the Trident demo version, with Maurice adding some bluesy licks (missing from later renditions). Take two will be the master take and it duly receives overdubs of bass and Mellotron (Maurice), drums (Colin), handclaps and vocals (Barry and Maurice singing the verses in harmony and the pair alternating in the overlapping chorus lines). By November 24th, the vocals will be sweetened further (by Robin) and Bill Shepherd will finish off the production with a luscious orchestral score (recorded in stereo).

1968

- Thursday, October 31, 1968

The Bee Gees open a month-long European tour tonight in Bremen, Germany.

- Friday, November 1, 1968

In Germany, the Bee Gees' tour travels to Kiel for a performance.

- Saturday, November 2, 1968

As the Bee Gees' tour reaches Hamburg—where they will perform two shows tonight (5:45 & 9:30) at the six-thousand seat Ernst Merck Halle—the NME publishes a revealing interview with Vince Melouney (who has been noticeably absent from the last month's worth of recording sessions). "I have never really felt 100% a Bee Gee," says Vince. "Because the talent that I have doesn't come up to the standard of the Gibb brothers' talent and I don't think I am adding as much as they are. Within the context of what I am playing I realize that my ideas don't augment their ideas."

Barry too seems to be showing strain, between tonight's shows he tells Disc's David Hughes: "It's all very well for Robert to fly to America saying, 'Take charge of the boys, Barry,' be he doesn't quite realize what a strain it can be. We've had no let-up for weeks, with the TV spectacular in Belgium, a hectic recording session and now this until the end of the month. Have you ever tried keeping your own brothers in order? Impossible! I'm so tired, I'm going home to bed early tomorrow morning." Barry will spend his day off tomorrow (Sunday) back in London. Maurice will also return to London to drive his newly purchased velvet green convertible Rolls Royce (purchased three days ago).

- Monday, November 4, 1968

In Germany, the Bee Gees are scheduled to perform in Munster.

- Tuesday, November 5, 1968

In Germany, the Bee Gees are scheduled to perform in Cologne. In the studio, masters are copied for the third and final volume of Rare, Precious & Beautiful (to be issued in February 1969).

- Wednesday, November 6, 1968

In Germany, the Bee Gees are scheduled to perform in Essen.

- Friday, November 8, 1968

In Germany, the Bee Gees are scheduled to perform in Stuttgart.

- Saturday, November 9, 1968

On BBC radio, Maurice appears in a taped interview with Keith Altham for the show Scene And Heard.

- Sunday, November 10, 1968

In Austria, the Bee Gees are scheduled to perform in Vienna.

- Monday, November 11, 1968

In Austria, the Bee Gees are scheduled to perform in Innsbruck. Back in Britain, Robert Stigwood confirms that guitarist Vince Melouney is leaving the Bee Gees. "There has been a musical disagreement between the Gibb brothers and Vince who prefers blues which is not the Bee Gees' bag. So he will be coming out of the group at the end of the German tour." Vince is now set to manage and perform with a group called Ashton, Gardner & Dyke (comprised of former members of the Remo Four and Creation). Stigwood says, "...Maurice Gibb will play lead guitar on sessions in the future."

"I didn't get along with Hughie Gibb," Vince will cite as his biggest reason for leaving in a 2006 interview with the author. "He was always treating me like an outsider. It never spilled out into an argument with the lads or anything like that. It was just a thing between Hughie and I. I thought this is a terrible way for this to go on. I've always been friends with the Gibb brothers and Colin, I don't want to be part of this anymore. It was just too much. After a while, I didn't have a life. I was just too young. Too fast, too young, too naïve."

- Wednesday, November 13, 1968

In Western Germany, the Bee Gees are scheduled to perform in Bochum.

• Thursday, November 14, 1968
In Germany, the Bee Gees are scheduled to perform in Düsseldorf.

• Saturday, November 16, 1968
In Germany, the Bee Gees are scheduled to perform in Braunschweig and will also be seen once again on television's *Beat Club* in a pre-taped, lip-synch performance of "I've Gotta Get A Message To You." Meanwhile, the *NME* reports that Vince might sign with the Beatles' Apple company once he officially splits from the group. The remaining Bee Gees will spend time completing their upcoming double album which the paper says is now titled *Masterpiece* and is due for January release.

• Monday, November 18, 1968
In Germany, the Bee Gees perform at Kongress-saal in Munich. Wonderland serves as the support opener for this date.

• Tuesday, November 19, 1968
In Germany, the Bee Gees are scheduled to perform in Nuremburg.

• Saturday, November 23, 1968
In the United States, the Bee Gees are seen as guests (in a pre-taped segment shot in September) on *Hollywood Palace* performing "Massachusetts" and "I've Gotta Get A Message To You."

• Sunday, November 24, 1968
During a break in their European tour, the Bee Gees rough mix some of their latest recordings at IBC Studio A. Titles include a master version of "First Of May," the now-sweetened "Melody Fair" and a demo of "Odessa."

"First Of May" was taped with just Maurice on piano and Barry singing lead. Prior to take one, the engineer asks the duo what the track is called and Maurice jokes that it is "Idea." Maurice's piano is heavily compressed (giving a similar effect as "Words") and for take one he will play an alternate introduction (as Barry sings along off-mic). This take falls apart when Maurice hits a wrong note on the piano part and Lulu (who is present in the studio) jokes about how involved everyone was getting in the performance. Take two will be the master and eventually receives overdubs of Barry's lead vocal, strummed guitar, bass, drums and Bill Shepherd's lush orchestration (which is more extensive than on the final LP mixes).

Also contained on the session tape for "First Of May" is an unknown, fairly short, Barry-led acoustic number announced by the engineer as "Catch Me When I'm Lonely" (the tape box calls it "Catch If I'm Lonely"). Before take two, an engineer from the control room remarks that the piano (played by Maurice and the only other instrument on this recording) doesn't sound in tune with Barry's twelve-string acoustic guitar. Take three will be the final rendition and it will receive overdubs of a second twelve-string acoustic guitar part. However, the production will go no further and little else is known about this unissued mystery track.

• Tuesday, November 26, 1968
In Germany, the Bee Gees are scheduled to resume their tour in Wiesbaden; however, this date will be cancelled. Tomorrow's edition of *Hamburger Abendblatt* roughly translated says: "The Bee Gees' Barry and Robin are in London sick with tonsillitis. Therefore the German Tour of this popular band has now ended. The tour should have continued yesterday in Wiesbaden after a one-week pause. The Bee Gees were supposed to appear in Wiesbaden, Frankfurt, Freiburg, Karlsruhe and Ulm. After that the group was going to disband because guitarist Vince Melouney and drummer Colin Petersen didn't extend their contracts. Therefore there is no chance that the cancelled shows will be rescheduled."

At London's Royal Albert Hall, the Bee Gees' RSO stablemates, Cream, perform their farewell concert. It is during this performance that Robert Stigwood later claims he receives a backstage phone call from Barry informing him that the Bee Gees are also splitting.

• Saturday, November 30, 1968
Disc reports that some dates of the Bee Gees' German tour may be rescheduled before shooting begins on their film, *Lord Kitchener's Little Drummer Boys*. *Disc* will later note that Barry invited Al Jardine and Mike Love from the Beach Boys to his flat this evening for an all-night guitar and vocal jam. So, perhaps reports of his tonsillitis are somewhat overstated.

• December 1968
In Australia, Johnny Ashcroft issues the Gibb composition, "Don't Forget Me Ida" as a single on (EMI) Columbia. Also Down Under, a group called the Brigade issues a cover of Maurice's composition "All By Myself" on Astor.

• Sunday, December 1, 1968
Today is Vince Melouney's last official date as a Bee Gee.

• Wednesday, December 4, 1968
Robin Gibb marries Molly Hullis at London's Caxton Hall register office. *Disc* reports that the couple won't get a honeymoon until after the Bee Gees' recording sessions end on December 18th (four days before Robin's 19th birthday).

1968

• Saturday, December 7, 1968
At IBC Studio A, rough mono mixes are completed of "Never Say Never Again" (with fuzz guitar), "Whisper Whisper," "Marley Purt Drive," "Edison" (still with some rough vocals), "Sound Of Love," and "With All Nations" (with the Bee Gees' vocals). Most of Bill Shepherd's orchestration is now in place on the various productions. In 2009, today's mixes of "Never Say Never Again," "Edison" and "With All Nations" will be included as bonus tracks on the Reprise reissue of *Odessa*.

"Never Say Never Again" was recently taped at IBC in two takes with Barry and Maurice on acoustic guitars. Take two will be augmented by overdubs of vocals (Barry on double-tracked lead, with Robin and Maurice on the choruses in three-part harmony), bass and drums. A fuzz-guitar overdub (probably played by Maurice) will later be erased in favor of orchestration from Bill Shepherd (added later in the month and recorded in stereo).

Another track made during this period will be the third and final recording of "Lamplight." The master track, like so many others from this era, will be built up from just Barry and Maurice on acoustic guitars. After two short false starts, the master—take three—will be captured. To this overdubs of bass, piano, drums, stereo orchestration and extensive vocal overdubs (including Robin's lead, with Barry and Maurice in three-part harmony on the choruses) will be skillfully added. This final master will be Robin's choice for the Bee Gees' next single release.

Later this month, productions of "Whisper Whisper," "Marley Purt Drive," "Edison," "Give Your Best" and "Sound Of Love" will be completed with new vocals overdubbed on the Atlantic session tracks from August. The album sessions will wrap with three further Bill Shepherd-led tracks: a remake of "With All Nations (International Anthem)" as an orchestra and choir number featuring no actual Bee Gees, "The British Opera" (initially titled "American Opera" and taped in three takes, possibly with Maurice on organ) and "Seven Seas Symphony" (taped in six takes with Shepherd's orchestra and choir playing live with Maurice on piano).

"There are two concertos in the album with a 60-piece orchestra," Barry will tell *Melody Maker's* Chris Welch. "The 'Seven Seas Symphony' in F major has Maurice playing piano. He was extremely nervous with all the musicians watching him. And there is a 'British Opera.'"

In the United States, the first volume of *Rare Precious & Beautiful* debuts on the albums chart. Over the next twelve weeks, it will hit a mild #99. In Britain, *Disc* publishes an interview with departed guitarist Vince Melouney. "I felt I wanted to play a different type of music," says Melouney, "Write my own material and do more production. When I was on stage, I felt guilty at getting applause because I wasn't adding anything to the group. When I was offstage I was paid for sitting around doing nothing while the Gibb brothers were working hard at songwriting. And the bigger the group has become, the less concerts there have been and the more time I've spent just twiddling my thumbs."

Barry tells the *NME*: "Vince has been a big blues fan since we started. He felt stifled because the rest of us are really only interested in playing commercial numbers and it's no good having somebody in the group who's not really with you. Obviously he'll be a great loss to us, but Vince will be a great gain to another group, because he's a brilliant guitarist..." Says Barry of the band's next project: "We're going to bring out a double LP in January. We thought of the double LP at the same time as the Cream, but everybody will say we're jumping on the Beatles' bandwagon again. We want to do a double album because we'll be able to develop our ideas and its more value for money. It won't have an over-all format, songs should be left separate with a beginning and an end and they should have heart. There won't be any sound effects, just ballads with an emotional message." As for the title, Barry explains: "In fact, it's *Master Peace*, P-E-A-C-E. Master as in recording the disc others are pressed from, and Peace. It's going to be a very unusual cover—red velvet with gold lettering."

• Saturday, December 14, 1968
In the United States, "I Started A Joke" enters *Billboard's* Hot 100 Bound listings at #103. It will ultimately rise to #6 over eleven weeks, becoming their highest charting Stateside single of the 1960's. Nevertheless, Robert Stigwood will refrain from issuing "I Started A Joke" as a single in Britain.

• Saturday, December 21, 1968
Disc & Music Echo reports that the Bee Gees have completed sessions for their fourth album, now called *Odessa*. Their next proposed single will be the title track ("described as an eight-

minute-long pop symphony"). The group is set for holidays until January 19th. Their motion picture debut (retitled *Lord Kitchener's Four Drummer Boys*) is slated to start shooting in March. Meanwhile, the *NME* pegs January 17th as the date for the single release of the title track from their album, "*Odessa*."

● Thursday, December 26, 1968
Barry Gibb arrives in Sydney at Kingsford Smith airport for a working holiday. "I've got to catch up on the Sydney pop scene," he tells The *Sydney Morning Herald*. "The market is ripe for a good male or female Australian singer in London at the moment. Should I find someone who is impressive during the next two weeks I intend signing them up for our manager, Robert Stigwood."

In Britain, the Bee Gees are seen on a special Boxing Day edition of television's *Top Of The Pops* performing "I've Gotta Get A Message To You."

● Saturday, December 28, 1968
In Britain, Maurice Gibb appears on his girlfriend Lulu's television program, *Happening For Lulu*. During the show, she announces they are engaged to be married. The couple also performs a song written by Donovan called, "What A Beautiful Creature You Are."

● Monday, December 30, 1968
In Sydney, a vacationing Barry suffers a theft of jewels and cameras (reported to be worth 8,000 pounds) from his suite at the Chevron Hotel. According to an interview later published in *Melody Maker* with Chris Welch, during this trip Barry hopes to possibly buy a hotel in Queensland.

● Tuesday, December 31, 1968
In Britain, Maurice falls ill with a throat infection. In Germany, the group is seen once more on television's *Beat Club* in a pre-taped segment of "I've Gotta Get A Message To You."

1969

● Wednesday, January 1, 1969
Jewelry stolen from Barry Gibb (on December 30, 1968) is recovered by police. Three men are charged with theft and receiving. The eighteen-year-old youth who broke into Barry's hotel suite will receive a two-year sentence in March.

● Saturday, January 4, 1969
The *NME* reports that the Bee Gees have decided not to release "Odessa" on January 17th as a single. Instead, it will kick-off their long player, to be issued on February 14th. The paper claims a new single will materialize when the Bee Gees return from a Japanese tour in mid-February.

In *Melody Maker*, Barry tells Chris Welch of the change in singles: "Robert makes the choice about which songs to release as singles. We didn't want to record 'Massachusetts' but he insisted and it was our biggest seller...We've just finished *Odessa*, which is a double album. We planned this six months ago, then the Beatles did their one, so we're not copying. Our next single was going to be eight minutes long but we cut that out because it would really have started a scene after 'Hey Jude.'

"The songs are varied and there is a hillbilly song we did in America. There are a couple of songs even I don't understand. The lyrics don't mean anything, so don't start looking for meanings. They are just words we like the sound of... I can't even remember the titles, there are so many tracks. Oh, one called 'Edison' is a comedy song all about the inventor of light bulbs.

"Film-wise all is going well. *Lord Kitchener* had to be postponed till February because Vince left the group and his part had to be cut out. I didn't want Vince to leave in the first place, but he wanted to play his own music and I hope he gets his group together, because he deserves success."

Speaking of Vince, *Disc* covers his current work with Ashton, Gardner & Dyke. "We are releasing our first single on January 24th, then doing about eight to ten college dates here before flying to America for TV appearances. Because I was a member of the Bee Gees it makes it easier to get these TV bookings so we may as well take advantage of the fact." As for the Bee Gees, Vince predicts: "They will either become really big, or they could fade right out."

In an interview with Richard Green, Lulu tells the *NME* that Maurice played on her recent release, "I'm A Tiger." In *Melody Maker*, Lulu's manager, Marion Massey, tells the paper that Lulu will cut down on personal appearances following her wedding to Maurice. "Lulu and Maurice want to see as much of each other as possible..."

- Friday, January 10, 1969
At IBC, the Bee Gees regroup to help Marbles tape two new Gibb-penned numbers for a potential single, "The Walls Fell Down" and "Love You."

- Sunday, January 19, 1969
In Britain, the group tapes two performances (one in color for the States and another in black and white for Europe) for an upcoming episode of television's *This Is...Tom Jones*. In both cases, they perform a unique medley of "I Started A Joke" and "First Of May."

- Thursday, January 23, 1969
Trixie Belmont, writing for the *Women's News Service*, interviews Lulu's manager, Marion Massey, who has advised Lulu to give up her career to be with Maurice. They are due to be wed following Lulu's appearance at the Eurovision Song Contest on March 29th.

- Saturday, January 25, 1969
The *NME* reports that the next Bee Gees single has been delayed to the end of February because of a special Continent-only release by the group ("I Started A Joke"). The paper says their next single will be "Lamplight." Shooting for their movie, *Lord Kitchener's Little Drummer Boys*, will reportedly start in Spain during March. If it is delayed any further, shooting will revert to South Africa (as originally intended). Their *Idea* television special has already been screened on the continent and may be picked up in Britain by ITV.

- Tuesday, January 28, 1969
At IBC Studio A, a final mono mix for the single release of "First Of May" will be completed. In 2009, this mix (which varies from the monaural dubdown included on mono pressings of *Odessa*) will be issued digitally on *The Ultimate Bee Gees* compilation.

- Saturday, February 1, 1969
The *NME* reports that the group's next single—"First Of May" c/w "Lamplight"—is to be issued on February 14th. The LP, *Odessa*, has been delayed until February 28th. Barry tells the paper that he expects to begin work on his Hollywood movie, a Western, next Christmas with Clint Eastwood. Barry says that Robert Stigwood will book Robin and Maurice into solo movie roles concurrently. Their oft-delayed group movie, produced by John Perrington, will now start shooting in April (with a three-month shooting schedule). It is said that the Bee Gees will not tour for another six months (in fact, it will be much longer).

- Wednesday, February 5, 1969
At IBC studios, Barry and Robin will tape acoustic guitar and voice demos of three new songs in mono. Barry says before the first of these, "Bury Me Down By The River," "We may change the title later." Robin adds: "It's called 'Lay Me Down And Set Me Free By A River...'" After a description of the character that is meant to sing the song, Barry will tell the engineer: "Ad lib lyrics. We'll finish these later, but this is the song." In fact, the whole tune is very close in structure to the version later taped for *Cucumber Castle*, with the notable distinction of Robin singing harmonies on the choruses.

Before the second song, "I Fell In Love With A Beautiful Woman," Barry directs Robin to, "Do it more Orbison styled." This medium tempo number will be sung by Robin after some rehearsal and coaching from Barry (who seems to have just composed the tune). The lyrical obscurity—"I was the king of a sociable crowd"—hints at Robin's input on the words, but this is unconfirmed.

The last of today's recordings, "My Woman," will be sung by Robin (with Barry adding some harmonies in spots). This song is the roughest in construction of the three taped today, though it is undoubtedly complete. All of today's recordings will remain unissued and only "Bury Me Down By The River" will be revisited (in a few months). Despite the comedic mood captured on tape between songs on this date, it will be Barry and Robin's last set of recordings together until August 1970.

● Thursday, February 6, 1969
At IBC studios, engineer Mike Claydon remixes "Nobody's Someone" (originally recorded October 3, 1968) to mono. Nevertheless, this track will be passed over for initial release.

● Friday, February 7, 1969
Barry is due at a party for David Garrick to launch his new Gibb-penned single, "Maypole Mews." However, a blizzard ultimately prevents his attendance.

● Saturday, February 8, 1969
The NME reports that Vince Melouney will travel to America next month to produce the Cowsills (though no recordings will emerge from this rumored collaboration). He also plans to work with Hungarian singer, Sarolta Zalatnay (once romantically linked to Maurice and managed by Robert Stigwood). The group Vince manages, Ashton, Gardner & Dyke, have a first release imminent on Polydor.

● Thursday, February 13, 1969
In Britain, the Bee Gees appear on television's Top Of The Pops to promote "First Of May" in advance of its official release tomorrow.

● Friday, February 14, 1969
In Britain, the single—"First Of May" c/w "Lamplight"—is issued. Maurice Gibb is a presenter at the Disc and Music Echo awards (appearing alongside his fiancée, Lulu) which is held at London's Seymour Hall.

● Saturday, February 15, 1969
Melody Maker reports that Robin is unhappy with the Bee Gees' current A-side, "First Of May." "I feel strongly about the whole thing. 'Lamplight' should come off the album and not be the B-side. I will go even further and take my songs off the album, if Mr. Stigwood doesn't want to see eye to eye. I think 'Lamplight' would be number one for weeks. 'First Of May' might make #10. I've never been wrong on singles. I felt dubious about 'To Love Somebody' and 'Jumbo.'"

In the NME, Barry talks of the Bee Gees' future: "I'd hope to do a tour definitely within the next six months. We'd have a completely new act, but the orchestra would remain because that is our symbol. But we'd have a lot more artists on the show. The mistake that artists have made, and we ourselves have made is that you cannot tour alone or with just two supporting artists." Barry says he would like to bring Marbles on tour.

● Tuesday, February 18, 1969
Maurice marries Lulu at St. James' Parish Church at Gerrard's Cross. Barry, Robin, Colin Petersen and about three thousand others converge on the wedding site.

● Friday, February 21, 1969
In the United States, the Bee Gees' appearance on television's This Is... Tom Jones airs for the first time (a British broadcast will occur February 23rd).

● Saturday, February 22, 1969
In Britain, "First Of May" enters the singles chart and will rise to #6 over the next eleven weeks. Robin tells Melody

Maker that the Bee Gees will "...stay together, because we're not like a pop group, we are writers and we like to perform and record the things we write...I hope we all stay together singing."

In the United States, *Odessa* enters *Billboard's* albums chart and will peak at #20 over the next twenty-five weeks. In *Disc*, Barry says of the album: "The composing credits still show it as having been written by all three of us, but like Lennon and McCartney, we often do a song entirely separate of each other. I'm very satisfied with the record, in fact as satisfied as with any singles we've done." Barry says he is still interested to move into acting because, "It's the only way still to be seen when you are past 30. You can't stay in a group at that age and I couldn't be a cabaret artist." As for the band's film, he says: "People don't believe it is ever going to be filmed, but the makers are still working out the budget. That's what is keeping us waiting. I aim to fill in the time by taking some acting lessons."

• Sunday, February 23, 1969
In Britain, the Bee Gees' appearance on television's *This Is... Tom Jones* will air (a U.S. broadcast already occurred on February 21st).

• Friday, February 28, 1969
In Britain, *Odessa* is issued.

• Saturday, March 1, 1969
The *NME* publishes an interview with Barry Gibb conducted by Nick Logan at Robert Stigwood's estate in Middlesex. "I see myself as an outsider now," says Barry, "Like Colin thinks he is. He doesn't say it but I know he feels this way." As for the selection of their current single and the issues Robin had with it, Barry says: "I had thoughts that it might be 'Melody Fair' from the *Odessa* album but if Robert says 'First Of May' then 'First Of May' it is, whether it is a flop or a hit. Because, I never try and pick our singles, I can't; I leave that to Robert. I can pick other people's singles; like I picked the two for Marbles. You know, that guy Graham Bonnet has got the most powerful voice I have ever heard." Barry's pick for the second Marbles single is issued this week: "The Walls Fell Down."

• Thursday, March 6, 1969
In Britain, the Bee Gees appear again on television's *Top Of The Pops* to promote "First Of May." Although Barry tells *Disc* that the atmosphere at the taping was "amicable," this will be the final time that Barry, Robin, Maurice and Colin will ever appear together in public. Robin's dissatisfaction with Stigwood's current choice of single will lead to his departure from the Bee Gees as a group.

• Saturday, March 8, 1969
Disc runs a two-part article "written" by Robert Stigwood. He says of Robin: "He has a private catalog of every song the Gibb brothers have written since the age of eight and he documents the chart returns from every country around the world...Of course he had a recent row with me over the decision not to put 'Lamplight' on the A-side of the new single. But I haven't released a single yet that the whole group have liked...'Odessa'...is, I think, one of the finest pop songs ever written."

As for Maurice, Stigwood says: "The way he can translate the songs they've written into the right field of recording amazes me. It's because of this that the other two can come into a recording studio and write a song and then Maurice will instantly arrange it for immediate recording."

• Monday, March 10, 1969
At Chappell Recording Studio, Robin Gibb works with engineer John Timperley on the production of his first solo recording (albeit with help from Maurice): "Saved By The Bell." The song will start life on 1" eight-track and is captured in just two takes. The basic track will feature an electronic rhythm box for drums, plus tracks of piano, bass and guitar (all likely played by Maurice). These basic tracks will then be bounced to a second ½" four-track machine at 30 i.p.s. for further overdubs including orchestra (conducted by Kenny Clayton) and tracks of lead vocals (Robin) and backing vocals (possibly both Robin and Maurice). To tape will be bounced to a third generation of production to double Robin's lead vocal track in sections. The completed recording will be issued as Robin's first single on June 27th.

During this period, Robin will also tape such songs as "Mother And Jack," "Alexandria Good Time" and "Janice." However, recording dates have yet to surface for these and many of Robin's other demos and studio recordings from this highly prolific period.

• Saturday, March 15, 1969
Robin informs Robert Stigwood he no longer wishes to be a Bee Gee. *Disc* later reports Robin making a statement that, "There is a rift between us. I am not talking terms with Stigwood." Molly, Robin's wife, adds that her husband is not getting enough credit for the Bee Gees' success.

The *NME* publishes an interview with Colin conducted by Nick Logan. Colin's admiration for the Band's debut album, *Music From Big Pink*, is reflected in some of the songs that appear on *Odessa*. "It was my idea that we do that sort of thing...I am trying to teach myself how to play [guitar] so I can write songs. I only know four chords at the moment, so the four songs I've written all sound the same." As for the future, he is committed to being a Bee Gee. "All we have to do this year is the film and I think that after this year the Bee Gees' work will be limited to recording. I might be wrong but I think that will be the case."

In *Record Mirror*, Colin tells Derek Boltwood of *Odessa*: "...there's only one track that really disappoints me, and that's 'Edison.' It's too much like the sound of the old Aussie Bee Gees...Originally we were going to do the whole album in the States, and the theme would have been America and the American way of life...I'd still like to do an album in America as we'd planned on that theme—I think it would be nice, especially for an English group to do...Of the tracks we did in England, I think I like 'Melody Fair' best. I would have liked it as a single—but then I'm never right about singles. I didn't think 'I Started A Joke' would be a hit, though I thought 'Jumbo' would have been massive."

Melody Maker reviews the newly-issued *Odessa*. "'It's going to be a sad album, but listen to the words,' Barry Gibb warned us recently. Indeed the mood of their monumental work—it's a double album—is basically one of despair and desolation. The strings surge over the Gibb brothers melodies, which are often very good indeed...arranger Bill Shepherd must be congratulated on his wide screen type scores which cope with all of the Bee Gees moods. The cover matches the general air of lush extravagance. It is probably the most tasteful and striking, produced in red velvet. The Bee Gees can be proud of their achievement, it moves pop forward along a totally different track from the basic 'underground' experiments and is equally worthwhile."

Fabulous 208 runs an interview with Barry (conducted by Julie Webb). "I never realized just how good they could be," he says of Marbles, "I'm definitely sticking with Marbles and I've got a girl group I'm going to record. They are four sisters from Australia unlike any girl group I've ever seen in my life. I just hope everyone thinks they're as good as I do!" Barry has been passing his time recently hiring movies to screen at home on a projector: "You can get good films now like *A Man For All Seasons*," he says. Next year, this film will inspire a song title for the Bee Gees (see August 20, 1970).

● Monday, March 17, 1969
According to *Disc*, Robin changes his phone number in an effort to separate himself from the group. The Stigwood Organization state that he cannot leave the Bee Gees at present since his contract with the group runs a further three years.

● Tuesday, March 18, 1969
According to *Disc*, Robin meets with Robert Stigwood and various legal advisors to discuss his departure from the Bee Gees (and to try and reach a settlement in regards to his contract). The remaining members also meet separately with Stigwood.

● Wednesday, March 19, 1969
Robert Stigwood issues a statement that he is suing Robin. "Solicitors acting on behalf of the Robert Stigwood Organization have issued a writ against Robin Gibb and Robin Gibb Ltd. claiming a declaration, damages and injunctions."

At IBC Studio A, Barry, Maurice and Colin attempt to record a new single: "Tomorrow, Tomorrow." The song is said to have been penned for Joe Cocker to cover, but instead the Bee Gees make their first run at the song. The basic track will consist of Barry on acoustic guitar, Maurice on bass and Colin on drums. The band will run through eight takes of the song before arriving at today's master. To this, overdubs are added of piano and Bill Shepherd arranged orchestration (recorded in stereo) and vocals. The results are complete, but judged as not good enough for release; the song will be remade on March 21st.

harmonies from Maurice). The completed production will be issued in the UK on May 30th in mono only (a separate radio edit will also be issued in the US—see May 24th). In 1990, Bill Inglot will create a stereo remix of the song for the *Tales From The Brothers Gibb* box set (which leaves in Barry's count-off, something that cannot be edited off after the fact, since he speaks over Maurice's opening bass note).

The Bee Gees will also lay down a new backing track for Maurice's "Suddenly" at this session. Announced by the engineer as a "TV track" this may be intended for use in the group's upcoming *Talk Of The Town* special. No vocals will be taped (so the band can sing them live) and the recording also lacks any kind of orchestration, employing instead a pad of Mellotron keyboard sounds. Excepting Colin's drum track, Maurice may be the only musician (playing guitar, bass, piano and Mellotron) on the track, which has a nice clean ending so the band can mime to it and finish cold (unlike the fade on *Odessa*).

• Saturday, March 22, 1969
In the United States, "First Of May" enters the *Billboard* singles chart. Over the next seven weeks, it will peak at #37.

In Britain, the Bee Gees' second composed-and-produced single for Marbles—"The Walls Fell Down" c/w "Love You"—enters the singles chart. Over the next six weeks, it will reach a peak of #28. It will be the Bee Gees' last production for the duo (as well as their last chart entry).

Melody Maker reports that Robin is going solo and will open a management organization called Bow and Arrow. Furthermore, Barry now refuses to appear in the group's long-awaited film, *Lord Kitchener's Little Drummer Boys*, which was due to start filming in April. On television, the Bee Gees (minus Robin) make a surprise appearance on the final episode of *Happening For Lulu* and broadcast a "get well" message to their brother. Apparently, Robin was given a doctor's certificate for nervous exhaustion, hence his absence.

Barry tells *Disc*: "Whether or not Robin goes, the rest of us—myself, Maurice and Colin—would definitely carry on as the Bee Gees. There's no question that we would go our separate ways." Robert Stigwood adds: "The Bee Gees are always having rows, but they always blow over. I am confident everything will be sorted out satisfactorily, but it may take a few days." As for their film, Barry now feels,

"I'm against group films. They're a bore. If we want to make films we should make them individually." Associated London Films may make *Lord Kitchener's Little Drummer Boys* with a fresh cast.

Also at this session, the band tapes three takes of the wistful "Sun In My Morning." The basic tracking will be done by Barry and Maurice on acoustic guitars. On the final take, overdubs will be added of Bill Shepherd orchestration (recorded in stereo and more extensive than heard on the final mix), vocals from Barry and Maurice, as well as a track of Mellotron keyboard. In order to open up enough room of the 1" eight-track tape for the orchestra, the previously taped tracks are combined in a process nicknamed a "ping pong" (moving and reducing the number of tracks from one channel to another on the same tape). This later leads to speculation that the Bee Gees have recorded a song called "Ping Pong," which is a misnomer. "Sun In My Morning" will be issued in mono on May 30th. In 1990, Bill Inglot will create a stereo remix of the song for the *Tales From The Brothers Gibb* box set.

• Friday, March 21, 1969
At IBC Studio A, the remaining Bee Gees work with engineers Mike Claydon and Andy Knight to record a second version of "Tomorrow, Tomorrow." The tracking line-up will consist of Barry and Maurice on acoustic guitars and Colin on drums. The first eight takes will be incomplete, false starts after which it is decided to roll back over the early takes and start again. The engineer announces, "Back to take one" and the trio will perfect the backing track in four takes. The basic results will be the same as far as the basic arrangement; however, the performance is far more polished rhythmically and vocally. To the basic tracks of guitars and drums, overdubs will be added of bass and piano (Maurice), orchestration from Bill Shepherd, and lead and backing vocals from Barry (with

• Sunday, March 23, 1969
Maurice and Lulu go on holiday preceding her appearance at the Eurovision song contest.

• Friday, March 28, 1969
In Madrid, Spain, Maurice and Lulu prepare for her appearance on behalf of Britain at the 14th annual Eurovision song contest. Tomorrow, she will perform "Boom-Bang-A-Bang" as the British entry. The unlikely result sees four countries all tie for first place; Lulu's entry is not one of those.

• Saturday, March 29, 1969
The *NME* reports that the Bee Gees are set to star in their own color television showcase to be filmed by the BBC at London's *Talk Of The Town* on April 27th. Still, much depends on Robin's membership in the group. Everyone concerned is hoping the issue of his break with the group can be settled amicably out of court.

Barry tells *Disc*: "We've been recording without him in the past few days in the hope of finding something suitable for a single, which shows that we are still determined to keep the group going whatever happens." Colin remarks: "It's such a great loss to the music industry...We can't take another member leaving, and, despite what Barry has said in *Disc*, I don't think the three of us...could carry on as a trio...to think that Robin's going to come back and say 'Let's swing again' is being more than optimistic." Hugh Gibb says: "They've got to show Robin they can do it without him. That's more likely to bring him back than anything."

• Saturday, April 5, 1969
In Britain, *Odessa* enters the albums chart for a single week, peaking at #10. *Disc* says that Robin is still suffering from exhaustion. Meanwhile, the remaining Bee Gees have "spent time in recording studios this week" though there is no specific evidence of these sessions. Back from Spain, Maurice and Lulu are due to leave Britain once again for their honeymoon on Monday.

• Saturday, April 12, 1969
The *NME* reports that the Bee Gees' BBC special is now confirmed, but director Michael Hurll notes: "I still don't know whether I shall be getting three or four group members!"

• Saturday, April 19, 1969
The *NME* says that despite writs being served on Robin by Stigwood, it is not proposed to take the matter to court at this stage. Robin is currently recovering from a minor breakdown. "The writs were purely an interim measure to prevent him and others from claiming he had actually left the Bee Gees," says a spokesman. The Bee Gees' BBC special is now set for a June 7th transmission.

Meanwhile, the paper notes, Vince Melouney has left Ashton, Gardner & Dyke, the group he joined upon his departure from the Bee Gees. "Ashton, Gardner & Dyke's music became too involved for me," Vince says. "I wanted to do a lot more commercial stuff and material with string arrangements. This wasn't the group, and we want to put them out for what they are. I felt it best to leave and concentrate mainly on producing and songwriting."

• Thursday, April 24, 1969
At IBC Studio B, mono masters are completed for the next Bee Gees' single: "Tomorrow, Tomorrow" c/w "Sun In My Morning."

• Saturday, April 26, 1969
Disc reports that Robin is still suffering from exhaustion. The Bee Gees apparently have a pending sixteen-date concert tour. The kick-off date is set for Montreal on August 27th. The *NME* names potential venues such as Los Angeles' Forum and New York's Madison Square Garden, and that the gigs will go on "with or without Robin."

• Sunday, April 27, 1969
In Britain, the Bee Gees (joined by Gibb sister, Lesley) tape a BBC spectacular: *The Talk Of The Town: The Bee Gees In London*. The program, now lost, features performances of "New York Mining Disaster 1941," "Kitty Can," "With The Sun In My Eyes," "Suddenly," "To Love Somebody," "Seven Seas Symphony," "First Of May," "Morning Of My Life," "I've Gotta Get A Message To You," "Spicks And Specks," "Sun In My Morning" and "World."

In 2012, Lesley will remark to UK's *Mirror*: "I loved it on the night. I know Robin watched it and he said he felt very choked up about it. I couldn't sound like Robin, of course, but our harmonies as Gibb family members sounded very much the same. He said he loved my performance, but I told him if he felt like that, why don't you just come back then?"

• Saturday, May 3, 1969
The *NME* reports that sister Lesley Gibb has been signed by Robert Stigwood to a personal management contract. Although she subbed for Robin in last week's television taping, they say there is no possibility that she will join the Bee Gees for their American tour in August. The *Talk Of The Town* special will now be screened in Britain on May 17th. "Tomorrow, Tomorrow" will be the Bee Gees' next single, but no release date has been set as yet.

In the same edition, an interview with Barry (conducted by Nick Logan at London's Revolution night club) is printed. "If Robin wants to come back," Barry says, "he will be welcomed with open arms. But I won't speak to him again unless he speaks to me first. And if he doesn't come back we will continue as a trio. There is no question of us breaking up." A recent interview with Robin published in the *Daily Mirror* has been key in upsetting Barry. "...I wondered what it was all about. I phoned him and I was told to b—r off. He wouldn't speak to me." Barry says Robin was invited by letter to the session for "Tomorrow, Tomorrow," but he's not sure if it ever reached him. "He still has one of the greatest voices I've ever heard. He has a far better voice than I have. And he is a great songwriter too."

● Wednesday, May 7, 1969
At IBC Studio A, the Bee Gees work on two new recordings. The first of these, "Who Knows What A Room Is," Barry will later describe as a homage to the Beatles (see September 13th). The basic track will be made by just Barry on acoustic guitar and Colin on drums. After two takes, Barry remarks: "I'm not getting the right drumming effect; I can't feel it. We seem to be slowing down." Colin replies: "It's hard with one guitar and drums." Barry says before take three, "I'll play less; I'm playing too heavy." Take three will be another false start, albeit an improvement; take four will be the master.

To this, tracks of bass, electric guitar, piano, and Mellotron (all likely played by Maurice) will be overdubbed; the production is capped by Barry's double-tracked lead vocals and Maurice's harmonies. This excellent production, tipped for their next long-player, will nevertheless remain unissued.

Also at this session, Barry pays tribute to Jim Reeves' style of country ballads with the song, "Don't Forget To Remember." The song will be tracked with Barry and Maurice playing acoustic guitars and Colin on drums. The first six takes will be in a different, somewhat more upbeat arrangement than the final production. The last take performed in this style will be treated to overdubbed piano, but no vocals will be taped. "Don't Forget To Remember" will be immediately remade with the final arrangement as take seven. This take lacks drums and Barry and Maurice will no doubt complete the production—recording it anew later at this or another undated session—sometime in the next month. The completed master of "Don't Forget To Remember" will be issued as a single on August 8th.

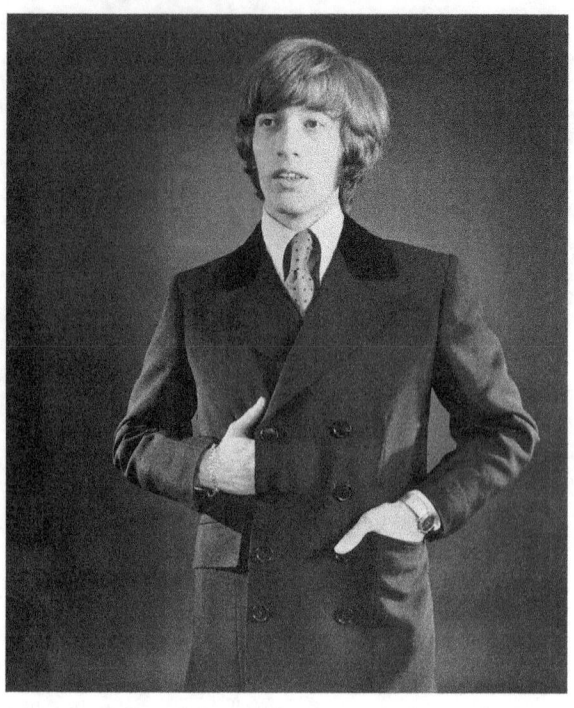

● Saturday, May 10, 1969
Robin announces his solo plans in the *NME*. A spokesman comments: "Robin tried to leave the Bee Gees in a peaceful way and bring about an amicable solution, but negotiations finally broke down last weekend." In lieu of a settlement, Robin will issue "Saved By The Bell" worldwide and let the matter be settled on the back end. RSO will take action against the release, noting that it contains the instrumental work of Maurice, and that he too will join them in stopping the release. Nevertheless, the single will still find its way into shops at the end of June.

● Sunday, May 11, 1969
This afternoon, Robin makes his first public appearance in two months before an audience of 10,000 at *NME*'s Poll Winners show held at the Empire Pool in Wembley. He will present Cliff Richard with an award and show off his new, shorter hair style (according to an *NME* report). Maurice (who accompanies Lulu to the awards) reconciles with Robin. "It was great to see Maurice again," Robin tells *NME*, "we hadn't been in touch since the split. I had the opportunity to tell him myself that, so far as I am concerned, we are still brothers—but I would not be returning to the Bee Gees. He said he understood that this was my decision, and he wished me luck...I wish them well with their new record and, despite what has been said, I hope they will not involve themselves in any attempt to prevent mine from coming out."

● Saturday, May 17, 1969
In Britain, the Bee Gees are seen in their own television special: *The Talk Of The Town: The Bee Gees In London*. Their next

single—"Tomorrow, Tomorrow" c/w "Sun In My Morning"—is scheduled for release on May 30th. *Disc* says the Bee Gees will seek a replacement for Robin to cover their upcoming American concert tour. *NME* says that Maurice is producing the debut single by a duo named Tin Tin (formerly Steve & Stevie—Australian pals of the Gibbs', Steve Kipner and Steve Groves). Meanwhile, Barry is working with Cheryl Gray, an Australian singer who came to Britain nine months ago and is now managed by Robert Stigwood—she will change her name to Samantha Sang for record releases.

In *Record Mirror*, Colin tells David Griffiths, "...we are in a twilight zone as Bee Gees. We don't know what to do about the future. Personally I can't see the group continuing without Robin. He's got such a strong voice. But I have nothing to do with the quarrel, it's a family matter to be decided among the brothers."

• Thursday, May 22, 1969
Barry grants an interview to *Disc* from his new flat in Eaton Square, Belgravia. "We are just about ready to hold auditions for a young guy singer with Robin's range, harmonies and ability to write. It may amaze people, but we were recently thinking of bringing in Jack Bruce to replace Robin! We had talks with him about it, but Jack felt that it wouldn't be his sort of music...We want to hear from people who would like to audition...If a young guy wants to audition, he can come round to my place and strum along just with me in the room."

• Saturday, May 24, 1969
In the United States, *Billboard* magazine reports that Atco has issued a specially shortened version of "Tomorrow, Tomorrow" as a promotional disc for DJs. This move is to aid the disc's chart chances in a climate of tight programming. The full-length version is featured on the flipside. The US release of this single precedes its appearance in Europe.

• Monday, May 26, 1969
In London, Maurice crashes his Rolls Royce in Belgravia and suffers a broken nose and two black eyes (according to *NME*). Maurice's passengers, Roberto Bassanini (the future husband of Cynthia Lennon) and fashion photographer, Brian Duffy, both suffered facial injuries. The trio had been out to dinner at Mr. Chow in Knightsbridge. According to *Disc*, Lulu collapsed with shock when Maurice ran in the house and it was left to Barry to drive the injured passengers to St. George's Hospital.

• Thursday, May 29, 1969
In Britain, host Alan Freeman welcomes the Bee Gees—Barry, Maurice & Colin— to BBC1 television's *Top Of The Pops*, where they will be seen performing "Tomorrow, Tomorrow." The exclusive audio mix of this performance (which differs slightly from the released version) will also be syndicated on the BBC World Service radio series, *Pick Of The Pops*.

• Friday, May 30, 1969
In Britain, the single—"Tomorrow, Tomorrow" c/w "Sun In My Morning"—is issued by the Bee Gees (with a label noting "Featuring Barry Gibb, Maurice Gibb and Colin Petersen").

• Saturday, May 31, 1969
In the United States, "Tomorrow, Tomorrow" enters the *Billboard* singles chart. Over the next six weeks, it will reach a peak of #54.

In Britain, *Disc* says Maurice turned down an offer to star in a film version of the musical *Hair* (Robert Stigwood is coincidentally one of the producers of the London stage version). Barry, who is considering the role of Claude, says: "Maurice doesn't like at all the idea of being seen nude on the screen and may back out of the film because of it. My own first reaction to the offer to appear in *Hair* was to turn it down as well, because I love stories, and there's no real story in this show. I also think that the bulk of the public hate hippies, which is what it's all about. Still, the show has been a huge success and I will do the film. But later on, I'd love to do a film with a real storyline." According to *NME*, RSO are currently bidding for rights to the film adaptation of the hit musical, but have stiff competition from other major studios. This story of Barry and Maurice's involvement in a film version may be a maneuver by Stigwood to be one up on his competitors.

NME also notes that negotiations are once again in progress between RSO and Robin's representatives. In regard to Robin's forthcoming solo disc, Barry tells *Disc*: "As for it being a very commercial hit record, I've heard it and frankly I just can't agree."

NME further reports that Colin has formed five show business related companies with his wife Joanne: Joanne Petersen Management, Slim Miller Entertainments, Carlu Records, Colin Petersen Productions and Hercules Music. Slim Miller is a comedian/neighbor of the Petersens who will run a variety firm under this umbrella. "Obviously the Bee Gees won't last forever," remarks Colin, "and whenever they do finish, I want to have this as a backbone to carry me on."

• Saturday, June 7, 1969
In Britain, "Tomorrow, Tomorrow" enters the singles chart and will peak at #23 over the next eight weeks. The NME reports that director Mike Mansfield has created a promotional film to help drive sales. It was shot on location in Dorset and on the grounds of Robert Stigwood's home (and in 2009 will be included on the DVD in the compilation The Ultimate Bee Gees). Mansfield is now set to direct Cucumber Castle, which the paper says will begin shooting in July.

• Thursday, June 12, 1969
At IBC Studio A, Barry Gibb produces a session (working with engineers Mike Claydon and Andy Knight) for his friend, P.P. Arnold, formerly a hit maker for the Immediate label, which will soon fold operations. Bill Shepherd will be on hand to direct a full band and orchestra for a rendition of Barry and Maurice's "Give A Hand, Take A Hand." Pat Arnold will sing live with all four takes taped today. The last of these will be marked as master and is subject to overdubs of background vocals (see August 16th). "Give A Hand, Take A Hand will be issued as the flipside of her cover of "Bury Me Down By The River" in October.

Also at this session, a backing track for a new Bee Gees song, "Between The Laughter And The Tears," will be taped. The production will be built around Maurice on piano, with backing from Bill Shepherd's orchestra (ala "Seven Seas Symphony"). Nine takes will be made of the song—broken only by a full orchestral performance of "Happy Birthday" (possibly in honor of Bill Shepherd)—however, the final performance will not feature a lead vocal and the production will remain incomplete (unless it is intended to be an Odessa-styled instrumental—something it sounds identical to).

• Tuesday, June 17, 1969
Robin returns to IBC to work with engineer Mike Claydon on mixing and completion of masters for his first solo single (which at this point is a coupling of "Saved By The Bell" and "Alexandria Good Time").

• Thursday, June 19, 1969
Barry Gibb arrives back in London from a trip to Australia and is reportedly fined for bringing a diamond-studded wristwatch into the country.

• Saturday, June 21, 1969
The NME says a series of concerts under the banner An Evening With Robin Gibb are planned later this year featuring Robin with a "large orchestra." A settlement was reached on Wednesday with RSO; Robin's solo debut release is now scheduled for June 27th. The single is still slated to be "Saved By The Bell" c/w "Alexandria Good Time." A five-year agreement allows for RSO to operate his new publishing company. Robin's discs will continue to be issued via Atco in the United States and Canada and Polydor in the rest of the world. Robin is apparently still committed to contractually work with the Bee Gees for part of each year. Chris Hutchins will act as Robin's personal manager on behalf of RSO.

The first single by Clare Torry—"Love For Living"—produced by Robin with Ronnie Scott is issued by Decca today. The NME says that the Bee Gees' follow-up single to "Tomorrow, Tomorrow" is likely to be "Bury Me Down By The River" (indicating that it was probably taped at an undated session during the last few weeks). Maurice tells the paper that he and Barry are "spending a lot of time writing and recording material" for a new album which they say is complete and is expected to be issued as soon as possible (though these sessions are largely undocumented). Vince Melouney, meanwhile, says that "things have really gone sour on me... everybody will be paid when I get things sorted out."

NME also runs an interview with Maurice conducted by Richard Green. Of "Tomorrow, Tomorrow" he says: "I don't think it's us; but I quite like it. We've got another one that we'll put straight out if it doesn't make it." This new one, "Bury Me

Down By The River," features vocals from P.P. Arnold and is described as a "gospel-type raver" without strings. "We know we don't want to split up," remarks Maurice, "maybe Colin will want to leave sometime in the future...but at the moment we're all happy with the way things are." As for Robin he says: "I hope his single is a hit. I wouldn't stop it. I read somewhere that I was supposed to be against it, but I wouldn't do that, he's my brother." On their next album Maurice says, "...I do six leads...before I think I only sang three...Barry keeps telling me to write harder music...I still think *Bee Gees' 1st* is our best album. In those days we were very ambitious and on cloud nine all the time. There must be at least a hundred songs at IBC we've done nothing with." Auditions for a Robin replacement have apparently transpired. "We've only seen two people," comments Maurice, "We're getting tapes from Wapping and Nottingham and Stoke and all over, but...we want someone who can sing nice, we can take care of the hair and clothes and all that."

• Friday, June 27, 1969
In Britain, Robin's first solo disc—"Saved By The Bell" c/w "Mother And Jack"—is due to be issued today. However, according to *Disc*, the single was not available until four days after the official release date. Fans apparently rang Robin's office to complain. The hold-up centers on Robin's change of heart on the flipside, which was initially to be "Alexandria Good Time." Polydor's pressing plant worked around-the-clock to meet the initial orders of nearly 100,000 copies.

Also in shops today, Tin Tin's Maurice Gibb-produced debut single—"Only Ladies Play Croquet" c/w "He Wants To Be A Star." Robert Stigwood will hold a Sunday afternoon croquet party with Maurice and Lulu to launch the disc.

• Saturday, June 28, 1969
Disc reports that the Bee Gees have given up on replacing Robin. Barry says he is no longer interested in working with his departed brother. "Maurice and I have star parts in a big movie that is to be made in three months time. It isn't *Hair*—that's all I can say at the moment." Robin says in the same issue: "The Bee Gees have a fantastic future and I wish them all the best. I think, for a start, their current single is great."

Top Pops runs an interview with Maurice conducted by John Richards: "Although I quite like the [current] single, I don't really think it's us, do you? We did the next one the other day and it's completely different to anything the Bee Gees have ever done. It's up-tempo with a soul feel and a bit of raving going on. We'll put it out straight away if necessary."

• July 1969
Barry recently worked with Japanese group the Tigers on a version of his "Smile For Me." The song will be issued this month on Polydor in the UK and Japan (the Japanese picture sleeve of which features a picture of Barry in a go-cart). Barry also recently made a cameo in the Tigers' film, *Hi London!*

• Saturday, July 5, 1969
Disc reports that Robin has received offers to appear on American television's *The Tonight Show*, as well as for a solo concert at Paris' Olympia. This could be part of a proposed world tour detailed in the *NME*, which the paper says will take in twenty-two countries. Robin's "Saved By The Bell" single officially hit shops last Tuesday after the B-side was changed to "Mother And Jack." Robin declined to comment on Barry's statement that he will not work with Robin again. A spokesman says, "Robin has no plans to do so anyway!"

Top Pops runs an interview with Robin conducted by Tony Norman. The paper says Robin will not be managed by the RSO-appointed Chris Hutchins and asks Robin what it will be like when he steps out on stage alone, for his first solo concert. "Well," Robin says, "I have done it before. There have been times in Australia when I've done it and the time Barry and I tried it in Germany. I mean there's no feeling of nerves about working alone." As for future projects, he says: "I'd like to go into films. I'd love to do something classical, possibly a real high class English gentleman who lived a couple of centuries ago. I wouldn't mind having a go at Julius Caesar!"

1969

● Tuesday, July 8, 1969
At IBC Studio A, engineer Mike Claydon makes mono mixes of two tracks that will ultimately be issued as the Bee Gees' next single: "Don't Forget To Remember" and their tribute to Johnny Cash, "The Lord" (recently taped at an undocumented session). Other recordings from this period include "I Lay Down And Die" (initially issued as the Canadian flipside to "Don't Forget To Remember" in a mix that differs from the one featured on the forthcoming *Cucumber Castle*), Maurice's "My Thing" (see July 12th), "Everytime I See You Smile" (completed and mixed in January 1970) and "I Was The Child."

● Wednesday, July 9, 1969
At IBC Studio A, another Barry Gibb-produced session for P.P. Arnold results in two new masters: covers of "Let There Be Love" and "Bury Me Down By The River." Backing is provided by Bill Shepherd's orchestra.

Also at this session, six takes will be made of a new Bee Gees track: "The Day Your Eyes Meet Mine." The final take will be treated to a lead vocal by Barry, but the results will remain unissued. Once again, the backing is provided by Bill Shepherd's orchestra. The song will later be offered to Andy Williams (see September 13th), and remade in March 9, 1970 for Barry's solo album, though this version will also remain in the can.

● Saturday, July 12, 1969
In Britain, Robin's solo single, "Saved By The Bell," enters the singles chart. Over the next sixteen weeks, it will peak at #2. Meanwhile, Barry Gibb has been voted best dressed pop star by Carnaby Street retailer John Stephen and Radio Luxembourg's 208 People Club at Youthquake. Today, he is awarded a statuette of Beau Brummel (valued at 500 British pounds) by actress Tsai Chin from a balcony overlooking the famed fashion district (and some five thousand onlookers). Newsreel footage will capture the entire event. *Disc* runs a feature on Maurice's Pyrrenean Mountain Dog, Aston de Maurice de Baeaudier. The paper notes that a recently taped song, "My Thing," on the Bee Gees' upcoming album is dedicated to him.

● Thursday, July 17, 1969
In Britain, host Tony Blackburn welcomes Robin Gibb to television's *Top Of The Pops* where he performs his single, "Saved By The Bell."

● Friday, July 18, 1969
According to the *NME*, Robin is scheduled today to front a ninety-seven piece orchestra and sixty-piece choir in recording "To Heaven And Back" (inspired by the Apollo 11 moon shot). A rush-release of this material is planned under the moniker Robin Gibb Orchestra And Chorus. This track will never surface commercially and the story is likely a publicity stunt, since recordings of this track (under the title "Moon Anthem") and another, "The Ghost Of Christmas Past" (see August 9th) are rumored to have been taped at Chappell Studios on June 27th.

● Saturday, July 19, 1969
Disc says that *Cucumber Castle*, the Bee Gees' television spectacular in talks for nearly two years, will finally go in front of cameras on August 11th. Maurice describes the production as a "Tudor period Laugh-In," and the *NME* notes that the script is now complete and the final film could run ninety-three minutes. Upon completion of *Cucumber Castle*, the Bee Gees are due in America. Barry and Colin are currently on holiday in Spain and Greece respectively.

In *Record Mirror*, Robin speaks with Ian Middleton: "I'm just finishing my first solo LP which has no title as yet. There'll be fourteen compositions on it. One of the tracks called 'Heaven And Back' is a musical piece of mine and features a hundred-piece orchestra and seventy-piece choir. It should have been a seventy-three-piece choir, but three were working at the time in Tooting!"

● Tuesday, July 22, 1969
At IBC Studio B, a series of stereo mixes for "Don't Forget To Remember" will be completed (though all of them are eventually rejected for commercial release).

● Wednesday, July 23, 1969
Robin flies to Stockholm to promote "Saved By The Bell."

• Thursday, July 24, 1969
In Britain, host Jimmy Savile welcomes Robin Gibb to television's *Top Of The Pops* where he performs "Saved By The Bell." Today, Robin will pick up his first advance from his new solo recording deal with Polydor.

• Friday, July 25, 1969
According to the *NME*, Robin sells his shares today in Abigail Music publishing to RSO. Abigail is the company formed in 1967 by Robert Stigwood to publish the Bee Gees' songs (among others). The label for Robin's first solo release credits his songs to a company called Saharet Music in the UK. He will switch publishers for future solo releases, though the Bee Gees (and Barry and Maurice individually) will remain Abigail writers through the end of 1972. With the copious covers of their songs worldwide, publishing will be the Bee Gees' biggest earner in this era (beyond record sales and personal appearances).

• Saturday, July 26, 1969
In the United States, a compilation, *Best Of Bee Gees*, enters the *Billboard* albums chart and will peak at #9 over the next forty-nine weeks.

In Britain, *Disc* runs an interview with Robin conducted by Bob Farmer. Of his first single Robin says: "It has been lying around my house for three months. It's been a long wait for my freedom." In addition to reportedly composing eighty new songs in past few months, Robin has been extraordinarily prolific since his split with the Bee Gees. "I've also written two musicals—one is Scrooge, based on Dickens' *Christmas Carol*, which is likely to be a TV musical and ideally Alec Guinness would be in the title role. The other is Henry VIII, and a German company already want to buy the film rights. It would be a great kick if they got Peter Ustinov to play the title role, he's my favorite actor. You see, it's not looks I go for in artists—it's ability."

Disc further notes that Robin has four hundred typewritten pages of stories and poems which form a book titled *On The Other Hand*. Working titles for his first solo long player currently include the monikers *All My Own Work*, *Face To Face* or possibly *Dead Or Alive*. As for his relations with the other Bee Gees, he says: "Do you know what? I haven't had a single word of congratulations from my brothers for 'Saved By The Bell.' Not a word." Though he notes, "I've got good friends around me and I can go over to Maurice and have a jam session like in the old days any time I like. What's been done is done and it's petty to keep bringing up the squabble again."

Robin also appears as the featured artist in this week's entry of *Melody Maker's* print series called *Pop Think-In*. Speaking on the day of the Apollo 11 moon shot (July 16th), he remarks: "I'm very interested in astrology and I'm a weather fanatic so I've followed the Apollo expedition in a sense. I'm not optimistic about their venture though, I've got no faith in their coming back." This despite the title of his recent song, "To Heaven And Back."

"An ordinary tramp in the street knows that there's a risk of this kind of thing the first time you do anything. I think they know themselves that they are not coming back and if they do they'll introduce into this world a lot of germs."

Of the Bee Gees, Robin says: "On their new album Maurice has dedicated a song titled 'My Thing' to his dog, Aston. On my new album I've a song that's a reply called 'So What.' You wait until you hear it."

• Monday, July 28, 1969
While visiting Hamburg, Germany for promotion, Robin grants an interview to Nick Logan of the *NME*. The paper duly reports that Robin has installed a studio in his home and even has a disc cutter on order to create his own demo acetates. Robin is in Germany for three days to do television plugs for his single, but plans to spend his nights writing new songs. Robin has recently been composing prospective songs for Tom Jones to record and he hopes to meet with the Welsh star upon his return to Britain.

• Tuesday, July 29, 1969
Variety reports that Robin is supposed to fly to the United States for television guest spots to promote "Saved By The Bell." The remaining Bee Gees are due to begin their film, *Cucumber Castle*, in the next few days.

• Saturday, August 2, 1969
NME reports a rumor circulating this week that Colin will leave the Bee Gees on September 1st. The rumor was denied by both Colin and Robert Stigwood on July 30th. Meanwhile, the guest cast for *Cucumber Castle* has swelled to potentially include Sammy Davis, Jr., comedienne Hermione Gingold and the legendary Vincent Price. Lulu, Richard Harris and Blind Faith are also currently on tap to appear. Robert Stigwood hopes to turn the film into a thirteen-week television series (and many of the guests named would likely be a part of the extended version of this special). On a side note, *Cucumber Castle*'s director, Mike Mansfield, was involved in a car accident July 28th and is currently recovering from a concussion.

Meanwhile, Robin has written the screenplay and score for a film titled *The Family Circle*. This comedy, set in 1886 London, is to be produced in autumn by the Rank Organization. The *NME* says that Robin may take an acting role in the production. He is also due to appear on three US television programs, *The Ed Sullivan Show*, *Kraft Music Hall* and the *Glen Campbell Goodtime Hour*, with a fourth, *The Andy Williams Show*, now likely. Robin's current manager, Chris Hutchins, is due in New York City to finalize the details of these appearances this week with Robin set to join him on the weekend. After this, Hutchins travels to Las Vegas to take his post as Elvis Presley's publicist at the International Hotel (and his involvement with Robin will consequently ebb).

Robin's solo concert tour of the UK is now provisionally being set for eight concerts from November 28th through December 5th. In Germany, Robin appears in a videotaped, lip-synch performance of "Saved By The Bell" on Radio Bremen's *Beat Club* (likely taped earlier this week).

- Tuesday, August 5, 1969

At IBC Studios A and B, multi-track copies will be made of the recent Bee Gees recordings "Don't Forget To Remember," "Then You Left Me" and "I Was The Child" (the latter two taped at undated sessions) for use in the *Cucumber Castle* television special soundtrack. "Then You Left Me" was initially tracked by Maurice on piano and Colin on drums in four takes. The last of these performances is the basis of the master, to which overdubs are added of Barry's voice, backing vocals, guitar, piano, bass and Bill Shepherd's orchestra (recorded in stereo).

Additionally, engineers John Pantry and Andy Knight work with arranger Bill Shepherd to tape the show's incidental score. These will be Shepherd's short instrumental orchestral versions of the Bee Gees' songs "World," "Massachusetts (The Lights Went Out In)," "I Started A Joke," "First Of May," two versions of "I've Gotta Get A Message To You," "Don't Forget To Remember," "New York Mining Disaster 1941," "Words" and "Holiday." Because shooting and production has yet to commence, not all of these cues will be utilized in the final show. Rather, they are taped as links for scenes should they be needed. Additional cues will be taped during this period at another session; the results will be mixed on August 8th.

Other Bee Gees productions from this period include "Twinky" (a catchy, unissued Barry sung song, possibly written for the movie of the same name and later covered by Andy Gibb), started by Barry and Maurice on acoustic guitars and captured in three takes. The multi-track features another vocalist besides Barry, so it is also possible that this excellent song was actually intended for another artist to cover. "Law" is a four-minute-plus, Maurice-led rock jam in the twelve-bar mode. No vocals will be recorded for this track, which remains incomplete and unissued. Lastly, the Bee Gees' own version of "Give A Hand, Take A Hand" is taped by Barry, Maurice and Colin and topped off by overdubs of organ, bass and piano. The completed production will be mixed in January 1970 for possible release on *Cucumber Castle*; instead, the Bee Gees will remake the song in January 1974 for their *Mr. Natural* album.

- Wednesday, August 6, 1969

Maurice joins his recent collaborators Steve Kipner, Steve Groves and his brother-in-law, Billy Lawrie, in a jam session that will produce a track titled, "Have You Heard The Word." On March 7, 1970, this track will be issued as a single credited to The Fut on the Beacon label (following its release, it will become fodder for early bootlegs of the Beatles, where compilers mistake or try and pass off the track as the work of John Lennon and company).

- Thursday, August 7, 1969

In Britain, host Pete Murray shows Robin Gibb in a repeat performance of "Saved By The Bell" on BBC1 television's *Top Of The Pops*.

- Friday, August 8, 1969

In Britain, the Bee Gees issue their single: "Don't Forget To Remember" c/w "The Lord." Also today, the Monkees' Davy Jones meets with Robin Gibb at his London home (likely to discuss Davy covering some of Robin's songs). According to *Disc*, Robin plays Davy "several previously unreleased songs and some new compositions." Robin's manager, Chris Hutchins, says: "They got on very well together. Davy liked a lot of what he heard. Of course they have one thing in common—both come from Manchester." Sadly, Davy will never cut any of Robin's material.

At IBC Studio A, mono music cues for the *Cucumber Castle* television special are compiled. These include unique mixes of "Don't Forget To Remember," "The Lord," "Then You Left Me," "I Was The Child," as well as Lulu's rendition of Simon & Garfunkel's "Mrs. Robinson" and Barry's "Morning Of My Life." Additionally, Bill Shepherd's incidental score is included in these preparations. For the record, his list of taped cues are "Cucumber Castle," "Holiday," "Massachusetts (The Lights Went Out In)," and shorter links of "World," "Massachusetts (The Lights Went Out In)," "I Started A Joke," "First Of May," "Don't Forget To Remember," "New York Mining Disaster 1941," "Words," "Holiday" and two different cues of "I've Gotta Get A Message To You."

- Saturday, August 9, 1969

Disc says that the Bee Gees' *Cucumber Castle* television series could feature such additional guest players as Eleanor Bron, David Hemmings, Arthur Mullard and Rita Tushingham. The paper further notes that Maurice will now be director of photography for the comedy sketches. Rumors continue to circulate that Colin is leaving the band. Maurice asks, "Who's putting these stories around? It's simply not true that Colin is quitting."

More *Cucumber Castle* production news comes from the *NME*, who report today that Joanne Steuer has been signed as choreographer for the fifty-thousand pound budgeted film. Hugh Gladwish is now the director, replacing Mike Mansfield (who will produce the project). Not to be outdone, Robin announces that he will star in his own forty-five minute television special this autumn (to be taped in early October). *Disc* says that Robin's next single will be credited to the Robin Gibb Orchestra & Chorus and is to feature a song called "The Statesman (Sir Winston Spencer Churchill)" coupled with "The Ghost Of Christmas Past" (a track from Robin's musical Scrooge), though neither track will surface commercially.

• Monday, August 11, 1969
In Britain, shooting begins on *Cucumber Castle* at Robert Stigwood's thirty-six acre estate in Stanmore, Middlesex.

• Thursday, August 14, 1969
In Britain, host Tony Blackburn welcomes the Bee Gees to BBC1 television's *Top Of The Pops* where they will perform "Don't Forget To Remember." The exclusive audio mix of this performance (a new vocal over the studio backing track) will also be syndicated on the BBC World Service radio series, *Pick Of The Pops*.

• Saturday, August 16, 1969
In Britain, "Don't Forget To Remember" enters the singles chart and will go all the way to #2 over the next fifteen weeks. *Disc* runs an interview with Maurice. "Robin had always wanted to go solo," he says, "so when it happened I wasn't really angry at all. I simply understood the situation.... recently I saw that Robin was appearing on *Top Of The Pops* and I'd heard he was a bit sorry to be losing contact with his brothers, so I rang up the studio and asked to speak to him...a couple of hours later there was a knock on the door and there was Robin, saying he'd heard I'd been trying to contact him. So we embraced, all emotional, sat down and had a drink and later we went round and Robin reunited with Barry like nothing had happened."

The *NME* says that Barry has formed his own record label, Diamond. He plans to focus on releasing music with a gospel and spiritual feel. His first signing is P.P. Arnold, who the paper says has already cut material with backing from singers Madeline Bell, Doris Troy and Rosetta Hightower. Her first release is to be her rendition of "Bury Me Down By The River" (which was initially tipped as the follow-up to "Tomorrow Tomorrow"). Filming of *Cucumber Castle* is underway; the paper says Mike Mansfield will not fly to Hawaii to film Blind Faith for the program (concert footage of the band performing "Well All Right" from their June 7th Hyde Park debut concert will be substituted in the final film).

1969

Robin tells Lon Goddard of his current activities in *Record Mirror*: "I've got fifteen tracks in the can for the LP, titled *Robin's Reign*. There isn't any universal theme to the tracks, just a series of my compositions. It should be out before long. I'm also doing a musical score for a film called Henry The Eighth and I'm making my own film called *Family Tree*. It involves a man, John Family, whose grandfather, Sir Catarac, is caught trying to blow up Trafalgar Square with a homemade bomb wrapped in underwear. He is taken away by ten policemen and left in a cage at the zoo, where after a considerable time he begins to enjoy his abode. The rest of his relations dislike seeing him in the zoo, so knowing his partiality for cages, John Family has one installed in his lounge at home and keeps the old man there. The theme of the film is John Family's attempts to get into his past and trace his ancestors."

• Thursday, August 21, 1969
In Britain, host Alan Freeman welcomes both Robin Gibb and his brother Bee Gees to BBC1 television's *Top Of The Pops*, where they are individually seen in respective performances of "Saved By The Bell" and "Don't Forget To Remember."

• Saturday, August 23, 1969
The *NME* reports that production on *Cucumber Castle* is running behind schedule due to inclement weather. Frankie Howerd and Spike Milligan have been added to the guest cast. The final sequences are scheduled to be shot on Thursday with Richard Harris and Friday with Sammy Davis, Jr. (although neither will appear in the final cut of the film). An April 1970 article in *Hit Parader* seems to hint that their scenes were at least scripted and possibly shot. Davis (according to the report) was in town on a London cabaret stint and snuck away to film a sequence portraying a duck hunter pursued by two very large ducks (Barry and Maurice). Meanwhile, Richard Harris is said to deliver the immortal quip: "What am I doing in this century, get me out of here."

Additionally, the production was blighted by theft last weekend when someone drove off with the Bee Gees' Ford transit van containing Maurice's Les Paul model guitar.

Meanwhile, Colin has formed yet another showbiz agency, signing Keith Potger and the New Seekers. Details of his departure from the Bee Gees will soon emerge.

In Britain, EMI's Parlophone label issues a single by Samantha Sang—"The Love Of A Woman" c/w "Don't Let It Happen Again"—written by Barry and Maurice and produced by Barry (who sings backgrounds on the disc). Bill Shepherd is the disc's arranger. In America, the disc is issued on Atco.

Record Mirror publishes an article by Hugh Gibb detailing his stalled communication with Robin. "It's been virtually impossible for me to speak to him for thirteen weeks," says Hugh. The piece chronicles Hugh's days managing his boys in Brisbane, while he juggled an eighty-pound-a-week job as a lawnmower salesman: "They have a lot of grass in Australia, you see." *Record Mirror* notes that eleven-year-old Andy Gibb, "might become the fourth Bee Gee when he grows up." In conclusion, Hugh says of Robin: "The door is wide open. We all hope and pray that Robin will come back. You've no idea how worried we are about what is happening to him. But I believe he will come back."

• Saturday, August 30, 1969
The *NME* confirms that Colin is no longer a member of the Bee Gees. The official announcement was made August 25th. "I received a letter from Barry and Maurice on Tuesday evening to the effect they no longer desire to be associated with me," remarked Colin. "I am a partner in the Bee Gees and as a result of getting this letter I have no alternative but to put this matter to my lawyers and ask them to dissolve the partnership heretofore known as the Bee Gees. I intend to continue under the name the Bee Gees even if it means forming another group."

The paper also publishes an interview with Robin conducted by Alan Smith. "I was a Bee Gee thirteen years and it's hard to forget, but I'm throwing myself into my work. I'm writing a one hundred page book. I'm doing a Christmas special of my own for ATV." In the studio, he has been working to complete an album (though these sessions are largely undocumented). "The tracks on the album are 'Alexandria Good Time,' 'The Flag I Flew Fell Over,' 'I'll Heard My Sheep,' 'The Man Most Likely To Be,' 'Love Just Goes,' 'Make Believe,' 'I Was Your Used To Be,' 'The Complete And Utter History,' 'Seven Birds Are Singing,' 'It's No Use Crying Anymore,' 'Sing A Song Of Sisters' and 'Beat The Drum.' I don't think I've missed any." *Odessa* is still on his mind and he remarks: "The others wanted to call the album *Masterpiece* (sic), you know, but I thought that was pompous."

In *Record Mirror*, Barry tells Valerie Mabbs about the Bee Gees' next album: "We have been working on our album, but it's got to be mixed yet. Two of the tracks are featured in the film, as well as the single and some music from Blind Faith."

Maurice, meanwhile, plays Mabbs tracks that he recently cut with his brother-in-law, Billy Lawrie. Mabbs describes the tape: "...the number that is planned for Billy's first single 'Visitor from America,' was written by him and arranged and produced by Maurice. It features a twenty-five-piece chorus and Lulu adding extra power."

- Thursday, September 4, 1969

In Britain, host Tony Blackburn welcomes the Bee Gees—Barry & Maurice—to BBC1's *Top Of The Pops* television program, where they perform "Don't Forget To Remember" sans Colin Petersen. In the meantime, Robin has switched management to Vic Lewis at NEMS, causing his father, Hugh, to threaten to make him a ward of the court. Robin's move has also prompted RSO to issue writs against Vic Lewis and NEMS Enterprises. Robin comments, "My father is making something of nothing. I have my own career and my own family. It is nothing to do with him." Hugh tells David Scan at *Record Mirror*: "I will only make him a ward of the court as a last resort. I will only do it if there is no other way out."

- Saturday, September 6, 1969

The *NME* reports that Colin's sequences will be cut from *Cucumber Castle* (which wrapped shooting last weekend). Barry says of Colin's dismissal: "It is a firm decision, and there is no going back on it. In any case, Colin was in no way involved in any of our songwriting."

In *Record Mirror*, Colin discusses the split with Ian Middleton. "I'm still very bewildered by it," he says. "After the Bee Gees did *Top Of The Pops*, everything was fine. Then I suddenly get this letter delivered by Robert Stigwood's chauffeur saying I'm out of the group. Just like that. No phone call or anything.

"From the other week backwards, we all got on well...Apart from the odd illness, I've always turned up for gigs and things, and I've always put the group first and foremost...In the two-and-a-half-years I've been with them, it's been like being a member of a family—and now I've been thrown out."

- Monday, September 8, 1969

Colin issues a statement protesting Barry and Maurice's recent appearance on *Top Of The Pops* without him. Colin has taken the advice of industry heavy Marty Machat, who has instructed him to take action on the Gibbs using the name Bee Gees sans his presence. RSO comments: "...the brothers Gibb have been appearing under the name of the Bee Gees—which are Barry Gibb's initials—for many years. The brothers Gibb have no objection to Colin Petersen performing under his own initials, or any other name."

- Friday, September 12, 1969

In Britain, Parlophone issues the debut single—"Denver" c/w "Son Jon"—of Jonathan Kelly. The disc is produced by Colin Petersen (who is also the publisher of both sides).

- Saturday, September 13, 1969

The *NME* reports that future Bee Gees recordings will appear on their own custom label imprint beginning in November. The previously mentioned name for Barry's label, Diamond, has been scotched by a label already operating in America (since 1961; Diamond Records will fold in 1972). P.P. Arnold's first disc (originally slated for September 12th release) will be held until the Bee Gees' label is up and running. Another artist slated for the roster is ex-Marble, Graham Bonnet (see October 4th). In other news, Barry has written a song for Andy Williams to record, "The Day Your Eyes Meet Mine," and Booker T. & The M.G.'s are said to be cutting a full album of Gibb songs (though neither of these ventures will result in releases).

The *NME* also notes that a track, "Who Knows What A Room Is," recently taped for the forthcoming Bee Gees album is a tribute of sorts to the Beatles. Barry describes it as, "the Beatles as they were—and as they are now." Another recent recording, "I Lay Down And Die," is described as a homage to Phil Spector. "I've positively captured the sound," Barry tells Richard Green, "which hasn't been captured before...I think I have found the secret, Maurice and I have found it, of where the [wall of] sound comes from. The whole studio was in an uproar when it was finished because it's not that studio.

"All the studios have got eight-track and sixteen-track machines. That's what you get by experimenting with machines. The album's called *I Lay Down And Die*. We've got to mix it into mono and stereo and it'll be out for Christmas, about November. First, there's *Best Of The Bee Gees* in October." Barry describes their current hit, "Don't Forget To Remember," as a tribute to country great, Jim Reeves. "The music I'm writing now...is country and western," says Barry. "Nobody realized 'Massachusetts' was a country and western song. My writing is changing all the time. There are lots of tributes on our new album, to the Beatles, Jim Reeves, Johnny Cash...Every track we put down has to be considered as a single."

1969

- Saturday, September 20, 1969

In the United States, "Don't Forget To Remember" enters the *Billboard* singles chart. Over the next three weeks, it will reach a meager #73 (compared to its huge chart placement in the UK).

In Britain, the *NME* reports that Colin has now issued writs against Barry, Maurice and RSO to cease any Bee Gees business until their partnership is wound up in the court. Colin wishes to prevent Barry and Maurice from performing as the Bee Gees without him. A hearing is expected to take place on September 24th.

- Monday, September 22, 1969

Barry and Maurice begin recording at a new location: Recorded Sound Studios Limited (27-31 Bryanston Street, Marble Arch, London, W1H 7AB). The Gibbs are likely lured to this facility by former IBC engineer Phil Wade (now employed here); it will later become known as Nova Sound, though not until 1971. Today they will tape a new song, "The Only Way." The basic track for the song will be built around Barry and Maurice strumming on acoustic guitars (Barry on twelve-string and Maurice on his "lute" six-string heard frequently during the London sessions for *Odessa*).

After tuning and rehearsal, the duo roll through five false starts before completing the master backing track, take six. To this, overdubs will be added of drums, bass and piano, as well as orchestration (recorded in stereo across two tracks). Vocals (including a lead from Barry and harmony from Maurice) will be added at a later, undocumented session. Though the completed production will not surface commercially, it is later bootlegged under the title "Every Morning, Every Night."

- Thursday, September 25, 1969

A second session at Recorded Sound Studios with engineer Phil Wade finds Barry at work on three songs. These include one take of the mid-tempo country ballad "High And Windy Mountain," the production of which will be completed at a later IBC session with Barry on vocals and full orchestration from Bill Shepherd. Another track from that undated IBC session, "Go Tell Cheyanne" (in the style of Maurice's recent jam, "Have You Heard The Word") features vocals from Barry with Maurice and Billy Lawrie. Both "High And Windy Mountain" and "Go Tell Cheyanne," remain unissued.

Also at today's session, Barry will lay down simple voice and guitar demos of "One Bad Thing" and "If I Only Had My Mind On Something Else." On March 23, 1970, Barry will tape a full-fledged version of "One Bad Thing" for a potential solo single release. "If I Only Had My Mind On Something Else" will be remade during October.

- Friday, September 26, 1969

Another productive recording date at Recorded Sound Studios (working with engineers Phil Wade and Eric David Holland) results in the master of "Turning Tide," issued on next year's *Cucumber Castle*. Barry will also lay down a simple voice and guitar demo of "Sweetheart." This track will be remade at a further session on October 7th.

Meanwhile at IBC, Robin mixes mono versions of his recent productions (from undated sessions): "One Million Years," "The Worst Girl In This Town," "Most Of My Life," "Down Came The Sun" and "Moon Anthem." It is also apparent that some additional production/recording work is completed on "One Million Years" during this session. Other Robin productions from this era include the multi-movement epic "Hudson's Fallen Wind" (later edited for the shorter "Farmer Ferdinand Hudson" on *Robin's Reign*), "Give Me A Smile" and "Weekend."

In court, Colin loses his bid to prevent Barry and Maurice from their continued use of the name Bee Gees. "Colin lost complete interest in the group," Barry tells the *NME*'s Richard Green today. "During the first week of the last recording [sessions] he didn't turn up once. He said, 'Call me if you need me.' A dedicated Bee Gee doesn't do that...He said the Bee Gees wouldn't survive when Robin left—I was never under the impression that Colin Peterson was a fortune teller!...Maurice and I could be the Bee Gees for the next five years."

The *Evening Standard* features more measured quotes from the Bee Gees in light of their court victory. "I have no hard feelings towards Colin Petersen," says Barry. "We wish him well in anything he may do in the future." Maurice, who is currently in Las Vegas with Lulu, adds: "The letters BG stand for brothers Gibb and always will do."

- Tuesday, September 30, 1969

In Britain, the Bee Gees appear on singer Dusty Springfield's television series, *Decidedly Dusty*. Dusty joins them for the opening lines of "I've Gotta Get A Message To You," after which they perform "Words" alone.

- Saturday, October 4, 1969

The *NME* reports that Barry and Maurice plan to tour Britain in early 1970 with a thirty-piece orchestra. "I want to get back on the road as soon as possible," says Barry. Meanwhile, *Cucumber Castle* director/producer Mike Mansfield has suffered through another auto accident, his second in four weeks, totaling his vehicle. In other news, Marbles have officially split. Graham Bonnet will record with Barry as producer and Maurice, the paper says, has penned some songs for Trevor Gordon.

In the same issue, Richard Green talks with Barry about their next single. "There's a few tracks which I have demos of. The ballad called 'If I Only Had My Mind On Something Else' is the one I'm very keen on at the moment. It's a long title, but it can't be any other...The new label will be out in November... Robert suggested G.G., just the initials for Gibb and Gibb the two brothers, you see. I thought of [calling it] Lord, [like] the flipside of the last single ['The Lord']—it doesn't have to mean God or anything like that. I'm concentrating on capturing the American sound here and everyone who's heard Pat Arnold's record in America has said, 'Is this Phil Spector's new record?' That's a great compliment."

○ Sunday, October 5, 1969
In Brussels, the Bee Gees' promo film for "Tomorrow, Tomorrow" is screened on television's *Tienerklanken*.

○ Tuesday, October 7, 1969
At Recorded Sound Studios, Barry works with engineers Phil Wade and Eric David Holland to tape a new version of "If I Only Had My Mind On Something Else." Playing twelve-string acoustic guitar, Barry will play through two takes (the second of which will be the master). To this overdubs will be added of a acoustic twelve-string second guitar, piano, drums and a lead vocal from Barry. Still the results are deemed insufficient and the song will be remade tomorrow.

Also at this session, Barry and Maurice will revisit "Sweetheart," taping three takes of the number with tracks of acoustic guitar and drums. Like "If I Only Had My Mind On Something Else," today's efforts on "Sweetheart" will be scrapped; the production will be remade on October 13th.

○ Wednesday, October 8, 1969
At Recorded Sound Studios, Barry and Maurice work with engineers Phil Wade and Eric David Holland to tape their next US and UK single A-sides. "If I Only Had My Mind On Something Else" is finally captured (after two prior aborted versions) in a single take. Following this, "I.O.I.O.," which was first attempted during the *Idea* sessions on June 12, 1968, will be perfected in two takes (the first being just a short false start). "I.O.I.O." will be issued as a single in the UK on March 13, 1970; "If I Only Had My Mind On Something Else" will be the US choice for an A-side that same month on Atco.

In the United States, *Variety* notes that *Popcorn*, a film including a clip of the Bee Gees from 1967, is ready for release in November.

○ Friday, October 10, 1969
At Recorded Sound Studios, Barry and Maurice work with engineers Phil Wade and Eric David Holland to tape the ballad, "The Chance Of Love." Maurice will play through eight mostly fragmentary takes of the song on piano as the basis for the track (directed by Barry, who sings the lyrics off-mic). After take two, Barry suggests that Maurice change the chord sequence because it sounds to him like the Beatles' "Hey Jude." Maurice jokes: "Don't worry, Humble Pie sounded like bloody 'Get Back' didn't it?" Take 8 will be the master, receiving overdubs of guitars, organ, drums, as well as Barry's lead vocal and orchestration from Bill Shepherd.

The latter part of the Recorded Sound session is taken up by five takes of a Maurice-led, electric guitar jam (with drummer Terry Cox) which will develop into the song "Julia." Barry remains in the studio directing the composition and by take three he will join the musical proceedings, singing and playing acoustic twelve-string guitar. Before take four, Barry comments: "Maurice, it can go for five minutes this track. Let it go. We're not doing blues. We're doing a tune too; we're doing a proper thing." Despite some lengthy takes, Barry and Maurice decide to start anew on "Julia" at another session on October 16th.

Meanwhile at IBC Studio A, Robin will work on solo recordings built from rudimentary tracks of rhythm box and piano (played by Robin); these are later embellished by arranger Zack Lawrence who provides orchestrations. Both "August October" and "Gone Gone Gone" will be captured two takes; "August October" will have an Italian vocal track as an option for the Italian record market.

The third song from this date is announced by Robin as "Lord Bless All, Lord Let All Be Blessed" and will be performed by the composer singing live to his own organ accompaniment in three takes (the first two of which are incomplete). The final performance will receive several overdubs of Robin's voice to build a choir effect.

The final Robin song from this date will be "One Million Years," a future single for Robin. The multi-track tape will again have an Italian language vocal track as an option for the record market in Italy. Notes from this recording date also indicate that stereo mixes will be made today of the following productions: "One Million Years," "Down Came The Sun," "Most Of My Life," "Storm" (possibly a working title for a known song), "August October," "Gone Gone Gone," "Lord Bless All," "The Worst Girl In This Town," and possibly "Give Me A Smile."

○ Saturday, October 11, 1969
The *NME* reports that a High Court judge, Mr. Justice Shaw, has ruled Colin Petersen was "a minor attraction with the Bee Gees," squelching Colin's bid to prevent Barry and Maurice from using the name Bee Gees in the future.

1969

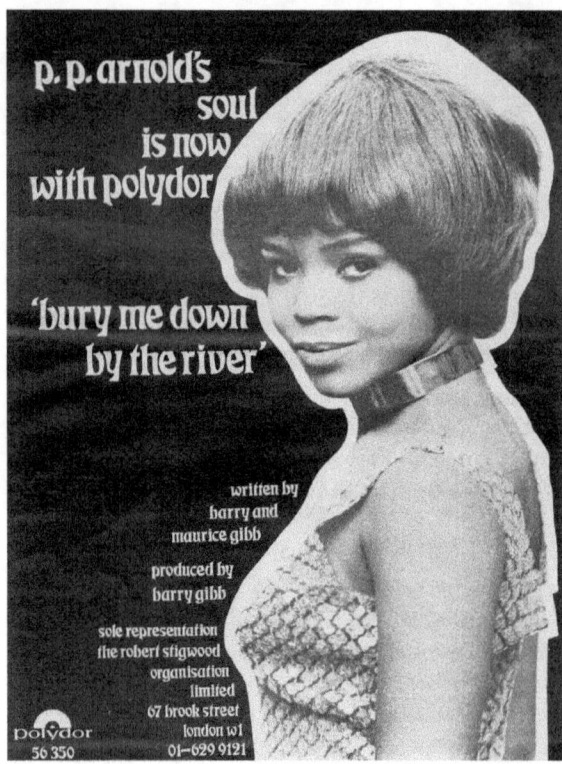

• Monday, October 13, 1969
Barry and Maurice remake "Sweetheart" in a single take; the results will be issued on the flipside of the Bee Gees' next British single in March 1970.

• Wednesday, October 15, 1969
At Recorded Sound Studios, Barry and Maurice work with engineers Phil Wade and Eric Holland on two recordings. The first of these is labeled "12 Bar," which is simply a fragment of a guitar and drum instrumental warm-up (and not really a song at all). The second recording will be a new version of Barry's "End Of My Song," a tune first demoed in 1967 as a perspective submission for Otis Redding to cover. Two complete takes will be made of the backing track, with the second pass selected as the basis for the master version (which will be treated to a substantial amount of overdubs, filling all eight tracks of the 1" tape). Although completed mixes of the song will be made on November 19th (and again in January 1970), the song will be passed over for commercial release and remains unissued (though it has circulated on bootlegs).

• Thursday, October 16, 1969
At Recorded Sound Studios, Barry and Maurice continue sessions with one take of the sinister rocker, "Julia" (composed at an October 10th session). Today's production will be completed with full orchestra and vocals but remains unissued.

• Saturday, October 18, 1969
The NME reports that the Bee Gees' proposed concert tour of early 1970 has been postponed, with Barry and Maurice now to focus on completing twelve further episodes of the Cucumber Castle television series. The initial show was already bought by television outlets in France, Germany, Italy, Scandinavia, Holland and Austria.

The only interruption to their filming will be a promotional tour of America where such artists as Mama Cass, Eddy Arnold and Janis Joplin are set to record Gibb compositions. The Bee Gees' own label is still in the works with releases planned from P.P. Arnold, Tin Tin and, of course, the Bee Gees. Maurice is currently recording Lulu's brother Billy Lawrie, whose rendition of "Roll Over Beethoven" is expected to be his first single. Graham Bonnet and Trevor Gordon's solo discs are also still in the works.

P.P. Arnold's long-awaited, Barry-produced-disc—"Bury Me Down By The River" c/w "Give A Hand, Take A Hand"—is now on release in Britain, as is Best Of Bee Gees, which has already proven a big seller Stateside.

• Friday, October 31, 1969
Barry works with Samantha Sang on a follow-up to her recent EMI release, "Love Of A Woman." Today, she is reported to have taped versions of "Please Don't Take My Man Away" and "The Day Your Eyes Meet Mine" with Barry at the helm as producer; neither track is issued but the singer will later find fame with the Bee Gees' song "Emotion" in 1977.

• November 1969
Maurice and Lulu make a promotional trip to Los Angeles late in the month. Harold Bronson conducts an interview with Maurice about the Bee Gees' current activities (published March 5, 1970 in the UCLA Daily Bruin). "Robin left quite freely," Maurice tells Bronson, "no arguments or anything. He said give me a year and see how I do, because he always wanted to be a bit of a soloist.

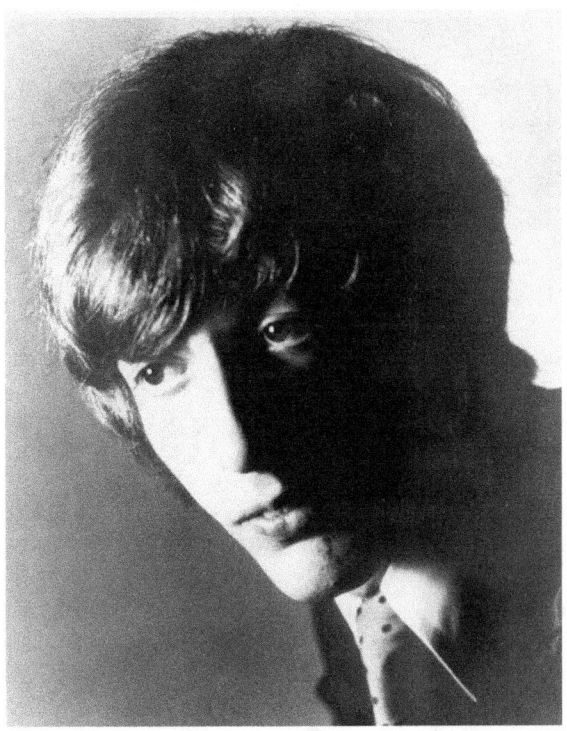

"He never got on with Vince or Colin at all, never. And there used to be a lot of friction everywhere we went. Vince wanted this or that done and Robin got mad on stage if he played something bluesy which didn't suit the songs. Robin got terribly annoyed on stage and afterwards he'd walk off and blow hell out of Vince. Vince used to say, 'Sit down little boy,' and all that crap. It was very tormentive and Robin couldn't stand that. After Vince had left the group, Robin said, 'If Colin is still with the group, I don't want in. Let me try a year and see how I do.'...he said he's coming back. He told us that..."

Maurice says the duo's next album will be called *Happiness* and will feature guest appearances from George Harrison and Eric Clapton. Maurice mentions "Julia" as one of the potential offerings. Of their previous LP he says: "*Odessa* was originally going to be called *The American Opera*. Each song was just going to help build up the history of America, from the beginning to the end.

"We started with the track 'Odessa' itself and if you listen to some of the words, it describes a young man living in America many centuries ago. And the song has words like, 'You haven't got your dog anymore,' which means 'you're out on your own, fella.' Start off the country on your own; get out there and make this into a great country."

• Saturday, November 1, 1969
The *NME* reports that Robin has been booked to appear on US television's *Andy Williams Show* (he is scheduled to travel to Los Angeles in January for this appearance). Robin's new manager, Vic Lewis, is negotiating for the release of a follow-up single to "Saved By The Bell" and a full solo album, which the paper says is now complete.

• Monday, November 3, 1969
Barry produces another session with singer P.P. Arnold, possibly for a future Gee Gee Records release. The date will turn out three covers—"Piccaninny" (an otherwise unrecorded Barry composition), "High And Windy Mountain" and "Turning Tide"—all of which remain in the can when the Bee Gees' label plans fall by the wayside (see November 26th).

• Friday, November 7, 1969
Billy M. Lawrie's first single—"Roll Over Beethoven" c/w "Come Back Joanna"—is issued in the UK. The disc is produced by Maurice.

• Saturday, November 8, 1969
In Britain, *Best Of Bee Gees* enters the albums chart. Over the next twenty-two weeks, it will reach a high of #7. The *NME* says the Bee Gees' own record label—now named Gee Gee—will make its public bow on November 21st. Barry and Maurice are currently trying to decide on which of their songs—"Sweetheart" or "If I Only Had My Mind On Something Else"—to issue as an A-side (so much for Robert Stigwood picking their singles!).

1969

• Saturday, November 15, 1969
In Britain, Robin's "Saved By The Bell" re-enters the singles chart for a single week at #49. The *NME* reports that Elvis Presley may issue a single of his cover of the Gibb composition, "Words." Australia's *Go-Set* runs an interview with Barry conducted by Ian Meldrum. "Elvis Presley's next single is 'Words,' this has elated me far above any feeling I ever had of us having our records a hit. The fact that he recorded 'Words' is enough for me, even if it never goes out as long as I have that copy to play at home I don't care if it is a hit or not.

"In February I start a movie with Vincent Price which will be the greatest thing that has ever happened to me. This will take three months. I have to go to America for this, while I am filming Maurice will be doing something else, I think it will be a film as well, but before the end of the spring we hope to be in Australia."

Meldrum asks Barry if the brothers will ever get back together: "Just because we are apart now doesn't mean we are enemies, we most certainly are not; most of what you read is for publicity sake. I never speak out against Robin, but Robin has a lot of fun speaking out against us...He has it in him to be a very big star. I want Robin to keep that up simply because he is my brother. There are no jealousies between us, he wanted to do this and I think it was just a matter of him doing it and he did it."

• Wednesday, November 19, 1969
At Recorded Sound, Barry and Maurice will lay down a single take of "New Song" with just their two (slightly out-of-tune) acoustic guitars. This production, a ballad, will remain incomplete; historically it is the final new recording by Barry and Maurice as a duo. Also today, engineer Phil Wade prepares stereo mixes of such recent productions as "Turning Tide," "End Of My Song" and "The Chance Of Love."

• Tuesday, November 25, 1969
Maurice and Lulu arrive in Sydney. Maurice comments to the press that he and Barry plan a tour down under next year.

• Wednesday, November 26, 1969
Variety reports that the Bee Gees have postponed plans for their own record label until early 1970.

• Friday, November 28, 1969
In Britain, Robin's second solo single—"One Million Years" c/w "Weekend"—is issued, but will surprisingly not chart.

• Saturday, November 29, 1969
The *NME* reports that the Bee Gees have complained to RCA over a mistaken label credit on Elvis Presley's latest US album: *Elvis In Person At The International Hotel*. The double album features Elvis' cover of their song "Words," but mistakenly credits songwriters Tommy Boyce and Bobby Hart, who had a hit with the same song title recorded by The Monkees (and distributed by RCA, hence the obvious mistake). The paper says the labels will be corrected for Britain and Elvis' version of "Words" may still be issued as a single. The Bee Gees are now set to visit America in January "for several promotional TV appearances."

• December 1969
Robin's current manager, Vic Lewis, issues a cover of the Paul McCartney-penned Badfinger hit "Come And Get It" with an intriguing flipside. Backing the disc is the song, "No Other Heart" with lyrics by Robin to a tune by Lewis and arranger Ken Thorne. The single will be issued next year in the US on the Epic label.

• Monday, December 1, 1969
In Britain, Barry Gibb announces that he is quitting the Bee Gees. The *NME* reports that Barry is, "Fed up, miserable and completely disillusioned." Barry plans to be a solo artist from this point on.

• Tuesday, December 2, 1969
In Britain, Robert Stigwood comments on Barry's departure from the Bee Gees. "We are not opposed in principle to Barry going solo, and we will be meeting with him and Maurice later this week—following Maurice's return to Britain—to discuss the matter."

• Saturday, December 6, 1969
The *NME* reports that with Barry's departure from the Bee Gees, plans for the Gee Gee record label "cannot be determined." However, plans for turning *Cucumber Castle* into a television series are now definitively scrapped. Rumors are that Maurice will focus his talents on working with Lulu. Meanwhile, RSO's dispute with Robin has been settled. Robin has agreed to relinquish his shares in the Bee Gees' publishing companies in exchange for his full release from

RSO. The *NME* say that Robin can now resume his career. It is possible that these recent disputes hurt the sales of Robin's latest single.

• Tuesday, December 9, 1969
Wasting no time, Maurice begins work today on a solo album (with help from Billy Lawrie) at Recorded Sound Studios. Exact session dates are not well documented, but between this first session and January 5, 1970, Maurice will tape the songs "Railroad," "Take It Easy, Greasy," "I've Come Back," "Laughing Child," "She's The One You Love," "Touch And Understand Love" and "The Loner." In the United States, *Variety* reports that the Bee Gees have sold twenty million singles, six million albums and collectively earned $7 million dollars annually.

• Saturday, December 13, 1969
The *NME* runs an interview with Robin, conducted by Richard Green. "I wrote three songs one night in my mind. I can write a complete song in my mind and never hear an instrument. The first time I hear an instrument is in the studio...I do all the mono and stereo reductions myself, that's what takes all the time."

• Saturday, December 20, 1969
The *NME* reports that Maurice Gibb has returned from Australia and is surprised by Barry's decision to leave the Bee Gees. Following their meeting, Barry commented that there is, "...nothing to stop them from working together in the future as the Brothers Gibb." As for a report that Barry has abandoned RSO's management, the paper says RSO, "...hoped the dispute will be resolved within a few days."

• Saturday, December 27, 1969
Music Now! publishes an interview with Robin conducted by Derek Boltwood. "I shall be writing some musical scores for films in the New Year," says Robin, "and I've also completed a book—called *On The Other Hand*—which is to be published soon. It's a collection of poems and stories, all very classical. I'm a great admirer of Dickens. All the stories are situations that could take place now, in the present, but in fact are based in the past. It's set in England...I really want to try and influence people towards a more patriotic feeling. The nearest I've got to it at the moment—as far as recording goes—is a song called 'The Statesman,' dedicated to Winston Churchill. It's not on my new album, but it's on a special album which is to be released early next year."

1970

• Thursday, January 1, 1970
Robin kicks off the new decade with a session at Recorded Sound Studios engineered by Mike Weighell and Eric Holland. Today he will tape the lyrically amusing "Sky West And Crooked," singing and playing twelve-string acoustic guitar. After a brief false start, the second take will be the master, to which Robin will add overdubs of his own backing vocals as well as some doubling of the lead vocal track.

A second song taped at this session, "A Very Special Day," is performed by Robin on piano. He will run through three incomplete takes of the song before accomplishing the master performance, take four. To this, Robin will add four tracks of backing vocals (spread across individual tracks of the 1" eight-track tape). Neither of today's recordings will be issued, as Robin stockpiles a great volume of material that will never see the light of day beyond collector's circles. Among those cut to acetate discs (a soft metal lacquer record used as a reference for studios and artists before the wider advent of cassette tape) from undated sessions during this period are such songs as "Sing Slowly Sisters," "Avalanche," "C'est La Vie, Au Revoir," "Everything Is How You See Me" and "Great Caesar's Ghost." The sheer volume of tunes and variety of acetates featuring this work will give rise to rumors of a great lost second album by Robin titled *Sing Slowly Sisters*. The reality is that there is no actual compiled and titled master featuring this material; this is just a series of sessions in the life of a very prolific writer.

• Saturday, January 3, 1970
NME announces that Maurice's solo single—"Railroad" c/w "I've Come Back"—is imminent. Barry is currently on holiday in Scotland, and upon his return, he will be consulted if Maurice's single should be issued. The paper says Barry is considering a possible reconciliation with Maurice. He has promised to give an answer this month. On British television, Maurice appears solo on BBC-1's new panel game program, *So You Think You Know The New Laws?* Earlier this week he was a guest with Lulu, singing on ITV's *Hogmanay*.

• Monday, January 5, 1970
At Recorded Sound, Maurice continues work on his solo productions for a potential album. Songs include "Railroad," "Take It Easy, Greasy," "I've Come Back," "Laughing Child," "She's The One You Love," "Touch And Understand Love" and "The Loner."

• Wednesday, January 7, 1970
In London, Polydor Records Studio prepares pressing masters for Robin's third solo single: "August October" c/w "Give Me A Smile." The disc is due to be issued on January 16th in the UK, where it will be available exclusively in mono as a 45. Outside of the UK, stereo versions will be serviced and produced; both tracks will appear in stereo on UK pressings of the *Robin's Reign* album.

• Saturday, January 10, 1970
The *NME* reports that Robin will fly to America next week to tape a spot on NBC television's *Andy Williams* show. However, it is unlikely this appearance is ever taped.

1970

● Friday, January 16, 1970
Robin's latest single—"August October" from the just-issued *Robin's Reign* album—is due for release today. Robin will be photographed visiting a session produced by his fellow former Bee Gee, Colin Petersen, for the song "Make A Stranger Your Friend" (written and performed by Petersen's protégé, Jonathan Kelly). This will lead to speculation that he appears on the single (issued by Parlophone on February 6th).

Meanwhile at IBC, engineer Ted Sharp prepares mono masters for the next Bee Gees single—"I.O.I.O." c/w "Sweetheart." However, today's results will be scrapped and remixed on February 26th. Mixing will also commence for the Bee Gees' next long player, *Cucumber Castle*. At sessions today (and continuing on January 19th) stereo mixes will be produced of "Sweetheart," "If I Only Had My Mind On Something Else" (this mix is rejected and will be redone), "Turning Tide" (this mix will also be rejected), "Who Knows What A Room Is" (a song that will remain unissued), "I Was A Child" (a rejected mix), "My Thing," "Bury Me Down By The River," "Then You Left Me," "Don't Forget To Remember," "Everytime I See You Smile" (an unissued track labeled as "not needed"), "The Chance Of Love," "End Of My Song" (another unissued track labeled as "not needed"), "Give A Hand, Take A Hand" (an unissued song that will be re-recorded for the *Mr. Natural* album in January 1974) and "I.O.I.O." (another rejected mix). These two reels of prospective masters will be cut to a stereo LP-length acetate for review at the close of the January 19th session.

● Saturday, January 17, 1970
At Recorded Sound Studios, Maurice continues sessions for his solo album. Tracks taped today include "Journey To The Misty Mountains," an instrumental number which will be captured in two takes under the working title "No Name Film Theme." Following this, an item initially labeled "Instrumental Rave Up," then "Soldier Johnny," "It Takes A Man" and finally "Insight" will be taped in one take. This obviously fluid production (based on the titling process) initially has a vocal, but this will replaced on the eight-track master by a brass overdub (making it another instrumental).

A third song from these sessions, "Triangle," may be intended for Tin Tin. The final number from this session, "Soldier Johnny," will be taped in two takes. All of today's productions are likely worked on at further, undated sessions based on the long list of engineers credited on the box and numerous items crossed out and revised. In any event, none of Maurice's solo productions from this date will be issued.

● Wednesday, January 21, 1970
In Britain, Robin is scheduled to appear on Granada television's *Lift Off*.

● Saturday, January 24, 1970
The *NME* reports that Barry and Maurice will continue to work together as the Bee Gees. "There was never a split," comments Maurice, "it's simply that Barry was bored and said the wrong things in the wrong way." Nonetheless, Maurice is now set to make his solo acting debut in a stage musical produced by Stigwood, *Sing A Rude Song*, opening at the Greenwich Theatre on February 17th. In preparation, Maurice is taking dance lessons and is set to shave his beard for the part.

In other news, *Cucumber Castle* may still be developed into a television series depending on Maurice's stage commitments. This week, Maurice tells *Record Mirror*: "...the Bee Gees are alive and well and living in London. I accepted the role because I was very bored. It came to a point where Lulu was so enthusiastic about her dancing parts on television that she was leaving the house at 8:30 in the morning. I didn't have anything to be enthusiastic about. All I was doing was staying home all day and doing nothing. So when I was offered this role I was delighted. Now I've got song and dance rehearsals all day, seven days a week."

● Monday, January 26, 1970
In Britain, Robin tapes a session for the BBC radio programme, *Johnnie Walker*. Unique performances of "Saved By The Bell," "August October," "Give Me A Smile" and "Weekend" will be aired on January 30th. Following this, Robin travels to New Zealand for his first solo concert.

● Saturday, January 31 & Sunday, February 1, 1970
In Auckland, New Zealand, Robin Gibb performs two solo sets (backed by a local orchestra) at Redwood Park, Swanson as part of New Zealand's first national rock music festival. NZBC footage of 'I Started A Joke' and 'Massachusetts' will survive; during the intro to the latter, Robin is pelted by a tomato (but continues his performance in earnest).

• Saturday, February 7, 1970
In Britain, Robin Gibb's third solo single, "August October," enters the singles chart. Over the next three weeks, it will peak at a mild #45.

• Tuesday, February 10, 1970
At IBC Studio B, further stereo mixes are produced to complete the next Bee Gees album, *Cucumber Castle*. These include the final mixes of "If I Only Had My Mind On Something Else," "I.O.I.O.," "The Lord," "I Was The Child" and "Turning Tide."

• Sunday, February 15, 1970
At IBC Studio A, Barry holds his first solo session with engineers Mike Claydon and Damon Lyon-Shaw. The first track taped, "I'll Kiss Your Memory," will be captured in three takes. The final pass will be the master and when completed, will be issued as the A-side to Barry's first solo single on May 29th. Also at this session (recorded on 1" eight-track tape) Barry will lay down four takes of "Victim," two takes of "Moonlight" (later covered by Jerry Vale) and one take of "Summer Ends." Except for "I'll Kiss Your Memory," none of today's tracks will be issued officially, though a different version of "Summer Ends" will later surface on a rare single made exclusively for the Barry Gibb Fan Club. In 1972, the group Co will issue a cover of "Summer Ends."

• Tuesday, February 17, 1970
At London's Greenwich Theatre, Maurice opens alongside Barbara Windsor in the musical, *Sing A Rude Song*. The production is a musical biography of Marie Lloyd, an English music hall star given to ribald renditions of otherwise innocent material. Maurice portrays Marie's third and final husband, Bernard Dillon, a champion jockey who won the Epsom Derby in 1910 and was legally married to her up to her passing in October 1922. Their stormy relationship is said to have contributed to Marie's downfall as a performer and ultimate demise.

• Friday, February 20, 1970
At IBC Studio A, work continues on Barry's solo productions. "I'll Kiss Your Memory," "Victim," ""Moonlight," "Summer Ends" will all be transferred from 1" eight-track to a new format, 2" sixteen-track. According to *Beat Instrumental*, IBC recently closed for a week to install this new tape machine, as well as Dolby noise reduction units and—for the first time—air conditioning to keep the musicians and rooms cool.

In particular, all of today's transferred productions will be augmented by added piano and various vocal overdubs to complete the masters (though "I'll Kiss Your Memory" will be the only master to officially surface). Also today, Barry will track two takes of a new song, "I Want To Take Care Of You."

• Sunday, February 22, 1970
At IBC Studio A, Barry works with engineers Mike Claydon and Damon Lyon-Shaw on further sessions for a potential solo album. Today, Barry cuts one take each of "A Child, A Girl, A Woman," "Mando Bay," "Born," "Clyde O'Reilly" (under the working title "Epitaph") and two takes of "Peace Of Mind." Despite all of the productions being completed, Barry's versions will never officially be issued. Next year, popular German singer Peter Maffay will cover "Mando Bay" for his album, *Du Bist Wie Ein Lied*.

• Thursday, February 26, 1970
At IBC Studio B, final mono masters are created for the next Bee Gees single—"I.O.I.O." c/w "Sweetheart." The disc will be issued on March 13th.

• Friday, February 27, 1970
At Recorded Sound Studios, Robin Gibb works with engineers Mike Weighell and Eric Holland on a new song, "Engines, Aeroplanes." This production will be completed with a full compliment of strings, guitars, bass and drums (performed by studio musicians). Like most of Robin's productions from this era, the results will remain unissued (though he will return to this recording for possible inclusion on *Trafalgar*—see April 7, 1971).

• Saturday, February 28, 1970
Melody Maker reports that a new Bee Gees single and album are to be "released shortly." According to the paper, the single will be chosen from two numbers—"Sweetheart" and "If I Only Had My Mind On Something Else"—and should be issued on March 13th. In fact, these are the choices for the duo's next Stateside release. Meanwhile, Robert Stigwood says the album, *Cucumber Castle*, will follow three weeks later. Today's session likely incorporates further Robin solo productions, but exact details are unknown.

NME reports that nine Bee Gees songs will be in a new feature film called *Melody* (starring Mark Lester and Jack Wild). The songs are expected to include "To Love Somebody," "Little Boy" (an otherwise unissued composition of which only a Trevor Gordon/Marbles version exists), "Melody Fair," "I've Gotta Get A Message To You," "And The Sun Will Shine," "First Of May," "I Started A Joke," "Give Your Best" and "Swan Song."

Melody will premiere in New York City on March 28, 1971 (and in the UK on April 21, 1971). The final cut will not feature the songs "I've Gotta Get A Message To You," "And The Sun Will Shine," "I Started A Joke," "Swan Song" or the speculative "Little Boy." The *NME* also notes that Jimmy Webb's Canopy publishing company will be the film's producers, though this too appears to be speculative; the final film's producers will include David Puttnam, Ron Kass and David Hemmings.

1970

• Thursday, March 5, 1970

At Morgan Recording Studios Limited (169-171 High Road, Willesden, London, NW 10), Ringo Starr records a version of "Bye Bye Blackbird" arranged by Maurice. This banjo and piano driven track will be issued next month on Ringo's solo debut album, *Sentimental Journey*.

• Saturday, March 7, 1970

The *NME* reports that Barry and Maurice will reunite to promote their new single, "I.O.I.O." (scheduled for release on March 13th). However, owing to Maurice's current run in *Sing A Rude Song*, their joint activities will be limited. The Bee Gees' album, *Cucumber Castle*, is now set to be issued April 3rd. Robert Stigwood is said to be on the cusp of announcing plans for airing of the parent television special. Another intriguing Stigwood/Polydor release this week is from Mike Wade, whose single "Happiness" is from the musical *Sing A Rude Song*.

• Monday, March 9, 1970

At IBC Studio A, Barry Gibb works on another solo session with engineers Mike Claydon and Damon Lyon-Shaw. Utilizing IBC's sixteen-track recorder, Barry tapes two takes of "What's It All About," the second of which is the master, though this will remain unissued. Following this, the B-side of his upcoming single, "This Time," is captured in three takes. The session will close with three takes of "The Day Your Eyes Met Mine," first taped for the Bee Gees on July 9, 1970. Neither version will ever surface commercially, though today's recording of "The Day Your Eyes Met Mine" will be mixed in September for a proposed October single release.

• Friday, March 13, 1970

In Britain, the Bee Gees' first single of the 1970's—"I.O.I.O." c/w "Sweetheart"—is issued.

• Saturday, March 21, 1970

The *NME* reports that Colin Petersen is searching for a lead singer to front his new group, Humpy Bong.

● Monday, March 23, 1970
At IBC Studio A, Barry wraps sessions for his solo album with engineers Mike Claydon and Damon Lyon-Shaw. Today three takes will be made of the potential single "One Bad Thing" (first demoed September 25, 1969). This track will be mixed in September for a proposed October single release. Also at this session, Barry tapes one take of "Happiness," a song he will perform at a solo radio session in June but ultimately never issues commercially (see June 8th).

Meanwhile at Recorded Sound Studios, Maurice takes a break from *Sing A Rude Song* to tape another session with engineers Mike Weighell and Eric Holland. "Please Lock Me Away" is a song composed by Maurice with Billy Lawrie and it will be taped in two takes. Following this, Maurice attempts a take of a song called "Going Where The Money Goes," but this production will be left incomplete without a vocal. Another one-take wonder, "Something's Blowing," is a song composed by Maurice with Billy Lawrie and Norman Hitchcock. This track will be fully produced with strings and a double-tracked lead vocal, but like the rest of today's efforts will remain unissued. This productive day closed out with two more Maurice and Billy Lawrie originals: "Did You Receive My Letter, Susan?" (recorded in three takes) and "Silly Little Girl" (recorded in two takes). Also today, Maurice appears (likely in a pre-taped segment) on BBC-2 television's *Young Generation Show* (alongside the band Arrival and singer Eartha Kitt).

● Wednesday, March 25, 1970
At Recorded Sound Studios, Maurice works with engineers Mike Weighell and Eric Holland to create stereo mixes of his recent productions. However, none of today's dubdowns of "It Takes A Man," "Please Lock Me Away," "Something's Blowing," "Silly Little Girl," "Journey To The Misty Mountains," "Soldier Johnny" and "Touch And Understand Love" will be considered the final masters. Mixing will continue in June.

● Saturday, March 28, 1970
In Britain, "I.O.I.O." charts for a single week at #49. In the United States, the choice of single—"If I Only Had My Mind On Something Else"—will not raise their fortunes further, peaking at #91 over the next three weeks. Also this week, *Rare Precious & Beautiful, Volume 2* enters the *Billboard* albums chart, reaching a high of #100 over the next eight weeks.

● Monday, March 30, 1970
Robin is scheduled to travel to Madrid, Spain for two days of Spanish television appearances.

● Thursday, April 2, 1970
Presumably back from Spain, Robin holds a solo session today at IBC Studio A engineered by John Pantry and Ted Sharp. The backing for today's recordings is provided by a small chamber group of strings and woodwinds conducted by Kenny Clayton, to which Robin will overdub his lead and background vocals on adjacent tracks of the eight-track tape. The first song recorded, the excellent "I've Been Hurt," will be captured in one take (to which Robin adds two tracks of vocals). Before recording the second composition, "Cold Be My Days," one of the engineers asks Kenny Clayton: "Is this 'Shipston-on-Stour,' Ken?," referring to the song's unique location in Warwickshire (ten miles south of Stratford-upon-Avon). The musicians chat and laugh about the location before the track title is again announced by the engineer as "Cold Be My Days In Shipston-on-Stour." This melancholy marvel will take three performances to perfect, with the final master receiving augmentation of harpsichord and two tracks of vocals from Robin. The final song from this session, the beautiful "Irons In The Fire," follows the same production format as "Cold Be My Days" and will be captured in one take.

Record Mirror reports on Maurice's recent activities and the recording "Railroad" (soon to be issued as a single) which they mention, "...was written by Billy Lawrie and Maurice some two months ago. The number was originally penned for the Bee Gees' album to be called *Happiness*. Brother Barry was uninterested in Maurice's original ideas for the number and did not want to include it on the album. With that Maurice took the number to brother-in-law Billy." Maurice comments: "Since that Bill and I have written a lot of material. I will probably be forming a group to work with me, there's something in the air. It will be a few lost friends, but I can't say too much about it." The article further notes that Maurice's production company has been working with a band called the Gambols.

● Friday, April 3, 1970
In Britain, the Bee Gees' *Cucumber Castle* album is scheduled for release. Meanwhile, Maurice works with the cast (including Barbara Windsor and Denis Quilley) of *Sing A Rude Song* to produce studio versions of the play's key musical numbers. On the final LP release of this material, Maurice only takes full lead vocals on one song, "Leave Me Here To Linger With The Ladies." Despite appearing on the LP cover and getting star billing, his role is predominantly a behind-the-scenes one for this session.

● Saturday, April 4, 1970
Barry works in the studio with P.P. Arnold to produce covers of his recent compositions, "Born" and "Happiness," as well as two recent Blood, Sweat & Tears cuts: "You've Made Me So Very Happy" and "Spinning Wheel." None of today's recordings will surface commercially.

● Thursday, April 9, 1970
At IBC Studio A, Robin's holds another solo session, his first employing the studio's new sixteen-track tape machine. The instrumental set-up for this date employs a live rhythm section (acoustic guitar, bass and drums), as well as a small orchestral

group. "Return To Austria" will be taped in two takes, with Robin overdubbing a lead vocal to the second performance. The second song taped at this date, "The Flag I Flew," is produced in the same exact fashion; it will be captured in two takes, with Robin overdubbing a lead vocal to the second performance (albeit over two channels of the tape).

Also today, "Make Believe" will be recorded in three takes, the first two of which are false starts. The final take will be treated to a lead vocal track from Robin. The final number taped today, the aptly titled "All's Well That Ends Well," will be captured in two takes (the first of which is simply a false start). Robin will add his voice to take two (which also features the unique sound of a piano accordion). Sadly, none of today's excellent productions will surface commercially.

- Saturday, April 11, 1970

The *NME* reports that RSO will produce a special promotional film for Maurice's forthcoming single, "Railroad," directed by Mike Mansfield. The paper also notes that Maurice is currently in the studio producing an album of songs from *Sing A Rude Song* (see April 3rd). This Original Cast Recording will be issued to coincide with the play's opening in London's West End.

- Thursday, April 16, 1970

In Britain, Maurice is scheduled to appear on television's *Top Of The Pops* performing "Railroad."

- Friday, April 17, 1970

In Britain, Maurice Gibb's solo debut single—"Railroad" c/w "I've Come Back"—is issued. At Recorded Sound Studios, Robin Gibb works with engineers Phil Wade and Eric Holland on three new recordings. In similarity to Robin's last session, the instrumental set-up will be a rhythm section of guitar, piano, bass and drums with a small orchestral group. However, this time out, Robin will sing live with each of the backing band's performances and will be further augmented on one song by a group of backing vocalists.

First up, "Anywhere I Hang My Hat Is Home," will be taped in two takes (both of which are complete, but only the second features a complete, double-tracked vocal from Robin). "Life" will be completed in four takes; beginning with take two a somewhat incongruous female backing vocal group will enter the proceedings. The vocal performances don't quite gel until the final pass, take four, and even then the two factions seem to fight each other for prominence. The final song, "Loud And Clear," is actually a rewrite of "I've Been Hurt" (recorded April 2nd) with some new lyrics and a slightly more upbeat arrangement. Despite today's efforts, none of Robin's material from this session will be issued. When he returns to record again in June, it will be with his brother Maurice.

- Monday, April 20, 1970

At Recorded Sound Studios, Maurice works with engineers Mike Weighell and Eric Holland on some new solo tracks. First up, "Alabama," will be taped simply with double-tracked piano, bass and vocals in a single take. The second song from this session, "This Time," will be tried twice. The first attempt will feature piano, organ and multiple guitar overdubs (both six and twelve-string). However, this will be scrapped in favor of a simpler production of just piano, organ, bass and drums; neither version will feature any vocals (and the second attempt may actually date from a later session on May 16, 1970). Today's final item, "No. 3," so named for its placement on the master reel, is another instrumental (and possibly dates from a later session on May 19, 1970). A mono acetate of "This Time" b/w "No. 3" will be cut at the end of this session, and though "Alabama" and "This Time" circulate amongst collectors, nothing from today's session will be issued commercially. Maurice will continue mixing and tinkering with selections from his solo sessions for the rest of the year. Nevertheless, his next round of recordings will be with his brother Robin.

On Atco Records & Tapes

• Saturday, April 25, 1970
The *NME* says that the BBC has purchased the rights to air the *Cucumber Castle* special. No transmission date has been set, but it could be shown some time next month. Maurice has been tipped to direct a new television comedy series about a crazy detective called Jumbo, which will be written by Ray Galton and Alan Simpson (*Steptoe And Son*). Maurice has also lined up a feature film directing turn on a project called Bunker, which is to star Stanley Baker and Lionel Jeffries as men trapped in a war time bunker. In addition to directing, Maurice will provide music for both ventures. The *NME* says he has already recorded some "...with a large orchestra," and that the theme for *Bunker* will be something that has been previously taped, but this may be completely speculative.

Maurice will later tell writer Karen de Groot of the *Bunker* project: "...it came out as definite in the *NME* news pages. It was just an idea, but people rush things so much. I've had a couple of film offers following the Bee Gees' work on *Cucumber Castle*...There's one film that Peter Ustinov has written called *Parson's Pleasure*, and another one by Tony Palmer, called *The Rise And Fall Of Jake Sullivan*, but after *Sing A Rude Song*, I'm exhausted!" Given these new projects and the delay in opening the West End stage version of *Sing A Rude Song*, Maurice questions returning to his stage role as Bernard Dillon. "In view of the delay," he says, "I am no longer sure that I want to do it."

• Saturday, May 2, 1970
Despite reports to the contrary, the *NME* says that Maurice will hit the West End as a part of the cast of *Sing A Rude Song* after all. The musical will open May 26th at London's Garrick Theatre for an indefinite run (though Maurice is only contracted for three months). The soundtrack album that Maurice has produced will be issued shortly by Polydor in Britain.

• Saturday, May 9, 1970
The *NME* reports that Barry will not be moving permanently to the United States (differing from a report they say was filed three months ago). "When I talked about leaving Britain," says Barry, "I was both restless and bored. But suddenly things have started to go right." Instead, Barry will undertake a promotional campaign for his first solo single in Britain. "I'll Kiss Your Memory" is scheduled for release on May 29th. The paper further notes that a full Barry solo album will follow on the heels of the single.

In the United States, *Cucumber Castle* enters the Billboard albums chart where it will peak at #94 over the next eight weeks. In Britain, the album places higher (at #57), but only charts for two weeks.

• Tuesday, May 26, 1970
In London, Maurice opens as Bernard Dillon in London's Garrick Theatre production of *Sing A Rude Song*.

• Saturday, May 30, 1970
The *NME* reports that Barry, Robin and Maurice have patched up their differences. A spokesman for RSO says, "There are no plans for reforming the Bee Gees. Nevertheless, the brothers are interested in working together again, and there is strong speculation that the Bee Gees trio will be reactivated this year."

1970

• June 1970
Perhaps hinting that his solo days are done, the Robin Gibb fan club informs its members that it will cease operations. "Unfortunately there wasn't a very big response to our drive for new members," Sally Bridge writes in the final newsletter, "and, after a lot of discussions, everyone concerned has agreed that the Club should close."

• Monday, June 1, 1970
At Recorded Sound, engineer Mike Weighell assembles stereo masters for Maurice's solo album (including "Touch And Understand Love," "Journey To The Misty Mountains," "The Loner," "Laughing Child" and "Silly Little Girl"). All of these mixes will be destined for a further master LP assembly on December 14th, except for "Touch And Understand Love" (which is rejected). On a side note, country singer, Myrna March, recently covered "Touch And Understand Love" for single release in both the US and UK.

• Sunday, June 7, 1970
At Recorded Sound Studios, Robin and Maurice team up to produce some new recordings together. The first tune the twins will tackle is the triumphant "Conquer The World," which is tracked simply by Maurice on piano (accompanied by a drummer). The two musicians will wind through four takes of the song, with the last performance being the basis of the final master. This will be augmented by overdubs of strings, brass, electric guitar, bass and a lead vocal from Robin (with Maurice harmonizing the choruses). Although this production is completed (and mixed in August), it will not be released.

Today's second duo track is announced by the engineer as "Distant Relationship," but it will eventually be transformed lyrically into the *2 Years On* cut, "Sincere Relation." "This song includes harpsichord, and is my tribute to my late father-in-law, George, who was sixty when he died unexpectedly a while ago," Robin will later tell Alan Smith in the *NME*. "He spent the last three days of his life in my house, and he told me he was going to die." Following his passing, Robin will revise the lyrics to this already recorded track in honor of George. The master basic track is take two and mixes with both sets of lyrics will be survive, but only "Sincere Relation" surfaces commercially.

A third song from this session, "We Can Lift A Mountain," is said to date from 1968. Today's production is captured in three takes and features a grand arrangement of brass, strings, tympani, guitar, piano, bass and drums (in addition to three tracks of lead and background vocal tracks with Robin taking lead). Despite receiving a final mix in August, "We Can Lift A Mountain" will remain unissued.

The final song from this session, Maurice informs the engineers, is titled "I Like Ya." "That's what Ray Stevens says," remarks Maurice, "and he's a Southern boy!" Indeed it is Maurice's tune from top to bottom, captured in a single take. However, it will be soon be retitled "Lay It On Me" and is to be featured on the next Bee Gees' long player. "It's sort of swamp soul," Maurice later tells Alan Smith of the *NME*, "and I recorded it at ten in the morning; I love the whole feel of it." Work on all of today's productions continues through June 13th.

• Monday, June 8, 1970
In Britain, Barry Gibb tapes a solo radio session for the BBC's *D.L.T.* show (hosted by DJ Dave Lee Travis). Songs include "Happiness," "This Time" and "I'll Kiss Your Memory." The results will be aired on June 14th, marking the only time Barry's version of "Happiness" is officially aired to the public.

• Wednesday, June 10, 1970
Tape logs indicate that Barry Gibb may again be in the studio producing singer P.P. Arnold today. Nevertheless, exact details of their work today are unavailable.

• Saturday, June 13, 1970
Record Mirror says the Bee Gees are once again talking, and that, "...Robin has taken the incentive to persuade his brothers to re-form the group." Barry, who has just returned from Spain, has some reservations: "...with my solo single only just having been released, I feel like I'd like to see how it goes, before committing myself to anything else." The paper says that while Robin is managed by Vic Lewis and Maurice is still with Stigwood, Barry manages his own affairs. "I don't think it would do any harm to wait a while," Barry says of the potential reunion. "The Bee Gees have existed for twelve years, nine years before Vince and Colin joined us."

• Sunday, June 21, 1970
At Recorded Sound Studios, Robin and Maurice work with engineers Eric Holland and Phil Wade on another set of duo tracks. The first item is called "Come To The Mission" (with Maurice on lead vocals) and will form the first part of an impressive three song suite. The second song in this medley is a wistful number called "Bluebird" sung by Robin (and displaying his unique rhyming sensibility). The final part of this seamlessly segued suite is the catchy "Whistle Me," also sung by Robin and again showing the trademarks of his whimsical lyrical touch. Despite the obviously impressive nature of this production (which has no real counterpart in the Bee Gees' catalog of songs), it will remain unissued.

Also at this session, Maurice will lay down an instrumental with the working title, "Call It What You Like," while Robin offers up his song "Belinda," which is melodically and lyrically reminiscent of much of his recent solo work. Undoubtedly equal or superior to such recent efforts as "August October" or "Alexandria Good Time," it will nevertheless become yet another of this year's copious outtakes.

● Sunday, June 28, 1970
Barry Gibb flies to Sydney to attend Australia's International Pop Awards.

● Tuesday, June 30, 1970
In Australia, Barry Gibb appears as a presenter at the *Go-Set* Pop Poll Awards. The event is scheduled to be filmed for television.

● Saturday, July 4, 1970
The *NME* reports that Vince Melouney has signed with the AMA agency and will be launched as a solo artist and record producer. Vince's new group, Fanny Adams (featuring Australian singer Doug Parkinson and New Zealanders Johnny Dick and Ted Toi), have signed a deal with the Uni label. Vince plans to produce two new artists—Donna Gaines and Ken Rodway—and hopes to use some of Barry Gibb's material in the process.

Go-Set publishes an interview with Barry conducted by John Halsall last month. "What people tend to forget is the fact that we'd been together for fourteen years when the split came," says Barry. "...One of the other things was the difficulty over composer's credits for songs. One of us would write a song which would go down on the record with B., R. and M. Gibb credited; that's okay, just the same as when Paul McCartney writes a song John Lennon automatically gets a credit. The problem comes when the song becomes a hit, then that person who actually composed it realizes that, not only is he missing all the prestige of having individually written a hit song, but he's also missing two-thirds of the royalties as well.

"Robin was the first to crack up and split and I followed, leaving Maurice on his own...It looks as if we're going to record together again; in fact, if all goes well, an L.P. and a single are scheduled. The Bee Gees are only kids so all this rubbish that everybody's talking that we're finished is all wrong, we can go on for another twenty years or more, who cares now who's the best singer or the best stage performer or the best arranger, all three names will be on future record labels and we're going to do live appearances and everything, when we busted up we didn't realize what we were losing.

"...We would very much have liked *Cucumber Castle* to have developed into a series, it was set in the 17th century and we would have done another set in Roman times, another in Robin Hood's period and another in the Stone Age and so on...We wanted to have a lot of overseas guest stars and really make it into something. Still, if we do get together again, it might possibly come off.

"...I've given up all thoughts about promoting other artists in favor of concentrating on my career and that of the others [Robin and Maurice]; besides, promoting other artists is a drag, as any record producer will tell you. One day they're bad tempered, the next day they've got a sore throat and so on, and so on. I'm going to stick to producing the Bee Gees and myself and on putting out the sort of record that the public want to hear, and from us that means simple, melodic ballads, put over with a lot of feeling, a la Roy Orbison."

● Tuesday, July 7, 1970
In Australia, an interview with Barry is aired on television's *GTK*.

● Saturday, July 11, 1970
In the United States, "I.O.I.O." charts for a single week on *Billboard* at #94.

● Thursday, July 23, 1970
At De Lane Lea Limited Sound Centre (75 Dean Street, London W1V 5HA), Maurice and his brother-in-law, Billy Lawrie, work with engineer John Stewart on scoring tracks for a film starring Richard Harris initially titled *Bloomfield* (released in 1971 in the United States as *The Hero*). Today they will produce four instrumental recordings including "Man Of Man" (not the same song as "Men Of Men" which was recorded by the Bee Gees during 1968). The song will be lead by Maurice on acoustic guitar and augmented by a beautiful score of strings, flute, French horn, trombone, drums and percussion.

The second order of business today is committing to tape two versions of a piece titled "Bloomfield." The basic instrumental line-up is the same as "Man Of Man," with Maurice again leading the musicians on acoustic guitar. "Version One" will be captured in two takes; "Version Two," which is somewhat moodier in feel, will take four passes to perfect. The final item taped, the subtle "Ballet Of Freedom," will be perfected in five takes. All of today's incidental items show an incredible maturity to Maurice's melodic scoring abilities and undoubtedly his talent in this area is under utilized commercially (though he will score one more feature film in 1984, *A Breed Apart*). On another note, Maurice obviously enjoys working at De Lane Lea, and it will become a key spot in general for Bee Gees recording activity over the next few months (replacing their mainstay IBC for a significant period).

● Saturday, July 25, 1970
The *NME* reports that *Sing A Rude Song* will close after a nine-week run at London's Garrick Theatre.

● Saturday, August 1, 1970
At Recorded Sound Studios, Robin and Maurice Gibb continue work on tracks as a duo. However, from this session on, the artist listed on the box is "Bee Gees" (perhaps hinting that the decision has already been made to reform in name). Today's first number, "I Can Laugh," is counted off by Robin (playing acoustic guitar on this session) accompanied by Maurice (also on guitar) and a drummer. After a false start, the second take will be the master and, like the recent recording "Sincere Relation," it will be lyrically revised as "2 Years On" to reflect current life events. The title is a somewhat exaggerated reference to the Bee Gees' time apart (though the time they spent apart is just a bit more than a year). Nevertheless, mixes will be made with both sets of lyrics for the choruses ("I Can Laugh" or "2 Years On"), but only "2 Years On" will surface commercially on their next LP of the same name. The song's a cappella intro will be taped separately and likewise the song's backing vocals, which feature Barry in harmony with Robin and Maurice. "This is a song Robin got together himself," Maurice later tells the *NME*'s Alan Smith, "It's kind of a mass of ideas on which we did a backtrack a while ago, although he changed the lyrics in the studio."

"It just happened to be a number we all felt we could work with," Robin explains to Smith, "We are perfectionists in the recording studios. The studio is our battleground. Our music is the sense of the unreal. In years to come, we want people to say that we made unreal music real music."

Next in this session, Maurice will tape four takes of a track labeled "BG Blues." No master will be achieved for this number (which is basically just bass and drum tracks); the tape box will bear the notation "Gave Up—No Master." The next song, "I've Been Waiting," is slightly more developed (featuring multiple keyboards, bass and drums), though it too is incomplete. The session continues with Robin's "I Wonder if You Wonder" (taped in three takes), a fully completed production featuring either Steve Kipner or Steve Groves from Tin Tin on guitar. This track, which features some nice lyrical twists from Robin, is sadly unissued. The final song from this session is another of Robin's compositions, the brief, acoustic-based "Sail At My Side." The basic track will be captured in six takes with one of the Tin Tin Steve's once again providing guitar backing and Robin singing live to the band's accompaniment. The final master, take six, features some lovely multi-tracked overdubbed vocals from Robin and Maurice, though this song will be left on the proverbial cutting room floor.

● Saturday, August 8, 1970
In the *NME*, composer Johnny Harris challenges a recent report published in their August 1st edition that Maurice is providing the entire musical score for the Richard Harris film, *Bloomfield*. In reality, there are a number of musical contributors to the project and Johnny Harris feels the incidental score is his alone. The truth might be somewhere in the middle, since Maurice is contributing a substantial amount of instrumental cues in addition to the title song.

● Friday, August 14, 1970
Sessions for the Bee Gees' reunion project move today to De Lane Lea where the group will work with engineer John Stewart on most of what will become the *2 Years On* album. However, the results are still largely the product of Robin and Maurice (without Barry).

Today's session opens with "Too Much To Think About," a lovely song featuring Robin on lead vocals. The basic track (which consists of piano, acoustic guitar, bass and drums from Geoff Bridgford) will be completed in four takes, with the last being considered the master. Nevertheless, the song (which is also mixed this month) will never be issued commercially.

Next at this session, two instrumental passes will be made of "Getting Back Together." The basic track for this will consist of two acoustic guitar and drums, but it will not progress any further. "You're Going Away," on the other hand, is a fully realized production. Started by Robin on acoustic guitar (and featuring Geoff Bridgford on drums), the song will captured in four takes. The final performance will feature Robin on lead vocals, as well as overdubs of tremeloed electric guitar, piano and layered backing vocals. The results will be mixed down in the next few days (and acetates will be cut), but will remain unissued commercially. Meanwhile, "The Way I Feel Today" is a Maurice led number which will be meander through four takes; work will continue on this song at another session on August 18th.

● Saturday, August 15, 1970
The *NME* reports that Engelbert Humperdinck's next single will be a version of "Sweetheart" (composed by Barry and Maurice) issued by Decca on August 28th. Humperdinck's reading of the song is fairly close to the Bee Gees' recording and will become the title song of his next long player.

● Tuesday, August 18, 1970
At De Lane Lea, Robin and Maurice once again work with engineer John Stewart. Work continues on "The Way I Feel Today" with Maurice playing electric guitar and providing off-mic vocals (to the live accompaniment of drums and two acoustic guitars). For the final performance, take six, Robin will take over on lead vocals (providing a fully realized set of lyrics). Still the results are somewhat uneven, and the track will be left as another outtake.

Maurice will take the lead on the next number, "Find Me A Woman", which will be captured in two takes. The instrumental set-up is much the same as "The Way I Feel Today," with Maurice chugging away on electric guitar to the accompaniment of two acoustic guitars and a set of drums. However, the production of "Find Me A Woman" could be considered unfinished and indeed this primitive composition will remain unissued.

Next up, the unissued "The Change I See," features Maurice on piano and Robin on lead vocals. More importantly, Barry can be heard from the control room commenting and eventually directing the proceedings, confirming the Bee Gees are now fully reunited. Only the final take of "The Change I See," take seven, will be a complete performance. Despite overdubs of electric guitar and layered vocals, this composition will never surface commercially.

The final item from today's session will be provisionally titled "All My Time," and features Maurice on some Creedence-styled swamp guitar. After two false starts, the song will be completed on its third take and eventually retitled "Back Home," the first number from these sessions to feature vocals from all three brothers. However, this may be on account of the fact that the lyrics are written at another session after the backing track is completed; indeed, work on today's productions will continue on September 28th. "We wrote this one at the time of one of the hijacks," Barry will later remark

in the *NME* to Alan Smith, "and it's all about that particular time. We more or less did it in the studio." A mass Palestinian hijacking on September 6th (known as the Dawson Field hijacking) is the likely inspiration.

Also during this period, the brothers will compose and record their next single—"Lonely Days" c/w "Man For All Seasons." At the earliest stage of production, "Lonely Days" is provisionally titled "No More Music Now," while "Man For All Seasons" (named after a 1966 film) features a totally different set of lyrics. Work on these productions will continue through October.

● Thursday, August 20, 1970
At De Lane Lea, engineer John Stewart prepares stereo mixes of some of the Bee Gees' recent productions: "We Can Lift A Mountain," "Sincere Relation" and "Lay It On Me." A more extensive reel also labeled with this date is likely misattributed; work on the album *2 Years On* will stretch through the next two months and De Lane Lea's dating of these sessions is often incorrect.

● Friday, August 21, 1970
This day is publicly given as the date the Bee Gees meet to discuss business at Robert Stigwood's office and finalize plans for their public reunion. In reality, recording sessions featuring all three precede this date, but that makes the occasion no less joyous or momentous. The public trading of RSO on the stock market is a key factor in the date the news of their official reunion is disseminated.

● Saturday, August 22, 1970
Billboard reports that Barry Gibb recently visited Switzerland where he taped an interview for Radio Zurich and made an appearance on television's *Europarty* (filmed in St. Gallen).

● Monday, August 24, 1970
Daily Variety reports that the Bee Gees have officially reunited on the eve of RSO going public on the London stock market this Thursday. The paper speculates that the return of Robin, "...cost Stigwood some fancy coin."

● Wednesday, August 26, 1970
The Bee Gees try a new recording venue—Morgan Studios—the location of recent sessions by Paul McCartney, the Kinks and Ringo Starr (where Maurice may have been present for a *Sentimental Journey* session). Accompanied by Geoff Bridgford on drums, the brothers compose three fantastic new songs. The first of these, "You Got To Lose It In The End," will be captured in just one take and features a joint lead vocal from Barry and Robin (as well as some nice Mellotron work from Maurice). The results are catchy and certainly on a par or better than most of the tracks so far taped for *2 Years On*.

1970

A second song, "Little Red Train," will require four takes to complete. It is built instrumentally upon the foundation of Barry and Maurice on twelve-string acoustic guitars (with Geoff providing drums) in a sound reminiscent of *Cucumber Castle* and *Odessa*, though decidedly more upbeat and catchy. Robin will add a lead vocal to take four with Barry and Maurice joining on the country-ish choruses in three-part harmony. Once again, the results outstrip many of the tracks included on *2 Years On*.

The final track from today's session, "Sweet Summer Rain," is built around Maurice on piano. After three brief false starts, take four will be complete and considered the master. For the vocals, Robin will begin the verses and is then joined Barry and Maurice in three-part harmony for the choruses. No other instrumentation (outside of Maurice's live piano track) will be incorporated. The results are sweet and somewhat melancholy, albeit somewhat less commercial than today's first two songs. None of today's recordings will be issued commercially, though all of them undoubtedly have great melodic potential.

- Thursday, August 27, 1970
Barry is officially divorced from his first wife, Maureen Bates.

- Saturday, August 29, 1970
Melody Maker reports on the Bee Gees' reformation. "We just discussed it and reformed," says Maurice. "We want to apologize publicly to Robin for the things that have been said. We just want to stop boring the public with our squabbles and do the music. We intend carrying on with our solo careers but we want to start things as a group again. There will just be the three of us and we will use a session drummer." The *NME* says that RSO's launch on the stock market offered two million shares and placed a three million pound value on the company.

Meanwhile, former Bee Gees drummer, Colin Petersen, is still assembling his new group, Humpy Bong. "I am still looking for a good lead guitarist and a pianist to finish the line-up." The group, which also features Petersen's protégé, Jonathan Kelly, hope to have an album out in mid-November with sixteen new songs.

- Sunday, August 30, 1970
The Sydney Morning Herald reports that retrieving Robin from his NEMS management contract cost Robert Stigwood fifty thousand pounds. A small price to have the Bee Gees reformed for the launch of RSO on the open market, which forecasts profits of half a million.

- Tuesday, September 1, 1970
In London, Barry Gibb marries Lynda Gray at Caxton Hall Register Office. Also this month, a second Barry solo single—"The Day Your Eyes Meet Mine" c/w "One Bad Thing"—is prepared at IBC Studio A.

- Tuesday, September 8, 1970
In Germany, Barry is seen on television's *Die Drehscheibe*.

- Saturday, September 12, 1970
The *NME* reports the Bee Gees' first single as a reunited unit will be issued on October 30th. The likely title is "Man For All Seasons," but it will not be confirmed until all the songs from the forthcoming album—due in November—are completed. Barry has a single—"One Bad Thing"—slated for issue on October 2nd. Both Barry as a solo artist and the Bee Gees are planning extensive plugging for their new discs and RSO are scheduling live dates for touring next year.

- Tuesday, September 29, 1970
At De Lane Lea, sessions continue for the Bee Gees' next album. Yesterday, some of the Bee Gees' previous productions were rough mixed and augmented and today the group will focus on taping a new song of Robin's, "I'm Weeping." "This is a song of mine I wrote on holiday in Madeira," Robin later tells Alan Smith of the *NME*, "and, as normal in my songs (I stick to a rule book!) I don't mention the title. I was thinking about my past."

Instrumentally, this downhearted song will be built around Geoff Bridgford's kick drum, Maurice's organ and Robin's voice. Barry will remain in the control room directing the proceedings; the simple production will be completed in three takes and is later embellished with overdubs of tambourine, strings and some closing vocal backgrounds from all three brothers. The final master will be featured as the closing track on *2 Years On*. Also at this session, Barry and Maurice work on a promising untitled guitar-based instrumental (with drum accompaniment). A double-sided acetate featuring a rough mix of this song idea, alongside "The Change I See" and "Back Home" (with finished lyrics, but lacking final instrumental sweetening) will be cut in the next day.

- Wednesday, September 30, 1970
At De Lane Lea, the Bee Gees work with engineer John Stewart on tracks earmarked for use on the soundtrack to the upcoming film *Melody*. First off, Barry's sumptuous "Morning Of My Life" (written and previously recorded in Australia under the title "In The Morning") will be taped in just one take. The final production, included on the soundtrack of *Melody*, will feature one of Bill Shepherd's finest orchestral arrangements (a perfect compliment to Barry's wistful lyrics).

Next up the band (Barry on acoustic guitar, Maurice on piano and Geoff Bridgford on drums) work through five takes of Barry's "Every Second, Every Minute." Barry will later tell Alan Smith of the *NME*: "This is another one of mine, a more aggressive, roll-on thing than some of the others I did. It was written for a film called *Melody*, but replaced by something else. I think it kind of builds." Despite its absence from the *Melody* soundtrack, it will find a home on the next Bee Gees' long player, *2 Years On* (augmented by Bill Shepherd's strings and Maurice's bass overdubs).

It is unlikely that the third item taped at today's session, the magnificent "The 1st Mistake I Made," is intended for *Melody*. Nevertheless, it will become one of Barry's two stand-out tracks from *2 Years On*. "It features a hook a lot of people play on," Barry will tell the *NME*, "but it's a natural, commercial hook. It's the story of someone who's gone through life and never knew his mother and father...and how everything he did in his life was the first mistake he made." The production will be built around Barry and Maurice on acoustic guitars and Geoff Bridgford on drums. This trio will strum through four false starts, before arriving at the master, take five. To this overdubs of electric guitar (filtered through a Leslie speaker), bass, piano, Bill Shepherd orchestration and two sets of lead vocals from Barry (featuring different drafts of the song's lyrics) will be added. Mixes will be made of both sets of lyrics, though only one will surface commercially on *2 Years On*.

The last item from today's date will be a new recording of Barry's Australian-era composition "Don't Forget Me Ida" (first recorded by Johnny Ashcroft). The song will captured in a single take and embellished by a lead vocal from Robin (with harmonies from all three brothers and Barry singing lead on the bridge), as well as Bill Shepherd's usual orchestration. The exact reason for recording this old-fashioned waltz number at this stage in the sessions is unknown, but the results will remain unissued (despite the completed production being mixed down during this period).

• Saturday, October 3, 1970
Billboard reports that the Bee Gees are due to "concertize" Australia and Japan in the New Year. *Billboard* further notes that a single of Barry's "One Bad Thing" was due for release in the UK this past Friday, October 2nd. The *NME* now says the single will be postponed until January at Barry's request. He feels that a record by the Bee Gees should come first. The Gibb brothers are at work on an album, with a single due out in late October.

• Monday, October 5, 1970
At De Lane Lea, the Bee Gees hold the final tracking session for their forthcoming *2 Years On* album (with John Stewart engineering). The first item taped, the aptly titled "Lost," is built around Maurice's piano and Barry's guitar. The two will run through three incomplete takes of the song, before completing take four. However, this performance is merely Barry sketching out the song's lyrics and calling out the chord changes to Maurice. "Lost" certainly has promise (with a nice tempo change midway through), but will go no further.

Next up, the band will lay down two takes of Barry's excellent "Portrait Of Louise," the first of which is simply a short false start (take two will be the master). This song is somewhat unusual for Barry lyrically since it doesn't feature the title as its hook (or indeed anywhere in the song). "I wrote this one," Barry will later tell the *NME*'s Alan Smith. "It's simply a song about love, but the title doesn't come into the words at all. The idea of the words is that if you fall in love with a woman, you're not interested in what's she's been. Musically, it's a slight tribute to the Searchers...not a take-off, just a tribute. They had some beautiful sounds."

Maurice will also record two takes of a number titled "Fantasy" at this session. A moody track featuring Maurice on lead vocals, organ, Mellotron and guitar (with some help from Geoff Bridgford on drums and tambourine), the results will be somewhat rough (though the track and melodic changes are intriguing, as is the song's extended ending). This production will go no further; the song will be revisited at a session on October 14th.

Meanwhile, Robin will contribute "Alone Again," which will be perfected in four takes. Barry will remain in the control room for the tracking, commenting on the proceedings while Robin sings live with each take to Maurice's piano and Geoff's drums. "I wrote this and Maurice plays piano, bass and lead guitar," Robin will later tell Alan Smith of the *NME*. "It was mixed in America. The facilities are no different over there, as far as we're concerned, except for maybe echo." Indeed, *2 Years On* will receive its final mix in New York City shortly after this session. The final production will incorporate group vocals (in three-part harmony on the choruses) and Bill Shepherd orchestration.

Closing out the album sessions will be Barry's "Tell Me Why." "I wrote this with Ray Charles in mind," Barry will later tell Alan Smith in the *NME*. "It was written just before a session—with the lights down." Following three short false starts, the band (Barry on guitar, Maurice on piano and Geoff on drums) will tape the master backing track, take four. To this, Bill Shepherd will add a fine orchestral score to complement Barry's overdubbed solo lead vocal (which is further supported by some overdubbed bass from Maurice). The final production will appear on side two of *2 Years On*.

• Friday, October 9, 1970
At De Lane Lea, engineer John Stewart will prepare stereo mixes of "Portrait Of Louise," "I'm Weeping," "Man For All Seasons" and "Lonely Days." However, none of these will be issued commercially; the final mixes will be done later at Atlantic Studios in New York City.

1970

• Saturday, October 10, 1970
At De Lane Lea, engineer John Stewart prepares mono masters for the Bee Gees' next single: "Lonely Days" c/w "Man For All Seasons." Though many countries have switched to stereo format 45's, today's mixes will indeed be used for the UK pressings of this single.

• Monday, October 12, 1970
At De Lane Lea, engineer John Stewart prepares three reels of stereo rough mixes of the Bee Gees' recent productions. These tapes include multiple mixes of "2 Years On," "Sincere Relation," "Lay It On Me," "The 1st Mistake I Made," "Morning Of My Life," "Don't Forget Me Ida," "Alone Again," "Tell Me Why," "I'm Weeping," "Portrait Of Louise" and "Every Second, Every Minute." None of today's dubdowns will be commercially issued.

• Wednesday, October 14, 1970
At De Lane Lea, the Bee Gees again work with engineer John Stewart. During this session, Barry will tape a shorter voice and guitar rendition of his "Morning Of My Life" (previously taped in a full band rendition on September 30th). The purpose of this recording (which begins with the song's second verse) is unknown, but it could perhaps be another request for the score of *Melody*.

Also at this session, another eight takes will be attempted of Maurice's song "Fantasy." The basic tracking will center on Maurice's piano (accompanied by some drums, presumably provided by Geoff Bridgford). It is possible that today's work is just to graft an ending onto the previous recording (from October 5th). No commercial release will surface of either of today's recordings.

• Saturday, October 17, 1970
The *NME* says the Bee Gees' next single will be issued November 6th and their album, *2 Years On*, will be completed this weekend. In December, the group is due to make a promotional trip to the United States primarily for television work, but it later transpires that *2 Years On* will be mixed in New York's Atlantic Studios during this period.

• Saturday, October 31, 1970
In Britain, the Bee Gees make their first reunited television appearance on DJ Kenny Everett's London Weekend Television program, *Ev*.

• Saturday, November 7, 1970
Music Now runs an interview with the Bee Gees conducted by Karen de Groot. "The last two tracks are being mixed now," says Robin of their forthcoming album. "We spent four weeks in the studios, and the first few days were the hardest. We had to feel our way in after the rift...it worked out well, in fact this is the album in which we have the most faith."

• Monday, November 9, 1970
In Britain, the Bee Gees tape a radio session for the BBC's *D.L.T.* show including unique renditions of "Man For All Seasons," "Alone Again," "Every Second, Every Minute" and "Lonely Days." The results will be aired on November 15th.

• Thursday, November 12, 1970
In Britain, the reunited Bee Gees appear on television's *Top Of The Pops* to perform "Lonely Days."

• Saturday, November 14, 1970
The *NME* runs a reunion special on the Bee Gees. Maurice has just returned from Ireland where he attended the premiere of Bloomfield, featuring his musical score. *2 Years On* is now scheduled for release in Britain on November 27th. The paper says the album was mixed recently at Atlantic Studios in New York City while co-producer Robert Stigwood "was holding business talks."

The BBC, which purchased the rights to *Cucumber Castle* in April, has been holding off broadcasting it for the time being. It was decided this week that it will be too costly to add Robin to the program. If it is expanded as a series, as once discussed, he will be a part of future installments. "It is a disappointment that I cannot be added to the show," Robin tells the *NME*. "I would have liked to be a court jester. But I hope when the fans see it that it does not mean we are back to two Bee Gees. I am part of it, in as much as the idea was formed long before the split, and the song was on one of our very early albums."

Also this week, *Record Mirror's* David Skan digs into the Bee Gees' break-up of last year. "I had got this idea into my head that Barry was going off into films," recalls Robin, "...I think he'd just had some offers and that Mo was going off to do his own music. But I never challenged them about it. I just sat and brooded. I got quite neurotic about it. I believed they were going to leave me high and dry...Then something snapped and I went off. I realize now that it was a very childish thing to do." Barry Gibb remains adamant that they didn't fire Colin in the aftermath, but rather it was the Stigwood office. Following this, Barry says, "I wanted to go solo. It seemed pointless us staying together as the Bee Gees when we weren't really achieving anything. That's why I went."

• Thursday, November 19, 1970
In Britain, the Bee Gees are seen once again on television's *Top Of The Pops* to perform "Lonely Days." Geoff Bridgford appears as their drummer, leading to speculation he has joined the band. "The Bee Gees will remain the three Gibb brothers," Maurice tells the *NME*. "In any case, Geoff has recently become the permanent drummer with Tin Tin, and from now on he will be busy working on promotion of that group's new single."

• Friday, November 20, 1970
In Britain, the first official release from Maurice and Billy Lawrie's Moby Productions unit is unveiled: a single by Tin Tin called "Come On Over Again." Tin Tin's previous discs were produced by Maurice before the Moby moniker was in place. "'Come On Over Again' is the first record by Tin Tin since they became a five-man group," says Maurice, "and as far as I am concerned, there couldn't be a better record to start Moby off."

• Thursday, December 3, 1970
At Recorded Sound Studios, Maurice tapes a new solo tune in two takes, "Danny." The results are lovely, with a sweet string quartet (recorded in stereo), and Maurice's typical, driving piano. Sadly, this promising production will not receive a commercial release.

• Saturday, December 5, 1970
In Britain, "Lonely Days" enters the charts. Over the next nine weeks, it will peak at #33. In the United States, it will peak thirty places higher at #3, their highest chart placement to date, during a run of fourteen weeks.

• Monday, December 7, 1970
At Recorded Sound Studios, Maurice works on a further set of solo recordings, as his LP, *The Loner*, nears completion. Today's session will produce six takes of a song initially labeled as "Everyone's Got To Be The Same," but retitled "Talk To The People." Six takes of this Maurice and Billy Lawrie composition will be made, the final take of which is treated to lavish overdubs of choir and orchestra. Billy Lawrie will take the lead vocal on this track; there is much crossover between his and Maurice's solo sessions at this stage. Also today, one take will be made of the drum and guitar instrumental "A Man In The Wilderness," as well as the piano and vocal tune, "Look At Me."

• Friday, December 11, 1970
At Recorded Sound Studios, Robin holds what will be his last solo session for quite some time. Today, he will tape six takes of an instrumental guitar demo of his song, "After The Laughter." The initial performances will be somewhat wayward and fragmentary; take six will be the master to which overdubs are added of two additional guitars (stylistically reminiscent of his production on the song "Avalanche," recorded earlier this year). Following this, Robin will tape one take of a voice and guitar demo of another song, "Why Not Cry Together." The production will feature a nice, echoed vocal effect. Nevertheless, "Why Not Cry Together" will never surface commercially.

1970

- **Sunday, December 13, 1970**
At IBC Studio A, the Bee Gees return to work with engineers Mike Claydon and Andy Knight on material for their next album. The first tune attempted, "Together," will be tried at least four times with the early takes rolled over to conserve tape on this 2" sixteen-track session. However, when "take one" is called anew, the results are complete and catchy. Barry will take the lead vocal on this track (which features his acoustic guitar, Maurice on bass, piano and electric guitar and Geoff Bridgford on drums). This completed production will not find commercial release.

Robin is not present vocally or instrumentally on "Together," but will surface on the second song from this session, "Over The Hill And Over The Mountains." Formed instrumentally around Maurice on piano and Geoff on drums, Robin will take the lead vocal on the third and final take of the song. Additionally, overdubs will be added of Maurice on electric guitar, organ and bass, as well as Barry on stacked, wordless harmony background vocals. Despite its obvious quality, this track will also be left in the vaults.

Following this, at least seven takes of the song "Merrily Merry Eyes" will be performed and then erased to conserve tape. When "take one" is called again, the song will be built instrumentally around Barry and Maurice's acoustic guitars. Take three will be the master and is soon treated to numerous overdubs including Maurice on bass, piano and electric guitar, Geoff on drums, Bill Shepherd-arranged orchestration and all three brothers on stacked harmonies (with Robin taking the lead on the song's verses). Though the song will be mixed and considered for release at some point, it remains unissued.

The last song from this session, "When Do I," will also be tried at least six times before it is decided to roll back the tape and start anew. Following this, Barry and Maurice lay down another three takes on their acoustic guitars (with Geoff Bridgford accompanying them on drums). The last of these takes will be considered the basis of today's master and is soon embellished with overdubs of Robin on double-tracked lead vocals and Maurice on piano. Initially, Maurice had tried a harpsichord on this track, but it was decided instead to move to the piano. This too will cause production problems, since it is out of tune with the basic track's acoustic guitars. This will cause today's rendition to be scrapped and "When Do I" will be remade on January 28, 1971.

- **Monday, December 14, 1970**
Masters for Maurice's solo album, *The Loner*, will be compiled today, though ultimately it will never be issued commercially. Barry's solo album from this year will share a similar fate.

- **Saturday, December 19, 1970**
In Germany, the Bee Gees are seen on television's *Wunsch dir was*. In Britain, *Record Mirror* runs an interview with the group conducted by Lon Goddard. "Our songs are still written as if they were conversation," remarks Barry, "as if we were talking to someone. We keep them melodic. Melody is my life. We still work closely with Bill Shepherd, who does all our arrangements. We advise him where we'd like little accents to go and he puts them into the orchestration and handles the production."

- **Saturday, December 26, 1970**
In Britain, BBC-2 television debuts *Cucumber Castle*.

1971

- **Saturday, January 2, 1971**
The *NME* runs an interview with the Bee Gees conducted by Alan Smith. "We were the first group to come along, man," says Maurice, "with a beautiful orchestra and a string section. And we went on stage with them and an R.A.F. band and a sixty-piece choir. So we've done that, so we won't do that again. We must try something else."

- **Saturday, January 9, 1971**
In Britain, the Bee Gees are guests on BBC-1 television's *Rolf Harris Show*.

- **Monday, January 11, 1971**
Maurice produces a session for his wife Lulu's next single release: "Everybody Clap" (written by Maurice and Billy Lawrie). The disc will be issued in May by Atlantic Records, but will not chart.

Another of Maurice's productions from this period is for singer Bev Harrell, who covers "Back To The People" (one of several songs composed by Maurice and Billy Lawrie). However, unlike the Lulu disc which is credited as a Moby Production,

Harrell's disc will be issued by Bell as A Winsak Production (so named for two songwriters, Bob Saker and Jack Winsley) and is arranged by J. Fiddy. Over the next few years, Bob Saker will work with Maurice on a variety of musical projects.

Reportedly, actor turned singer, Richard Harris, also works with Maurice on some sessions in this era, but few definitive details are known. Harris recently starred in *Bloomfield* (renamed *The Hero* outside of the UK) for which Maurice provided a significant amount of the scoring.

○ Sunday, January 17, 1971
In Australia, *The Sydney Morning Herald* holds a Surf And Sand Spectacular at Queenscliff featuring Vince Melouney's group, Fanny Adams (who the paper says formed six months ago).

○ Monday, January 18, 1971
At Recorded Sound Studios, engineer Eric Holland prepares a stereo mix of "Morning Of My Life," presumably for use on the forthcoming soundtrack album to the film *Melody*. The other Bee Gees-performed tracks included in the soundtrack album will utilize prior mixes from the *Odessa* album ("Melody Fair," "Give Your Best" and "First Of May") and *Bee Gees' 1st* ("To Love Somebody"). The actual film, however, features mono mixes of the songs, which in the case of "Give Your Best," may be unique.

○ Thursday, January 28, 1971
At IBC Studio A, the Bee Gees begin a new year of recording at a session working with engineers Mike Claydon and Andy Knight. The first song taped will be the Barry-led ballad, "We Lost The Road." The instrumental track will be based around Barry and Maurice's acoustic guitars and the drumming of Geoff Bridgford. The first four takes will be incomplete, false starts; take five will be the master. These basic tracks will be embellished with overdubs of bass, piano, handclaps, full orchestration and alternating lead vocals from Barry and Robin. The finished production will appear on 1972's *To Whom It May Concern*.

The second song produced during this session will be a remake of last year's "When Do I." Following just one false start, the master will be achieved on the second pass. To this basic track of Barry's acoustic guitar, overdubs will be added of bass, piano, drums, full orchestration and lead vocals from Robin. The finished production will be featured on the Bee Gees' next album, *Trafalgar*.

The third song from this date will be the song, "How Can You Mend A Broken Heart" (which the Gibbs will boast was written alongside "Lonely Days," at their first writing session together in 1970.) The song itself is a one-take-wonder: an instant classic. The finished production will become the Bee Gees' next single and shares a similar instrumental set-up to today's other productions. Barry's acoustic guitar (double-tracked in this case) will be the musical foundation for overdubs of Maurice's bass and piano, as well as Geoff Bridgford's subtle drumming. The whole thing will be topped off by one of Bill Shepherd's finest orchestral arrangements for the group. Although an early mix of the song (later issued by mistake on some early copies of 2001's *The Record* compilation) features Barry on lead vocals throughout, the final rendition will alternate between Robin on the opening verses and Barry on the choruses (with Maurice adding the third part of the vocal harmony in sections).

A fourth song cut at this session will be the unissued "If I Were The Sky," which will also be completed in just one take. Although this Robin-sung number will feature an impressive orchestral arrangement from Bill Shepherd, it will remain unissued (despite being mixed for release this year). Following this, another outtake, "Irresponsible, Unreliable, Indispensable, Blues" will be taped in one pass under the working title "Bring Out The Thoughts In Me." A basic rock number reminiscent of last year's "Every Second, Every Minute," this track will be passed over for release. It is however given a mix during this period (and later widely bootlegged); Maurice will attempt a variation on this song at a session on March 29th.

The final item from this session will be yet another outtake, the traditional "Ellan Vannin." As Barry will explain to engineer Mike Claydon before taping the piece, the Bee Gees initially intend "Ellan Vannin" to be a "tag" (or coda) to another song (possibly "If I Were the Sky") on their forthcoming album. The song's title comes from the Manx-language name for their birthplace, the Isle Of Man. Before the one and only take of the song taped today, Maurice will note: "'Ellan Vannin,' theme tune from the Isle Of Man." Robin quickly adds: "It's like 'If I Were the Sky.'" To which Barry quips, "The Isle Of Man pub song!"

Maurice will provide organ backing as the brothers sing this ninety-second piece (originally composed as a poem in 1854 by Eliza Craven Green). The production will be topped off by a simple string score courtesy of Bill Shepherd, but this recording of "Ellan Vannin" will be left unissued. In 1998, the Bee Gees will revisit the song in a lengthier reading, which will initially find release via a CD in charitable support of the Manx Children In Need fund.

1971

● Saturday, January 30, 1971
In Britain, NME runs an interview with the Bee Gees conducted by Alan Smith. Among the details discussed, Maurice is said to be producing some sessions with Kenny Rogers & the First Edition (though nothing from these surfaces commercially).

In the United States, 2 Years On enters the Billboard albums chart and will peak at #32 over the next fourteen weeks.

● Saturday, February 6, 1971
The NME reports that US sales of "Lonely Days" have topped a million and earned the Bee Gees a gold record award. According to the paper, the Bee Gees are supposed to be in the studio recording a new single (likely completing the production of the already taped but as yet unannounced, "How Can You Mend A Broken Heart"). NME & Record Mirror also state this week the brothers will be backed on their upcoming US tour by former Toe Fat members, Alan Kendall and Brian Glascock.

● Thursday, February 11, 1971
In the United States, the Bee Gees open their first full-fledged American tour at the Palace Theater in Albany, New York.

● Friday, February 12, 1971
In the United States, the Bee Gees' tour continues with two shows at New York's Philharmonic Hall with openers the Staple Singers (also managed by RSO). Billboard will publish a rave review in their February 27th issue noting: "It was incredible...impeccably perfect." The show, promoted by Ron Delsener, grosses $32,500 with tickets priced at $7 (according to Variety; Amusement Business pegs this number significantly lower). A press party for the group is briefly interrupted by a scurrilous phoned-in bomb threat in which the caller says the members of the group are "fascist pigs."

● Saturday, February 13, 1971
In Owings Mill, Maryland, the Bee Gees perform at the Painter's Mill Music Fair. The NME reports that Tin Tin, whose latest single "Shana" was issued last week, have postponed promotional work since their drummer Geoff Bridgford is on tour with the Bee Gees. "I have been assured that two weeks will not seriously hamper our promotion campaign," says Bridgford. Meanwhile, Record Mirror notes that Radio Luxembourg will conduct a live interview with the Bee Gees from America in which the group shall speak to DJ's David Christian and Paul Burnett.

● Sunday, February 14, 1971
On Valentine's Day, the Bee Gees appear at the Auditorium Theater in Chicago, Illinois.

● Thursday, February 18, 1971
In the run-up to their Los Angeles area concert tomorrow evening, the Bee Gees appear live on The Tonight Show starring Johnny Carson. Johnny's other guests include George Burns (later to appear alongside the Gibbs in their motion picture version of Sgt. Pepper's Lonely Hearts Club Band), George Gobel, Della Reese and Jo Anne Worley.

● Friday, February 19, 1971
In Santa Monica, California, the Bee Gees perform twice tonight at the Civic Auditorium with openers the Staple Singers (minus Pop Staples, who is in the hospital suffering from pneumonia). Rolling Stone later reports the second house is less-than-half-full. Val Mabbs of Record Mirror will question the band about the success of this date a few months later. "Both shows at Los Angeles were well attended," says Geoff Bridgford. "They'd had an earthquake there and people were still recovering from the shock of that anyway," added Robin referring to the San Fernando quake that rocked the area ten days earlier. "Some people came in again for the second show because they liked it, and a lot of people from the entertainment world were there for the second show."

1971

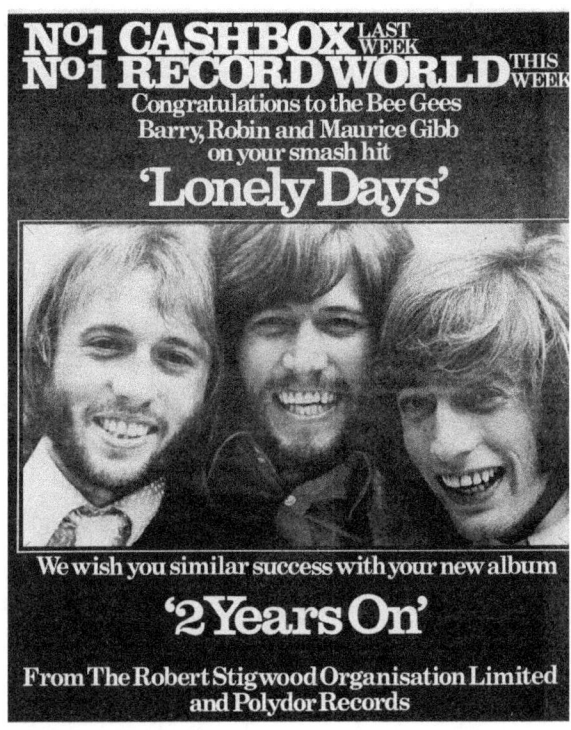

● Saturday, February 20, 1971
In Vancouver, the Bee Gees perform for the first time in Canada at the Agrodome ice rink.

● Saturday, February 27, 1971
In Portland, Oregon, the Bee Gees' tour concludes at the Paramount Theater.

● Sunday, February 28, 1971
Maurice and Lulu take off for a short skiing holiday in St. Moritz; Robin returns to Britain to rest and Barry stays behind in America for a short spell.

● Saturday, March 6, 1971
Billboard reports that Robert Stigwood hopes to use the band's US tour as a driver for getting more artists to cover Gibb compositions. Additionally, Peter Brown, president of Stigwood New York states that there is renewed interest in the film *Cucumber Castle*, which has thus far only been screened on British television. On US television, the Bee Gees will be seen tonight on *The Andy Williams Show* performing "Lonely Days" and "Man For All Seasons."

NME reports that the Bee Gees will soon tour in Israel, Hong Kong, Singapore, Thailand and Australia. However, in the paper's America Calling column, Nancy Lewis writes that at least one of the dates for the group's recent US tour was scrapped due to poor ticket sales.

● Monday, March 15, 1971
At Recorded Sound Studios, Maurice works with engineers Eric Holland and Phil Wade to tape "Trafalgar" on the studio's 1" eight-track recorder. Billy Lawrie will initially be listed as producer on the tape box (though this is crossed out and replaced with Maurice's name). Take one of the song will be an incomplete pass with Maurice playing an acoustic twelve-string guitar to some intermittent drumming. Take two will be the master take and will receive overdubs of a second twelve-string acoustic guitar, lead electric guitar, bass, piano, organ and three tracks of vocals. On April 7th, this master will be transferred to 2" sixteen-track tape at IBC for further sweetening. However, the final production will actually remain in the same state it left Recorded Sound, with no further production embellishment. No doubt having it on the same format as the Bee Gees' other recent productions paves the way for simpler mixing and "Trafalgar" becoming the title track of the band's next album. "It's a song about a very lonely guy who lives in London and spends a lot of his time feeding the pigeons in Trafalgar Square," Maurice will later explain to John Halsall in *Go-Set*. "In fact, a lot of people are going to think that the album has a general historical theme running through it because, apart from 'Trafalgar,' there are other titles like 'Waterloo' but I'm afraid that it's slightly misleading because none of them have any bearing on history at all."

● Tuesday, March 23, 1971
At IBC Studio A, the Bee Gees return to work on sessions for *Trafalgar* with engineers Mike Claydon and Andy Knight. They will first attempt to tape the song "Dearest" but will immediately decide to scrap the results (after rolling over at least three early takes of the song). Instead, they will move on to a sinister rocker called "Deep In The Dark Of The Day," featuring a joint lead vocal from Barry and Robin and fascinating, possibly improvised lyrics. The song, propelled by a heavy electric guitar riff and huge drums, is certainly their most rocking track from this entire era. Unfortunately, the Bee Gees will decide to leave it in the can (despite numerous tracks of overdubbed vocals). There is some discussion of it being too long—it does stretch out over five minutes—to which Barry quickly remarks: "It sounds incredible, who cares?"

Work soon returns to the more sedate piano ballad, "Dearest." Maurice remarks that he could play it better if they had a harpsichord at the studio instead of the piano, but Barry feels it will be fine. Barry will lead Maurice through six takes of "Dearest" (singing off-mic) before landing on the master, take seven. To this track a variety of vocals from Barry and Robin will be overdubbed; Bill Shepherd (who is present in the studio for most of this session) will add a finishing touch of strings. The final production will be featured on the Bee Gees' forthcoming *Trafalgar*.

1971

To close this session, the Gibb brothers tape three whimsical compositions in mono showing their satirical/comedic side. Robin introduces the first of these, "I'm Only Me," to which Maurice will quip, "Thank God! Can't see two of 'em." Robin adds, "It's a roughie," referring to the fact that this is simply a demo. To a backing of Barry on acoustic twelve-string guitar, Robin sings lead (with some added harmonies from Barry and Maurice as the song progresses). While introducing the second demo, "There's Something I Want To Tell You," Robin indicates that there will be dialogue to precede it, after which Barry mentions some actors (like Rex Harrison) who might sing these songs in a fantasy film project. Nevertheless, for this version of "There's Something I Want To Tell You," Robin will take the lead. The final number from this trio of tracks will be titled "Amorous Aristocracy" and features alternating vocals from Barry and Robin (with Maurice joining on the choruses) all to Barry's acoustic twelve-string backing. The results are similar to some of the comedy numbers from their childhood nightclub act (and are less bawdy than the title might imply). None of these three compositions will be heard from again.

Sometime during this period, the group will record three further songs for their next LP at an undated session. The multi-movement "Somebody Stop The Music" is initially titled "Today I Saw The Sun" and will be based, like so many earlier productions, around Barry and Maurice's acoustic guitars. After three false starts, the master will be captured on take four, which will feature some inventive overdubbed bass work from Maurice. Meanwhile, the simpler "Lion In Winter" (featuring some rather enigmatic lyrics) will be cut in just one take after some instruction from Barry on how to fade in the drums. After a short false start, the Robin-sung ballad "Remembering" will be captured on take two. All three of these masters will be included on *Trafalgar*.

- Sunday, March 28, 1971
The motion picture, *Melody* (featuring a number of Bee Gees composed and performed songs), opens in New York City. It will go into release next month in the UK.

- Monday, March 29, 1971
At IBC Studio A, studio work continues on *Trafalgar* with engineers John Pantry and Bryan Stott recording the proceedings. Today's session will open with an instrumental announced as "Maurice's Jam." However, before the band (featuring two electric guitars, bass, drums and cowbell) begins, Maurice tells the engineer the title is actually "Lumberjack," tying it to a lyrical reference in the previously taped (but rejected) "Irresponsible, Unreliable, Indispensable, Blues." Take one will be complete (running near five minutes in length), if a little sloppy in spots; take two will sound like an entirely different song (and lacks bass guitar—which was likely overdubbed in take one). "Lumberjack" by any title will not progress beyond a rock jam.

The second song logged at this session will be the incomparable "Walking Back To Waterloo." The basic track will be started by Barry on his acoustic twelve-string guitar and completed in three takes. The stunning final production will feature lead electric guitar, Mellotron, stereo piano, bass, drums, strings and five tracks of vocals and when completed, the master is undoubtedly a highlight of the soon-to-be-issued *Trafalgar*.

The final song from this session, "A Word Of Love," will be built around a piano track from Maurice. After a full run-through on take one, take two will be considered the master track to which layers of vocals will be overdubbed. Barry will sing lead on this ballad, which will never surface commercially.

- April 1971
American producer, A&R man and musical artist, Lou Reizner issues an album featuring covers of Barry's heretofore unissued "The Day Your Eyes Meet Mine," as well as "Morning Of My Life." In 1976, the Bee Gees will work with Reizner on the soundtrack to the film *All This And World War II* (covering three Beatles songs and presaging their own 1978 Beatles-related project, *Sgt. Pepper's Lonely Hearts Club Band*).

- Saturday, April 3, 1971
In the US, Tin Tin's "Toast And Marmalade For Tea" (produced by Maurice) enters the *Billboard* singles chart. Over the next eleven weeks it will peak at #20, marking the first time a non-Bee Gees performed Gibb production clicks in America.

● Tuesday, April 6, 1971

At IBC Studio A, the Bee Gees tape three new songs with engineers John Pantry and Bryan Stott. The first of these, "God's Good Grace" carries an anti-war message and will be captured in three takes. Musically, the track will be built around Maurice's piano with added instrumentation of acoustic guitar, bass, Mellotron, drums and tambourine. The production will be completed with four tracks of both strings and vocals. However, on the surviving period mix of this song, only a single track of Robin's vocals will be utilized. The results will remain unissued (though this track will be widely bootlegged).

Also at this session, the flipside to the group's forthcoming single, and a Maurice showcase number, "Country Woman" will be taped in two takes. This catchy track (perhaps Maurice's most commercial to date) will be built musically around two tracks of acoustic guitar, some solid bass, stereo piano (on the instrumental break), congas, tambourine, drums and four tracks of brass. The final touch will be a fine lead vocal track from Maurice (though rough mixes will survive with scratch vocals featuring all three brothers on backgrounds).

Barry's ballad, "The Greatest Man In The World," will require six takes to complete. The final production will be spread across all sixteen channels of the 2" master and features stereo drums, two channels of acoustic guitar, a track of bass, stereo piano, five channels of vocals and four tracks of Bill Shepherd-arranged strings. The master will be featured on *Trafalgar* (for which sessions continue tomorrow).

● Wednesday, April 7, 1971

At IBC Studio A, sessions conclude for *Trafalgar* with a final day of tracking engineered by John Pantry and Bryan Stott. The first of the songs attempted, Barry's "Israel" will be recorded in two takes as a heartfelt tribute to a country that Barry obviously admires (and it will be subsequently be issued in Israel as a single as a result of a Bee Gees appearance there—see May 22nd).

After a couple of false starts, Maurice will lay down his impressive tune "It's Just The Way" (with take three being the master). Sounding not unlike a track for Tin Tin, "It's Just The Way" shows his full maturation as a solo writer has undoubtedly arrived. Production-wise, it will feature four channels of drums (a stereo track, plus a stereo tom-tom overdub), stereo piano, multiple tracks of acoustic and electric guitars, percussion, bass, brass and strings.

Next up, Robin's "Engines, Aeroplanes" (recorded February 27, 1970) will be transferred from 1" eight-track to 2" sixteen-track for remixing. No actual changes to the original recorded material will be made, though surviving mixes from both eras display a different stage of the vocal overdubs. Despite this step of transfer and mixing, "Engines, Aeroplanes" will remain unissued.

The final song taped for *Trafalgar* will be Barry's epic "Don't Wanna Live Inside Myself," reportedly inspired by the work of Neil Young. Opening with Maurice's piano (not only recorded in stereo, but double-tracked over four channels), the production will build with Geoff's drums (taped in stereo) and tracks of tambourine, bass, organ and strings (again in stereo). Vocally, the song's powerful arrangement will be spread across four channels. The grand outcome will ultimately be issued in edited form as a US single to follow-up "How Can You Mend A Broken Heart" (see October 23rd).

● Thursday, April 8, 1971

At IBC Studios, engineer John Pantry prepares rough mixes of some of the Bee Gees' recent productions including "Country Woman," "The Greatest Man In The World," "God's Good Grace" and "Remembering."

● Thursday, April 15, 1971

Rolling Stone runs an article by Robin Green with interviews dating from their US tour this past February. "This may sound corny," Robert Stigwood says of the Bee Gees' appeal, "but it's their poetry. These boys are completely uneducated. They don't even know how to spell. They write lyrics spelled out phonetically. And the simple poetry of the words appeals to the public."

"It's like a spiritual thing when we write," says Robin. "We know what the other one is thinking, as if we had a language between us. 'Lonely Days' was written in ten minutes. It was quick."

● Wednesday, April 21, 1971

The film *Melody* opens in the UK where it will adopt the alternate title *S.W.A.L.K.* (standing for "sealed with a loving kiss"). Seemingly, this title change will be rather last minute, resulting in UK copies of the soundtrack album being restickered with the new title over the existing cover artwork.

● Saturday, April 24, 1971

The *NME* reports that the Bee Gees are putting the finishing touches on their album, *Trafalgar*, which is provisionally planned for late spring release. A follow-up single to "Lonely Days" will be selected from the album masters.

● Monday, April 26, 1971

At IBC Studio A, stereo mixes are prepared for "Walking Back To Waterloo," "We Lost The Road" and "How Can You Mend A Broken Heart."

● Saturday, May 1, 1971

In Britain, the Bee Gees are seen on television's *The Dick Cavett Show*. This is the first episode of this American program to be taped on British soil.

1971

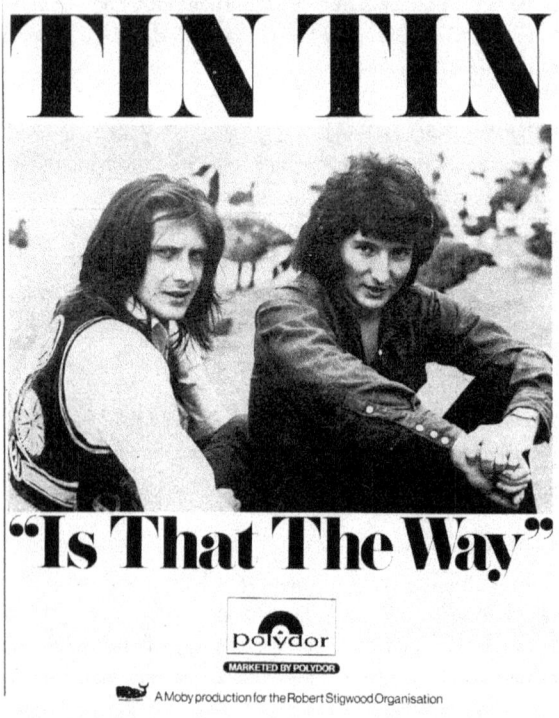

○ Sunday, May 2, 1971
At the newly renamed Nova Sound (formerly Recorded Sound Studios), Maurice prepares a stereo mix of his "Country Woman" with engineer Richard Dodd. The tape box seems to indicate that in addition to the basic tracking done at IBC, some additional production work on this tune was finished at Nova Sound.

○ Tuesday, May 4, 1971
In the United States, the Bee Gees' appearance on *The Dick Cavett Show* is screened.

○ Thursday, May 6, 1971
At IBC studios, attempts are made to mix "When Do I" into stereo (from the 16-track master).

○ Saturday, May 8, 1971
Disc & NME report that Geoff Bridgford is now a permanent member of the Bee Gees. The paper also notes that "...an additional guitarist is also being considered."

Geoff will later tell John Halsall in *Go-Set*: "I was gigging around with Tin Tin and, at the same time I was doing a lot of session work for the guys, I played on all of their solo albums whilst the break-up was in force. When they got back together again I played on *2 Years On* and the single 'Lonely Days.' It just seemed natural that we should stick together for a tour but I was surprised when they asked me to become a permanent member, I'd expected to be on sessions with them but not a fully fledged Bee Gee.

○ Saturday, May 22, 1971
The *NME* reports that the Bee Gees will return to the United States on September 1st for their most extensive tour to date. "Prior to this, the Gees will play a string of concerts in Israel, as a part of that country's 25th anniversary celebrations. A specially written song titled 'Israel,' penned by Barry Gibb, will be released there within the next few weeks. The group is also in line for a nine day concert tour of Australia in July."

○ Friday, May 28, 1971
In Britain, the Bee Gees issue their single "How Can You Mend A Broken Heart" c/w "Country Woman."

○ Wednesday, June 2, 1971
At IBC's tape copy room, various mixes from the Bee Gees' recent sessions are assembled, including outtakes from *Trafalgar*: "Engines, Aeroplanes," "Country Woman" (destined to be a B-side), as well as alternate mixes of "The Greatest Man In The World," "Don't Wanna Live Inside Myself" and "We Lost The Road."

• Saturday, June 5, 1971
Record Mirror publishes an extensive interview with the group conducted by Val Mabbs. Robin says of their forthcoming album: "It will knock spots off every album we've done." Maurice adds, "It's as good as *Bee Gees' 1st.*" Robin is still sensitive about the split and reasons that, "...nobody gave me any sort of justice after the Bee Gees split up, they still didn't think I was any good, even after 'Saved By The Bell.'

"'Saved By The Bell' only happened because I had so much publicity from the break up of the Bee Gees. But then Maurice and Barry didn't get any help on their singles because they came out later." Robin reasons that issues with Polydor's computer system that tracked distribution orders failed them all during this period. More than anything, the article expresses the desire of the band to be successful again in Britain. "I'm all Churchill and the Union Jack," says Robin, "and I'd like to have a number one in my country."

NME reports that Tin Tin will serve as openers for the Bee Gees' next US tour which opens September 1st and is due to take in 38 dates. On British television, the Bee Gees will be seen performing "How Can You Mend A Broken Heart" and "I've Gotta Get A Message To You" on *Whittaker's World Of Music*.

• Saturday, June 12, 1971
At Nova Sound, Maurice records a version of Tin Tin's "Is That The Way" (written by Steve Groves, Billy Lawrie and Steve Kipner) with a slightly rearranged introduction. It is unknown exactly why Maurice has chosen to cover this track, which he recently produced for Tin Tin with partner Billy Lawrie and which will soon become a US hit single (see August 8th). Nonetheless, the band, featuring electric piano, acoustic guitar and drums, seem quite serious about nailing a good backing track (or saving tape) since two sets of takes will be rolled over at the outset of the session (at least ten takes in all) before "take one" is called for a third time. Take five will be the master, but despite some added piano and percussion, no vocals will be taped and this rendering remains unissued.

The second song taped today, Maurice's own "You Know It's For You," will be finished with greater alacrity. After a false start, he will complete this wonderful song on take two incorporating six tracks of vocals with two tracks each of bass, drums, electric piano and acoustic guitar, as well as individual tracks of tambourine and Mellotron. The completed production will be Maurice's now customary solo spotlight track on 1972's *To Whom It May Concern*.

• Saturday, June 19, 1971
In Australia, *Go-Set* reports that: "...on the 9th of July the Bee Gees will arrive in Sydney to commence a one week tour of all capital cities. This is the first time the group as a whole has returned to Australia since they left for England four-and-a-half years ago. Accompanying them on their tour will be ten British musicians and their musical arranger, Australian born, Bill Shepherd. It is believed that the group will be backed by a thirty-piece orchestra."

• Saturday, June 26, 1971
In the United States, "How Can You Mend A Broken Heart" enters the *Billboard* singles chart and will eventually reach #1 over the next fifteen weeks: the Bee Gees' first US chart-topper. In Australia, *Go-Set* publishes an interview with the group conducted by John Halsall. "The new album has a gatefold sleeve and when you open it up it reveals the famous 'Death of Nelson' scene which we all posed for," remarks Maurice. "The album cover really doesn't have any bearing on the music except that the title track is called, in fact, 'Trafalgar.'

"What I will say, though, is that this is our best ever album. *2 Years On* which we made just after we got back together again was just an experiment to find out whether all of the tensions which caused the original break-up had gone, so we were all a bit wary about giving our best on that album. Gradually, throughout the session, the tensions and hang-ups disappeared and, as a result, the whole scene's back together again as it should be."

Robin adds: "I think that we were given a pretty hard time by the press when we broke up; I mean look at Free, they break up and their record goes straight to the top of the hit parade, when we broke up the whole industry sort of forgot that we existed."

• July 1971
Ronnie Burns and the group New Horizon each issue cover versions of Barry's heretofore unissued composition, "One Bad Thing." Meanwhile, Vince Melouney's group, Fanny Adams, have a self-titled, debut album now available on the MCA label.

• Thursday, July 8, 1971
In Australia, after two lightning Sydney press conferences and a reception from the Lord Mayor, the Bee Gees fly to Brisbane to prepare for their first concert.

• Saturday, July 10, 1971
In Australia, the Bee Gees are scheduled for a performance in Brisbane at Festival Hall.

• Sunday, July 11, 1971
In Sydney, Australia, the Bee Gees appear for two concerts (2pm & 8:30pm) at State Theatre. The show opener is Russell Morris and the Bee Gees are backed by a twenty-five piece orchestra. The second show will be filmed for broadcast and includes the songs: "New York Mining Disaster 1941"; "To Love Somebody"; "Really And Sincerely"; "Every Second,

1971

Every Minute"; "Lay It On Me"; "Jingle Jangle"; "Morning Of My Life"; "Holiday"; "I Can't See Nobody"; "Words"; "How Can You Mend A Broken Heart"; "I Started A Joke"; "I've Gotta Get A Message To You"; "Massachusetts (The Lights Went Out In)"; "Lonely Days"; "Spicks And Specks." *Go-Set* says of this date: "...the applause was still deafening almost ten minutes after the Bee Gees had left the theatre and were on their way to their hotel!"

• Monday, July 12, 1971
In Australia, the Bee Gees perform in Canberra. *Go-Set* says of this date: "Canberraites have rarely been known to show such overwhelming enthusiasm for a visiting act of any sort."

• Tuesday, July 13, 1971
In Australia, the Bee Gees return to Sydney for a show at the Capitol Theatre.

• Wednesday, July 14, 1971
In Australia, the Bee Gees are scheduled for a performance in Hobart, Tasmania.

• Thursday, July 15, 1971
In Australia, the Bee Gees perform at Melbourne's Festival Hall. *Go-Set* says: "In Melbourne an extra concert was arranged to cope with the huge demand for tickets, and the crowd reaction was spectacular."

• Friday, July 16, 1971
In Australia, the Bee Gees are scheduled for a performance in Adelaide.

• Saturday, July 17, 1971
In Australia, the Bee Gees are scheduled for a performance in Perth.

• Monday, July 19, 1971
In Australia, the Bee Gees are seen in an interview on television's *GTK* (which stands for "Getting To Know").

• Saturday, July 24, 1971
According to the *NME*, the Bee Gees are due back in Britain today from their Australian tour. *Go-Set* runs an interview with the band conducted during their tour down under. Robin speaks about why they left Australia at the dawn of '67: "We were tired of being ignored, a new Bee Gee record would come out, and the record people would take it 'round to the radio people, and they'd say, 'Oh yeah, another Bee Gees song.' We were still seen as a bunch of kids who played on *Bandstand*, while we were already full of ideas. We have an album planned of material we wrote here in Australia."

As to an allegation of their records being too same-y, or overproduced, Robin responds: "We have our style of music—it's classical-folk—and we are perfectionists at doing it. We don't want to produce different sounds just for the sake of being different."

• Saturday, August 8, 1971
In the US, Tin Tin's "Is That The Way" (a Moby production from Maurice and Billy Lawrie) hits the *Billboard* singles chart. Over the next six weeks it will rise to a mild #59 (despite Tin Tin serving as openers for the Bee Gees, next US tour, which hits the States in a few weeks).

• Thursday, August 19, 1971
On a break from touring, Maurice works at IBC Studio A with engineers Andy Knight and Richard Manwaring on a new song, "And For You." He will tape four takes of the song (which features guitar, bass, piano and drums). Although he will embellish the final pass, take four, with four tracks of lead and backing vocals, this production (and song) will remain unissued.

• Saturday, August 28, 1971
In Nashville, Tennessee, the Bee Gees kick-off their second American tour of the year at the Municipal Auditorium (backed by members of the Nashville Symphony). Tin Tin serve as openers for this and the rest of the tour dates. In Britain, the Bee Gees are seen in a pre-taped segment on Lulu's latest television series, *It's Lulu*.

1971

• Monday, August 30, 1971
In Gaithersburg, Maryland, the Bee Gees' US tour continues at the Shady Grove Music Festival.

• Tuesday, August 31, 1971
In Philadelphia, Pennsylvania, the Bee Gees are scheduled to appear at the Spectrum (this date is also rumored to take place on September 16th).

• Wednesday, September 1, 1971
In Ohio, the Bee Gees were due to open their tour of the United States at the Blossom Music Festival in Cleveland. They have cancelled, and their former Atco labelmates, Sonny & Cher, fill the bill in their absence.

• Thursday & Friday, September 2 & 3, 1971
In Atlantic City, New Jersey, the Bee Gees appear for two days at the Steel Pier.

• Tuesday, September 7, 1971
In the United States, the Bee Gees make their second appearance on television's *The Tonight Show starring Johnny Carson* alongside Carson's guests John Byner, Bernadette Peters and Monti Rock III.

• Thursday, September 9, 1971
In Trenton, New Jersey, the Bee Gees are scheduled to appear at the State Fair.

• Friday, September 10, 1971
In Saratoga Springs, New York, the Bee Gees are scheduled to appear at the Music Fair.

• Saturday, September 11, 1971
In Syracuse, New York, the Bee Gees are scheduled to appear at the War Memorial Auditorium.

• Monday, September 13, 1971
The Bee Gees appear for the first of three concerts at New York's Philharmonic Hall. The band is accompanied by the Mican Forrest Orchestra (as directed by Bill Shepherd). The set includes "Massachusetts," "New York Mining Disaster," "Lonely Days" and "How Can You Mend A Broken Heart." Noted rock critic Lillian Roxon will report that the shows are packed.

• Friday, September 17, 1971
In Charleston, West Virginia, the Bee Gees appear in concert tonight with openers Tin Tin at the Civic Center (in a show produced by National Shows). A review in the *Charleston Gazette* says the crowd for this show is "medium" and not as big as most of the summer's concerts. Tin Tin's set includes: "Take A Message To The Station"; "Jenny B."; "The Cavalry Is Coming"; "Astral Taxi"; "Elementary Hardtime Girl"; "Spanish Shepherd"; "Toast And Marmalade For Tea." The Bee Gees' set features: "Lay It On Me"; "Morning Of My Life"; "Jingle Jangle"; "How Can You Mend A Broken Heart."

• Saturday, September 18, 1971
In Little Rock, Arkansas, the Bee Gees are scheduled to appear at Barton Coliseum.

- Sunday, September 19, 1971
In Memphis, Tennessee, the Bee Gees appear in concert at the Mid-South Coliseum. A reported audience of 2,500 witnesses the Bee Gees perform with backing from a 20-piece orchestra.

- Monday, September 20, 1971
In the United States, the Bee Gees are seen on television's *The David Frost Show* (this appearance is televised on different dates in various regions of the country).

- Tuesday, September 21, 1971
In Wichita, Kansas, the Bee Gees are scheduled to perform at the Henry Levitt Arena.

- Wednesday, September 22, 1971
In Kansas City, Missouri, the Bee Gees are scheduled to perform at the Soldiers & Sailors Auditorium.

- Thursday, September 23, 1971
In Des Moines, Iowa, the Bee Gees appear in concert backed by Mican Forrest Orchestra at Veterans Memorial Auditorium. Tonight's show opens at 8pm with a performance from Tin Tin. *The Des Moines Register* says approximately fifteen-hundred fans turn up for this gig at $3 a head—another less than stellar draw. The set includes: "New York Mining Disaster 1941"; "To Love Somebody"; "Words"; "How Can You Mend A Broken Heart"; "Lonely Days"; "Spicks And Specks."

- Saturday, September 25, 1971
In the United States, *Trafalgar* enters the *Billboard* album charts and will rise to #34 over the next fourteen weeks. Tonight, the Bee Gees are scheduled to perform at the Arie Crown Theater in Chicago, Illinois.

- Sunday, September 26, 1971
In Davenport, Iowa, the Bee Gees are scheduled to perform at the Veterans Memorial Auditorium.

- Friday, October 1, 1971
In Columbus, Ohio, the Bee Gees perform in concert at St. John Arena.

- Saturday, October 2, 1971
In Evansville, Indiana, the Bee Gees perform in concert at Roberts Stadium (University of Indiana).

- Sunday, October 3, 1971
In St. Louis, Missouri, the Bee Gees' tour concludes at Kiel Auditorium.

- Tuesday, October 12, 1971
Maurice returns to some production work (as a part of Moby with Billy Lawrie) composing jingles and producing Jimmy Stevens.

- Wednesday, October 13, 1971
At IBC Studio A, the Bee Gees demo some new songs with engineers Damon Lyon-Shaw and Bryan Stott. The first of these, "What Could Have Been Done," will be captured in three takes. This simple number will be based around Barry's acoustic guitar and Geoff's drums, but will not go much further. It will remain incomplete and unissued.

The second song from this session, "Goodbye Blue Sky," will be in much the same mode instrumentally. However, it will reach further completion with a lovely set of rough vocals and another of the Bee Gees' incredible melodic hooks. This Barry-sung number (with Robin taking lead on the final verse) could have been a great album track or cover for another artist, but it will remain unissued.

The last song demoed on this date will actually become the Bee Gees' next single, "My World." Taped in just two takes, this breezy number will begin just like today's other tunes: with Barry's acoustic guitar and Geoff's drums. Nevertheless, take two will soon fill up all sixteen channels of the two-inch master. Overdubs will include bass, double-tracked piano, organ, tympani, percussion, flutes, brass and stereo strings. The production will be topped off by a wonderful Robin lead vocal (with stacked group voices on the choruses and vocal backgrounds); Barry takes the lead on the final A section verse. The results will be issued on January 14, 1972, bringing the Bee Gees back to the British charts.

- Saturday, October 17, 1971
Go-Set reports that Vince has left his most recent group, the Cleves, and is now playing with a new band in Melbourne. "It was like Vince Melouney and the Cleves," their guitarist, Rob Atkin, comments. "Now it's back to the Cleves."

- Wednesday, October 21, 1971
At IBC Studio A, the Bee Gees work on another prospective single with engineers Bryan Stott and Damon Lyon-Shaw. First up, the slow piano ballad "Alive" will be captured in four takes. The final production will incorporate four tracks of strings, stereo piano, flute, bass, percussion, stereo drums (plus a separate kick drum track) and double-tracked vocals from Barry. The final production will be issued as a single a full year from now (see November 11, 1972).

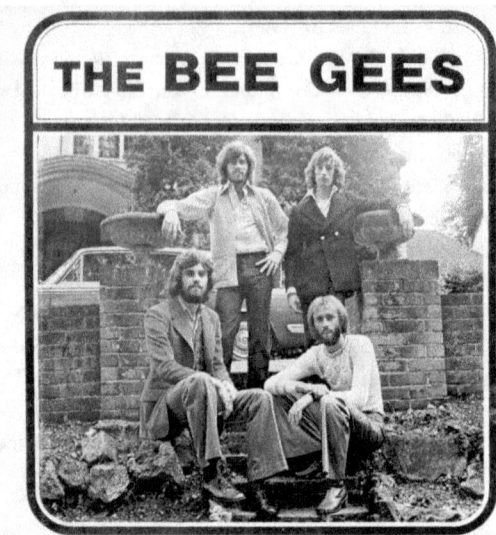

SOUVENIR PROGRAM $2.00

The second song from this session, Maurice's "On Time," will be featured on the flipside of the Bee Gees' next single ("My World"). Produced in one take (though this may be after three abortive takes have been rolled over), this swampy number will feature four tracks of guitar (electric and acoustic), four tracks of vocals, three tracks of drums, and individual overdubs of congas, tambourine, piano, bass and strings. The results will be issued to the public on January 14, 1972.

• Saturday, October 23, 1971
In the United States, the epic (albeit edited) "Don't Wanna Live Inside Myself" reaches a disappointing #53 on Billboard's singles chart during a seven-week chart run.

• Monday, November 8, 1971
At Nova Sound Studio A, Maurice tapes two new songs. Instrumentally, "Anymore" will be built upon Maurice's piano (recorded in stereo), live vocals from the composer and Geoff's drums (recorded across three tracks). The master will be take five, to which overdubs will be added of a second stereo piano, bass, tambourine, double-tracked trumpet and an echoey, double-tracked lead vocal from Maurice. Like so much of Maurice's material from the last few years, this production will remain unissued, despite the intriguing quality.

The second song from this session, the swampy "Saturday Morning, Sunday Night," will be taped in four takes. The instrumental track will be built on Maurice's acoustic guitar and Geoff's drums. The master, take four, will be treated to overdubs of a second full set of drums, a second acoustic guitar track, tambourine, shaker and two tracks of rough vocals. The results will remain unissued.

• Friday, November 12, 1971
In Britain, the album Trafalgar is issued. In the studio, Maurice and Billy Lawrie work with songwriter Norman Hitchcock. This will be the first of two sessions with Hitchcock (the second occurring on an unknown date early in the New Year).

• December 1971
The Barry Gibb Fan Cub issues a single of three acoustic demos—"King Kathy" c/w "Summer Ends" and "I Can Bring Love." These unique performances have never been reissued.

• Thursday, December 2, 1971
At IBC Studio A, engineer Bryan Stott assembles stereo masters of future single sides "On Time," "My World" and "Alive."

• Friday, December 3, 1971
In Britain, the Bee Gees film a promotional performance of their next single, "My World."

● Saturday, December 11, 1971
Record Mirror runs an interview with the Bee Gees conducted by Val Mabbs. "If we had another hit we would probably do a tour of England," says Maurice. "But at the moment it's not really worth the audience coming to see us, because they would be living on the memories of each song, and they'd be coming to see what we did. I'm sure we would draw an audience though."

Following their contributions to *Melody*, the Bee Gees were asked to contribute to another film. "We were supposed to write for *Little Lord Fauntleroy*," says Maurice, "which was going to star Mark Lester again, but we haven't heard any more about it yet." The group is planning another television series for an American audience, with the Gibbs starring as cowboys and Geoff Bridgford as the sheriff. Maurice plans more Moby productions in the future with Tin Tin and Carl Groszmann.

1972

● Saturday, January 1, 1972
Billboard magazine reports that the Bee Gees' music has been made officially available in Russia for the first time. A mini-album of selections on Bulgarian Balkantone is being distributed by the country's Melodiya label. Meanwhile, this month in the UK, Pye Records will issue a single by the Bloomfields (a.k.a. Maurice and Billy Lawrie) performing their song "The Loner," tagged as coming from the soundtrack of the film Bloomfield. A US release of this soundtrack, under the title *The Hero*, will appear on the Capitol label in September (see August 12th).

● Monday, January 3, 1972
At IBC Studio A, the Bee Gees' first session of 1972 produces the rather odd concoction, "Paper Mache, Cabbages & Kings." The off-beat title is given to the engineer (Bryan Stott) by Barry who has to repeat it three times for it to get properly notated (to which Maurice quips—"you illiterate sod").

Geoff asks, "What are you going to do for an intro, Maurice? Are you going to intro it?" Maurice replies, "Trust me, son." Barry adds, "Really nice, so Bill [Shepherd] can do something around it. Why don't you do the whole chorus then?" Robin begins to make some suggestions that don't have to do with the intro and Maurice reminds them all they are only recording the track now and they can worry about that later. The first two takes are short false starts and the track is purely piano and drums. Take three is fairly complete, but falls apart after the song's slow intermediate section. After three more false starts (takes four through six), a master, take seven, is completed which will receive numerous overdubs (including a chanting intro a la "Every Christian Lion Hearted Man Will Show You" as well as a wild, pitchy mandolin part). The song will be completed and issued as both a single side and album track late in the year.

The session's second song, "Passport," is an unfinished instrumental idea featuring Maurice on a Baldwin electric harpsichord (with the damper engaged for most of the song) and Geoff on drums. It follows a simple, almost 12-bar chord pattern, but it is never embellished beyond these basic tracks and will remain unissued.

● Saturday, January 15, 1972
In Australia, ABN 2 air part one of a television special called *Spicks And Specks Of Our Lives*.

● Friday, January 14, 1972
In Britain, the Bee Gees' first single of 1972—"My World" c/w "On Time"—is issued.

● Saturday, January 22, 1972
In Australia, ABN 2 air part two of *Spicks And Specks Of Our Lives*.

● Sunday, January 23, 1972
In Britain, the Bee Gees are seen on ATV's *The Golden Shot*.

● Thursday, January 27, 1972
In Australia, the Bee Gees arrive in Sydney to kick-off their second Australian tour. They will appear at a press conference; various footage survives of this event.

1972

● Saturday, January 29, 1972

In Melbourne, the Bee Gees perform in concert at the Kooyong Tennis Centre. Meanwhile back in Britain, their latest single—"My World"—brings them back to the charts for the first time in a full year. Over the next nine weeks, "My World" will reach a high of #16 (their biggest charting disc since 1969's "Don't Forget To Remember"). In the United States, the disc will also reach #16, charting on *Billboard*'s singles listing for eight weeks.

● Sunday, January 30, 1972

In Sydney, at 3pm the Bee Gees will appear with a twenty-piece orchestra in concert at the RAS Showground. A sell-out crowd of 11,000 is expected; Melbourne singer Colleen Hewitt and a group called No Sweat will open the show.

● Tuesday, February 1, 1972

In Australia, the Bee Gees are scheduled to perform in concert at Brisbane's Festival Hall.

● Thursday, February 3, 1972

In Australia, the Bee Gees are scheduled to perform in concert at Memorial Drive Park (a "tennis venue") in Adelaide.

● Friday, February 4, 1972

In Australia, the Bee Gees are scheduled to perform in concert at Subiaco Oval in Subiaco (a suburb of Perth).

● Saturday, February 5, 1972

Go-Set reports: "For the second time within a year the Bee Gees will play to capacity houses throughout their Australian tour. Originally it was planned that there would be only one concert in Melbourne and Brisbane but because both were sold out on the first day of bookings, promoter Paul Dainty decided to include extra concerts in both cities. An amazing effort when you consider that the Bee Gees first tour was only in July last year."

● Friday, February 25, 1972

In Amsterdam, Holland, the Bee Gees appear at the Grand Gala du Disque Populaire. In Australia, the band is seen in their own television special on Ten Channel 10.

● Saturday, February 26, 1972

Record Mirror runs an interview with the Bee Gees conducted by Lon Goddard. "We're up shit creek if people don't like our songs," says Barry, "But we'll go on doing them until we drop." "The Bee Gees that made 'World' and 'Massachusetts' are the same ones here today," remarks Robin. "Colin Petersen never sang and Vince Melouney hardly ever played. In the backbone sense, it's the same band." "Even to me," concludes Geoff, "They're still a three-brother group with their own style."

• Monday, February 28, 1972
The Bee Gees fly to Rome for promotion and concert appearances. They are scheduled to tape a forty-five minute program titled *Bee Gee Special* and a spot on the show *Teatro 10* (lip-synching to "My World" and "Lonely Days" in a monochrome video production before a live studio audience).

• Wednesday, March 1, 1972
In Bologna, the Bee Gees appear in concert at the Palazzo dello Sport.

• Thursday, March 2, 1972
In Rome, the Bee Gees appear in concert.

• Saturday, March 4, 1972
In the *NME*, Chris Van Ness writes in his Los Angeles column that the Bee Gees will go into production next month on a United States television series. The show was briefly discussed last year in *Record Mirror* (see December 11th), and Van Ness offers only the detail that the Western spoof series will not be musical. The Gibbs may contribute a theme song, but will have no further participation in the production's score (or lack thereof).

Sometime later, the Bee Gees will once again be tipped for making their dramatic debut in a feature described as a "comedy western with music." *The Bull On The Bar Room Floor* is said to be created by Bob Carroll and Madelyn Davis (of *I Love Lucy* fame), and set to be produced by RSO for America's NBC network. Like many of the Bee Gees' previous cinematic aspirations, this project will never reach fruition.

• Saturday, March 18, 1972
The *NME* reports that the Bee Gees are to tape a color television special in Tokyo. Although it is planned for Japanese broadcast, the paper says it will also be offered to Britain and America. Not reported, but apparent when they reach the Far East, Geoff Bridgford has departed the band. He will be replaced on tour by Chris Karon. From this point forward, the Bee Gees will remain the Gibb brothers and will never officially incorporate another outside member.

• Sunday, March 19, 1972
In Hong Kong, the Bee Gees are scheduled to perform in concert.

• Monday, March 20, 1972
The Bee Gees and their entourage (including Hugh Gibb and Lulu) arrive in Tokyo, enroute from Singapore.

• Tuesday, March 21, 1972
In Japan, the Bee Gees enjoy a day off in Tokyo.

• Wednesday, March 22, 1972
In Japan, the Bee Gees hold a press conference at the Tokyo Hilton. During the event, Polydor Japan will present the band with the gold discs for the *Melody* soundtrack. According to tabloid reports of the press conference, the Bee Gees said that what they knew about Japan was "samurai" and the baths where women wash men. Following this conference, *Music Life* conducts an interview with the Bee Gees.

• Thursday, March 23, 1972
In Japan, the Bee Gees appear in concert at Shibuya Kokaido Hall. Their set includes the rarely performed "Melody Fair" (at the request of Polydor Japan), beginning a tradition of including this song in their Japanese repertoire for years to come.

• Friday, March 24, 1972
In Japan, the Bee Gees perform in concert at Budokan Centre in Tokyo. Their set includes "My World" and "Melody Fair."

• Saturday & Sunday, March 25 & 26, 1972
In Japan, the Bee Gees perform in concert at Osaka Festival Hall. Saturday's soundcheck will include Maurice and Alan Kendall jamming Led Zeppelin's "Whole Lotta Love." On Sunday, Maurice, Lulu, and Robin watch the Four Leaves, Japan's current top boy band, playing at Festival Hall. During the Bee Gees' evening concert, Maurice will comically impersonate the Four Leaves, raising a round of laughter.

• Monday, March 27, 1972
In Japan, the Bee Gees travel back to Tokyo.

• Tuesday, March 28, 1972
The Bee Gees depart Tokyo, bound for Kuala Lumpur.

1972

- Sunday, April 2, 1972

The Bee Gees are scheduled to perform a concert in Jakarta, Indonesia.

- Monday, April 10, 1972

Back from touring, the Bee Gees begin work on a new album, *To Whom It May Concern*. Today they work on Robin's "Never Been Alone," Barry's beautiful ballad "I Can Bring Love" (first heard on his Barry Gibb fan club disc) and an unknown number called "It's All Wrong." Replacing the departed Geoff Bridgford will be popular British sessioner, Clem Cattini, who will provide the drums on this month's sessions.

- Wednesday, April 12, 1972

At IBC Studio A, the Bee Gees work with engineers Mike Claydon and Andy Knight to produce three new songs, including their next single. "Run To Me" will be taped in four takes, with the final pass being the master (topped off by a fabulous Bill Shepherd arrangement).

"Bad Bad Dreams" will be recorded in just one take. "Please Don't Turn Out The Lights" will require four takes to complete. Also at this session, the backing track for "Lonely Days" is copied over possibly to create some vocal-less mixes to use in television performances of the song (where the band will sing along live).

- Monday, April 17, 1972

After a weekend break, the Bee Gees return to IBC's Studio A to work with engineers Mike Claydon and Damon Lyon-Shaw. The first song taped, "I Held A Party" will be captured in eight takes (after rolling over at least five early abortive false starts). Of these, only the fourth and eighth are complete performances. Take eight will be the master and feature some of Maurice's fine harpsichord work, harkening back to the band's sound on *Bee Gees' 1st*.

The second song taped today, "Sea Of Smiling Faces," was actually written sometime earlier (likely 1968) and will be completed on take two, after a short false start. The finishing touch of Bill Shepherd's luscious orchestral arrangement places this among the Gibbs' most underrated compositions. Of particular note, this is Shepherd's final arrangement for the group. His involvement in their live shows (as conductor) has now been wound down and when the group moves their recording activity to the United States later this year, he will be a part of their past.

The final song from this session, "Sweet Song Of Summer," is essentially a Maurice Moog odyssey. "I had the first mini-Moog synthesizer," Maurice told Ken Sharp in 2001, "with wires and cables going everywhere. It was the same one that Quincy [Jones] used on the theme for Ironside (laughs). And it was huge, massive. I used it on our album called *To Whom It May Concern*. It showed you where our heads were at (laughs)."

Taped in one take, the recording features Barry on guitar, Clem Cattini on drums and Maurice on bass and Moog synthesizer. The brothers' haunting vocals are spread across five tracks of a 2" sixteen-track master (though one of these performances will not be used in the final mix).

- Friday, April 21, 1972

At IBC Studio A, the Bee Gees work with engineers Damon Lyon-Shaw and Richard Manwaring on a final day of recording for *To Whom It May Concern*. First up, they will tape seven takes of the boogie number, "Road To Alaska." The track will be built around Barry and Maurice's acoustic guitars, a drum track and live vocals from Robin for every take. To complete the production, overdubs of bass, electric guitar, piano, handclaps (in stereo) and background vocals will be added. Robin will also replace his original live tracking vocal with a newly overdubbed version (featuring some slight lyrical revisions).

The second musical idea explored during this session will be a short unissued piano and vocal piece, titled "Lay Down And Sleep." Robin will sing thirty-three takes of this brief possible link or interlude piece in an unusual high-pitched vibrato. It is unlikely that Robin and Maurice (who is also present on the tape) get what they desire, and the idea will be left on the cutting room floor.

- May 1972

Maurice and Billy Lawrie (under the guise of Moby Productions) complete work on an album for Jimmy Stevens, *Don't Freak Me Out*. Maurice will also contribute to albums by Mike Berry (Drift Away) and Bob Saker (They've Taken Back My Number) this year. Next month, Richard Harris will issue a single featuring "Half Of Every Dream" (produced and arranged by Maurice at an undated session).

- Thursday & Tuesday, May 4 & 9, 1972
At IBC Studio A, engineers Damon Lyon-Shaw and Richard Manwaring will work for two days preparing stereo mixes of material for the Bee Gees' upcoming *To Whom It May Concern* album. On May 4th, mixes will be attempted of: "Run To Me" (four acetates will be cut of this mix, one of which will be sent to Maurice on May 5th); "Road To Alaska" (six mixes—three of which are complete); "Bad Bad Dreams" (four mixes—with only the final take being complete); "Please Don't Turn Out The Lights" (which will be completed in two takes, the second of which will the master for this session). On May 9th, mixes will be made of: "I Held A Party" (seven mixes—two of which are complete); "Sea Of Smiling Faces" (eight mixes—of which only the final pass is complete); "I Can Bring Love" (three takes—of which only the final mix is complete); "Never Been Alone" (one mix only). It is possible that an attempt is also made to mix "We Lost The Road" at this session; it will be included in the master mixes assembled from these two sessions.

At the end of the May 9th mix session, Damon Lyon-Shaw will compile a reel of the past two days completed master mixes for review. After living with the results for a few weeks, the Bee Gees will decide to remix the entire album beginning June 6th.

- Tuesday & Wednesday, June 6 & 7, 1972
At IBC Studio A, a second round of mixes will be prepared for the forthcoming *To Whom It May Concern*. On Tuesday, engineers Damon Lyon-Shaw and Andy Knight will dubdown songs including: "Sea Of Smiling Faces" (six mixes—the last of which will be the only complete pass and considered the master); "I Held A Party" (two mixes—the second of which will be complete and considered the master); "Paper Mache, Cabbages & Kings" (two mixes—the second of which will be complete and considered the master); and one mix each of "Sweet Song Of Summer," "Nobody's Someone" (a 1968 outtake revived but not revised from the *Odessa* session, this will be the most commonly circulated mix of the track until its official issue in remixed form on *Sketches For Odessa*); "You Know It's For You"; "Please Don't Turn Out The Lights" and "Bad Bad Dreams" (which will be remixed at tomorrow's session).

On Wednesday, engineers Damon Lyon-Shaw and Richard Manwaring will prepare stereo mixes for "Never Been Alone" (which will be remixed June 14th) and six mixes of "We Lost The Road," the last of which will be the only complete pass and considered the master). A further mix session for *To Whom It May Concern* will be held at IBC Studio B on July 6th.

- Saturday, June 10, 1972
In Britain, the Bee Gees are seen performing "Morning Of My Life" and "Walking Back To Waterloo" on television's *2G's And The Pop People*.

- Wednesday, June 14, 1972
It is very likely that a further mix session for *To Whom It May Concern* will be held today at IBC studios. The only result from this date that is known is a remix of "Never Been Alone," though it is likely other titles are worked on during this period.

- Thursday, July 6, 1972
At IBC Studio B, engineers Damon Lyon-Shaw and Richard Manwaring prepare a rare set of mono mixes of some *To Whom It May Concern* tracks (for BBC radio use, in lieu of the Bee Gees recording exclusive radio session versions of these numbers). These will include: "Run To Me" (issued as a single tomorrow); "Bad, Bad Dreams"; five mixes of "Alive" (the last of which will be the only complete pass and considered the master); "Never Been Alone" (two mixes—the second of which will be complete and considered the master); "You Know It's For You" (lacking orchestration) and "Road To Alaska."

- Friday, July 7, 1972
In Britain, the Bee Gees' single—"Run To Me" c/w "Road To Alaska"—is issued.

- Monday, July 10, 1972
At IBC Studio A, the Bee Gees tape a new song, "The Happiest Days Of Your Life." The track, which will remain unissued, is a fully completed production in the Bee Gee pot-boiler mode: a slow Robin-sung piano section of several verses, shifting into a more aggressive Barry-led chorus and outro.

1972

• Saturday, July 15, 1972
The *NME* reports that the Bee Gees "are to star in a feature film for the cinema, for which shooting will commence in September." The Gibbs are said to have strong dramatic roles in the picture, but it will not be a musical. They are, however, currently writing songs for the soundtrack.

• Monday, July 17, 1972
In Britain, the BBC logs in a new radio session for the group, but these are merely the exclusive July 6 mono mixes of "Bad Bad Dreams," "Never Been Alone," "Alive" and "Run To Me" which are broadcast on the *Jimmy Young* show on July 24th.

• Saturday, July 22, 1972
In Britain, the Bee Gees return to the charts with "Run To Me." Over the next ten weeks it will reach a peak of #9, the band's first Top 10 placing since "Don't Forget To Remember."

• Saturday, July 29, 1972
In the United States, "Run To Me" enters the *Billboard* singles chart. Over the next twelve weeks, it will peak at #16.

• Saturday, August 12, 1972
Billboard reports that independent producer/composer, Neely Plumb, has re-signed with Capitol and as a part of his multi-album deal with the label, he has brokered a US release of the soundtrack to *The Hero*, featuring Maurice's music. No mention of Maurice is made in the article (which only notes the involvement of composer Johnny Harris and the group Heads, Hand and Feet). The soundtrack will be issued next month.

• Tuesday, August 22, 1972
Variety reports that the Bee Gees will star in *Castle X*, a medieval horror yarn, which is to be shot in Yugoslavia. The film is to be produced for Virgin Films by Ned Sherrin and set to be directed by Ridley Scott. Shooting is scheduled to commence on September 15th and the Gibbs are supposed to score the incidental music. The screenplay, written by Scott and John Edwards, has a shooting schedule of ten weeks.

• September 1972
In Los Angeles, the Bee Gees record a new album to be titled *Life In A Tin Can*. Sessions will be held at the Record Plant (8456 W. 3rd Street, Los Angeles, California) and these produce just eight songs: Barry's "I Don't Want To Be The One," "South Dakota Morning," "While I Play" and "Come Home Johnny Bride," as well as the group compositions "Saw A New Morning," "My Life Has Been A Song," "Method To Madness" and "Living In Chicago."

Having already recorded a magnificent long player (*To Whom It May Concern*) amidst extensive touring, this latest offering is not fully baked. It does however include such highlights as the epic "Saw A New Morning" (which will be the album's single). Spurred by the impending debut of Stigwood's new custom label imprint, RSO, the Bee Gees will go one further and create a third full album of material in Los Angeles next month to fill the commercial pipeline.

• Wednesday, September 6, 1972
At IBC Studio A, engineers prepare two new mono mixes of "Run To Me" to aid in the group's television promotion of the song. The first of these lacks both the lead vocal track (but features all the backing vocals) and Bill Shepherd's orchestration. The second mix includes the strings (but still lacks the lead vocal track). This allows the Bee Gees to sing live over the track when played back at a television studio.

• Tuesday, September 19, 1972
At the Record Plant, arranger Johnny Pate works from 8pm to midnight with a fourteen piece orchestral group (including Jerome Richardson, Israel Baker, Gordon Marron, Haim Shtrum, Arnold Belnick, William Kurasch, Leonard Malarsky, Carl LaMagna, Tibor Zelig, Armand Kaproff, Dennis Karmazyn, Raymond Kelley, Edgar Lustgarten and

Harvey Mason) to sweeten tracks for the upcoming *Life In A Tin Can* album. Pate will add overdubs to the tracks "I Don't Wanna Be The One," "Living In Chicago," "Method To My Madness" and "Saw A New Morning." After this sweetening session, work will more or less be completed on the LP. Regardless, Robin will return to Britain in few days to meet his newly born son, Spencer (who arrives earlier than expected on September 21st).

• Saturday, September 23, 1972
The *NME* reports that *Castle X* has been shelved. The film project that was supposed to begin shooting this month has been put aside while the Bee Gees record in Los Angeles. MGM say they do not know if the picture will be reactivated.

• October 1972
In Los Angeles, the Bee Gees return to the Record Plant to tape their third album of the year, *A Kick In The Head Is Worth Eight In The Pants*. Despite the pressure to generate another set of songs after the scant and less-than-stellar *Life In A Tin Can*, the ever-prolific brothers produce perhaps the best of their three albums this year (and their first with all group compositions since their 1970 reunion).

Masters produced during this month (and completed in November—see November 9th) include: "Elisa," "Wouldn't I Be Someone," "A Lonely Violin," "Losers And Lovers," "Home Again Rivers," "Harry's Gate," "Rocky L.A.," "Castles In The Air," "Where Is Your Sister?" and the first version of "It Doesn't Matter Much To Me." Despite their best efforts (and some additional recording in early 1973), this album project will be stillborn after the lukewarm reception afforded *Life In A Tin Can*.

"Wouldn't I Be Someone" c/w "Elisa" will be issued as a single in the middle of 1973 to little airplay, leaving most of the rest of this album in the vaults. However, the first version of "It Doesn't Matter Much To Me" will surface by mistake in 1974 on a UK budget release on the Contour label titled *Gotta Get A Message To You*. It was intended that this release should feature a second recording of this song (taped January 4, 1974), but this earlier recording is used in error. Elsewhere, Graham Bonnet will cover "Castles In The Air" for an RCA single issued in 1973; a snippet of the Bee Gees' version will appear on a 1978 promotional only publishing sampler, *The Words and Music of Barry Gibb, Robin Gibb and Maurice Gibb*. Following this set of recordings, the Bee Gees will take a new stylistic approach to their music and begin another chapter in their story.

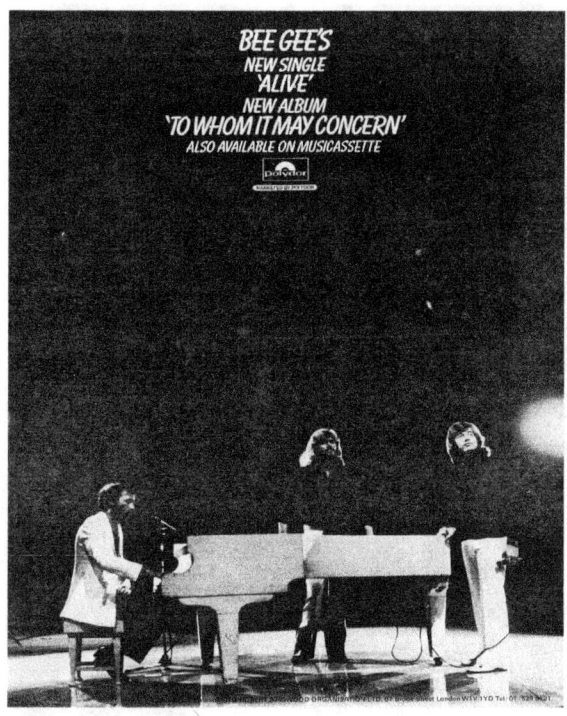

• Saturday, October 14, 1972
Disc reviews the Bee Gees' latest LP, *To Whom It May Concern*. "The master exponents of pop with orchestra strike again with an album which, when you open it out has the three heroes pop up in cardboard figures. Hmm! Is that significant? The sleeve lists thirteen tracks, the record plays only twelve and the one missing is their hit single, 'Run To Me.'

"What annoys me is that I took this album to review specifically because I liked the hit single and it was listed on the sleeve. Had I bought it for that reason I would have been banging on Polydor's front door after having found out how to invoke the Trades Description Act.

"A spokesmen for Polydor said: 'The Bee Gees decided to withdraw the track at a time too late to rectify the album cover. By the time the album reaches the shops a sticker either blocking out the track title or letting everyone know that the single is not on the album will be added.'"

• Friday, October 27, 1972
At IBC Studio B, engineer Damon Lyon-Shaw prepares a reel of exclusive mono mixes for use on BBC radio programmes (in lieu of the group taping new, live performances). Three songs will be produced: "Sea Of Smiling Faces" (lacking Bill Shepherd's orchestral overdubs), "Alive" (lacking orchestration) and "Massachusetts (The Lights Went Out In)" (a remix of the 1967 track without orchestration).

1972

The Bee Gees rehearsing at Memorial Coliseum, Los Angeles, 1972 (photos by Bobby Furst—courtesy of Saul Davis).

• Monday, November 6, 1972
In Britain, the BBC logs in a new radio session for the Bee Gees, but this is in fact just the receipt of the exclusive mono mixes from October 27th. "Sea Of Smiling Faces" will be broadcast on the *Jimmy Young* show.

• Thursday, November 9, 1972
At the Record Plant in Los Angeles, arranger Jimmie Haskell holds the first of two sweetening sessions for the album *A Kick In The Head Is Worth Eight In The Pants*. Today, Haskell employs a twenty-piece group for three hours (from 8pm to 11pm) to augment the songs "Wouldn't I Be Someone," "Elisa" and "Rocky L.A." Musicians for this session include: Sid Sharp, Paul Shure, Leonard Malarsky, Tibor Zelig, Stanley Plummer, Henry Ferber, Robert Konrad, Wilbert Nuttycombe, Joseph Reilich, Philip Goldberg, Harry Hyams, Margaret Aue, Joseph DiTullio, Jerry Kessler, Jesse Ehrlich, Peter Mercurio, Don Bagley, Timothy Barr and Jim Bond.

• Saturday, November 11, 1972
In the United States, *To Whom It May Concern* enters the *Billboard* album charts. Over the next fourteen weeks, it will rise to #35. In Britain, a new single—"Alive" c/w "Paper Mache, Cabbages And Kings"—is issued (this 45 is already available in the States).

• Friday, November 17, 1972
In Los Angeles, arranger Jimmie Haskell holds a second sweetening session at the Record Plant. Haskell will employ a twenty-piece group for four-and-a-half hours (from 7pm to 11:30pm) to augment the songs "Where Is Your Sister," "Lonely Violin," "Castle In The Air," "Harry's Gate," "Home Again" and something titled on the union sheet "Na Na Na." Musicians for this date include: Sid Sharp, Henry Ferber, Harry Bluestone, Tibor Zelig, Leonard Malarsky, William Kurasch, Ronald Folsom, Harry Hyams, Samuel Boghossian, Joseph Reilich, Wilbert Nuttycombe, Myer Bello, Jesse Ehrlich, Armand Kaproff, Jerry Kessler, Raymond Kelley, Timothy Barr, Peter Mercurio, James Hughart and Jim Bond.

• Saturday, November 18, 1972
In the United States, "Alive" enters the Billboard singles chart. Over the next seven weeks, it will reach a peak of #34.

• Saturday, November 25, 1972
In Los Angeles, the Bee Gees appear in concert at The Ultimate 'ROQ' Concert/Festival at the Memorial Coliseum. Sponsored by radio station KROQ (started only three months ago by entrepreneur Gary Bookasta), the show, which draws a paying audience of 32,848, is staged to benefit Los Angeles' Free Clinic. Other performers taking part include The Fabulous Rhinestones, Sha Na Na, Love, Batdorf & Rodney, Stevie Wonder (introduced by Keith Moon of The Who), Raspberries, the Four Seasons, Chuck Berry, Merry Clayton and Sly & The Family Stone.

Sadly, the show will be plagued by sound and site problems. In particular, the Bee Gees set is interrupted by a phone call from Yoko Ono played over the sound system (apologizing for her and John Lennon's absence and saying the show is "a beautiful project"). Nevertheless, the band is filmed in performance and portions of their set—"I Started A Joke," "Alive" and "Lonely Days"—will be screened on television in July 1974.

The Bee Gees recording at the Record Plant in Los Angeles, 1972 (photos by Bobby Furst—courtesy of Saul Davis)

AFTERWORD

"Run To Me" would be the final major hit in the Bee Gees' original sweeping ballad style. Successive singles such as "Alive," "Saw A New Morning" and "Wouldn't I Be Someone" were melodically splendid, but commercially lacking. In 1973, the group continued their worldwide touring schedule; however, they still found trouble drawing audiences even after chalking up a dozen or so well-known hits. While they made a conscious transition of changing arrangers and moving recording activity to Los Angeles, they stylistically remained in the same musical bag through 1973. By the end of the year, they were back recording at IBC studios but were now working with an outside producer, Arif Mardin, for the first time since the dismissal of Ossie Byrne in late 1967.

Sessions with Arif Mardin stretched into early 1974, producing the *Mr. Natural* album: a fan favorite but still a lackluster seller. It wouldn't be until 1975's *Main Course* (and another change in recording environment to Miami, Florida) that group were restored to the top commercially. In fact, the success the Bee Gees enjoyed for the rest of the decade would completely eclipse the reception afforded their early work. "Jive Talkin'" would become the Bee Gees' first #1 single since "How Can You Mend A Broken Heart" and ushered in the disco era of their career (which produced more than a dozen major hits, including seven more #1 singles).

While there was a marked difference in approach to the genre in which they were now working, the Gibbs' songwriting remained spontaneous and inventive in every note they produced. By the end of the decade, the Bee Gees had broken sales records and were cemented as popular music icons. Nevertheless, such intense exposure created a critical backlash (and the band had never been justly lauded for their work in the first place). A failed movie, *Sgt. Pepper's Lonely Hearts Club Band*, and a very public break-up with their mentor Robert Stigwood spelled the end of their mass appeal. But the Bee Gees kept writing and after years of trying, at last became solid hit writer/producers for other artists such as Barbra Streisand, Dionne Warwick and Kenny Rogers. The Gibbs never lacked for songs and their work remained pervasive in the mainstream.

For the next two decades, the Bee Gees flirted with the charts, scoring sporadic sizeable worldwide hits and even chalking up another round of solo successes for Robin and Barry. Maurice remained behind the scenes, as always; he would never again top his prolific run as a solo writer/producer in the early 1970's, though his talents remained unfettered. A final group album in 2001, *This Is Where I Came In*, attempted to turn back the clock and reignite their brotherly collaborations, but there was little group energy left.

The Bee Gees officially ended on January 12, 2003 with the death of Maurice (from a heart attack brought on by intestinal complications). The creative friction that had always existed between Barry and Robin became insurmountable in the absence of Maurice; the sadness of his loss created a distance that could not be reconciled. Random reunions and award presentations kept Barry and Robin in intermittent contact, but plaudits and family ties would not create the desire for Barry to publicly lead the tribe. Robin maintained a high media profile until he too succumbed to illness and passed away on May 20, 2012.

Barry Gibb is all that remains of the Bee Gees. In February 2012, he performed his first public US solo concert. The show was a success on many levels and he has talked publicly of undertaking further performances. There is no doubt that Barry can excite and impress audiences, but whether he will once again tap into the creative headspace of songwriting remains the final chapter in this remarkable story of family, fame and enigmatic artistry.

Regardless of what is written in the future, the Bee Gees will have left behind one of the most varied and vast catalogs in the history of popular song. Their personal exploits and chart positions will always remain a distant relation to their real role in popular culture: as brilliant fantasists who explored a spontaneous creative telepathy that can never be recreated or accurately described. In the end then, we are left with just their everlasting words and melodies, an elusive chemistry that created a singular voice.

AUTHOR'S NOTE

Every effort has been made to accurately transcribe and credit those involved in the Bee Gees' story. Nevertheless, there are bound to be omissions and errors. If you have something to add or correct in the chronology, please email the author: beegeesbook@aol.com

Sources: All quotes unless otherwise noted, come from interviews by the author and are Copyright 2006 by Andrew Sandoval; Further research was culled from *Amusement Business; Australian Women's Weekly; Billboard; Australian Cashbox; Everybody's; The Sydney Morning Herald; Music Maker; Disc & Music Echo; Fabulous; Variety; Beat Instrumental; New Musical Express; Record Mirror; Melody Maker; Muziek Express; Los Angeles Times; Rolling Stone; Radio Times; Bravo; Go-Set; Top Pops; Music Now!; Hit Parader; Teenset* and Joe Brennan's brilliant Bee Gees website: http://www.columbia.edu/~brennan/beegees/

Respect and acknowledgements to my friend David Leaf for the only authorized biography of the Bee Gees: 1979's *Bee Gees—The Authorized Biography* by Barry, Robin and Maurice Gibb as told to David Leaf. And last but not least, Melinda Bilyeu, Hector Cook, Andrew Mon Hughes, Joseph Brennan and Mark Crohan's for their indispensable *Tales Of The Brothers Gibb* (published by Omnibus in 2000).

ABOUT THE AUTHOR

Andrew Sandoval is a Grammy-nominated producer and engineer. For the past twenty years, he has been the architect of comprehensive reissues covering such artists as the Bee Gees, the Kinks, the Beach Boys, the Band, Elvis Costello, the Everly Brothers, Left Banke, Beau Brummels, and the Monkees, in addition to crafting entries in Rhino's long-running Nuggets compilation series.

His writing has appeared in such publications as *The Hollywood Reporter*, *Record Collector* and *Shindig!* Sandoval's first book, *The Monkees: The Day-by-Day Story of the 60s TV Pop Sensation*, was issued to universal praise in 2005. His association with the band led to personally managing the Monkees and overseeing their artistically and commercially successful concert tours.

Known as a connoisseur of all things rare, precious and beautiful, in 2006 Sandoval turned his extensive music collection into a weekly radio program called "Come To The Sunshine" (www.cometothesunshine.com) that can be heard live or as a podcast.

As a singer/songwriter, he has issued five critically acclaimed albums of his own material (*A Beautiful Story*, *Happy To Be Here*, *What's It All About?*, *From Me To You* and *33*), as well as enjoying a stint touring and recording with Rock And Roll Hall Of Fame inductee, Dave Davies (of the Kinks).

www.ingramcontent.com/pod-product-compliance
Lightning Source LLC
Chambersburg PA
CBHW081418300426
44109CB00019BA/2340